THE PORCUPINE

THE
PORCUPINE

The Life of
Algernon Sidney

John Carswell

JOHN MURRAY

To Lewis Arnold Dralle
Scholar and Lover of English History

Text © John Carswell 1989

First published in 1989
by John Murray (Publishers) Ltd
50 Albemarle Street, London W 1X 4BD

British Library Cataloguing in Publication Data
Carswell, John, *1918–*
The porcupine: the life of Algernon
Sidney.1.   England.   Politics.   Sidney,
Algernon, 1623–1683
I. Title
942.06′092′4

ISBN 0–7195–4684–2

Printed and bound in Great Britain by
Butler & Tanner Ltd, Frome and London

Contents

Illustrations

Between pp 146 and 147

Credits

1,2,7, Viscount De L'Isle, VC, KG, PC; 3, Fitzwilliam Museum, Cambridge; 4, The Lord Barnard; 5, British Architectural Library, RIBA; 6, Statens Museum for Kunst, Copenhagen; 8, from an early edition of Clarendon's *History of the Rebellion*; 9, The Historical Society of Pennsylvania; 10, The Library, Friends House, London NW1; 11, the London Library; 12, the Earl of Leicester, photograph from the Courtauld Institute of Art; 13,14, British Museum.

Table of the Sidney Kin

1 This table is intended to illustrate family connection, not inheritance of titles. Primogeniture, though observed as much as possible, has therefore taken second place where necessary to bring out important marriages. Thus Isabella Sidney, though a younger daughter, has been placed before her elder siblings to accommodate the Smythe marriage.

2 Capitals mark the arrival of a new family name in the connection.

3 Names underlined show persons who were alive in Algernon Sidney's lifetime.

4 It should be noted that some titles reappear without having been inherited (e.g. Warwick, Leicester). This is due to fresh creations of extinct or forfeited titles.

TABLE OF THE SIDNEY KIN

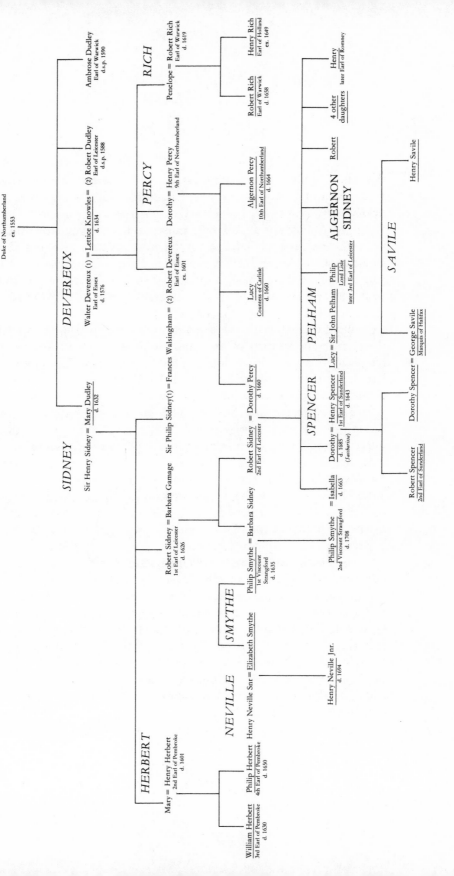

Preface

Algernon Sidney, in his last message, gave me the title of my first venture into the history of the seventeenth century – *The Old Cause* – nearly forty years ago. He seemed to emerge from obscurity into a spotlight of history and, I felt, must have a longer story linking in some way the turbulence of the mid-century with the steady foundations of Whig Britain. But no account of him was available, and ever since then I have wanted to discover the biography of the man who was the hero of English liberty till Macaulay expelled him from history for more than a century.

What follows is intended as a straightforward biography setting the man in the context of his time, rather than as an assessment of his place in the history of ideas; but to give enough account of the latter to show its originality, for it is hard to find a character whose thinking is more closely integrated with his personal experience.

The materials for Sidney's life are exceptionally abundant, though they leave many gaps and riddles; and are in great measure unpublished. These include two substantial works which have been discovered by historians in the last twenty years (*The Character of Sir Henry Vane* and *Court Maxims*) and the remarkable series of letters he wrote from the Tower of London during his last imprisonment. To these must be added a mine of information about him in the archives of the Sidney family preserved in the De L'Isle Papers, and much in other collections.

My thanks and acknowledgements are therefore wide-ranging, but notably to Viscount De L'Isle and Dudley and Viscount Hampden for access to archives in their ownership and permission to quote from them. The guardians of many collections have also been unfailingly helpful – those of the Warwickshire, East Sussex, and Kent County Record Offices, the Public Record Office, the Department of Manuscripts of the British Library. And I owe a particular tribute to the Librarian of the Public Library of Nérac and Mlle Bourrichon for a letter which throws a flood of light on Sidney's life in exile.

I have discussed this undertaking with several historians of the period, but particularly with Dr Blair Worden and Dr Jonathan Scott, both of whom have shared with me their interest in the period and in Sidney. With Dr Worden I have had invaluable discussions, and have drawn much on his pioneering work. When Dr Scott and I discovered our common interest in Sidney it led to most fruitful contacts, and I am glad to make clear, as he does in the first part of his study, which has recently appeared, that we have not been hesitant in willingness to exchange discoveries, as scholars should, even if our approaches and interpretations have sometimes differed.

The biography of Sidney has never been written fully till now, so that his biographer is rather in the position of the tourist agent offering an unspoilt beach with apologies for the lack of modern conveniences. In a word, he is faced with a special problem of references. In Sidney's case this is further complicated by the fact that those of his works and letters which have been printed appear very often in several different printed texts with varying pagination and wording. A complete system of references would involve not only annotation but a discussion of reliability of evidence or text. There is much scholarly work ahead here, but to attempt it in a general biography such as this would suffocate the reader. I have therefore limited my references to what is needed to support direct quotations, and (though I have usually consulted the documentary source where it exists) have given reference to a printed text if one is available. I have added a note on my main sources, with some discussion of Sidney's texts and their history.

Although, therefore, I cannot claim to have drawn two neat red lines at the bottom of this remarkable life, and the account in this sense remains open, it is enough to be able to say that a major figure has been reintroduced to English history – and not only English, for as I show, the transatlantic influence of Sidney and his ideas has been his most lasting achievement.

A porcupine is the crest of the Sidney coat of arms, and could not have been more appropriately chosen, for they were a spiny family, and none was spinier than the central figure of this work.

J.P.C.
Berins Hill
September 1988

Prologue

On 7 December 1683 a tall grizzled man of about sixty, soberly dressed and escorted by a small knot of officials, walked from the gates of the Tower of London to a scaffold just outside. He had a military bearing and probably a slight limp from a wound received in a cavalry charge forty years earlier. Simple beheading had been substituted for the sentence of physical devastation passed a month earlier, but that had been the only response to influential appeals for mercy, and was primarily a recognition of his high birth.

Although it was a bitterly cold day there was quite a large crowd which included an observer whose business it was to send full details of the event across the Atlantic as soon as possible to the President of Harvard. A speech would have been usual. However, the victim refused the opportunity, saying he had come not to speak but to die. Instead he handed over some sheets of paper remarking that they contained what he would have said and, when the Sheriff expressed the hope that they contained nothing critical of the Government, replied testily that if they were not liked he would take them back and tear them up. The Sheriff thought it best to keep them, and later in the day they were laid before King Charles II and his brother James.

No chaplain was present and no prayers were said, but as the victim put his head on the block the executioner noticed a slight movement which might mean the intention of a last word, and asked deferentially 'Will you rise again, Sir?' 'No,' was the reply, 'not till the last judgment', so the axe fell and ended the life of Algernon Sidney.

At the same time it created one of the most potent political martyrs in English and American history, whose name passed not only into the triumphant Whig tradition but into the origins of the United States, on which his political ideas had more influence than any thinker's but Locke's. Military hero, thinker, and martyr are not a common combination, and in the year of Independence the Commonwealth of Massachusetts added Sidney's iron motto to its coat of arms:

Manus haec inimica tyrannis
Ense petit placidam sub libertate quietem.

The sixth President of the United States, John Quincy Adams, took
four lines to put Sidney's terse couplet into English:

This hand to tyrants ever sworn a foe
For freedom only deals the deadly blow,
Then sheathes in calm repose the deadly blade
For gentle peace in freedom's hallowed shade.

No friend or relative accompanied Sidney in the last scene of
his life except his valet-cum-secretary Joseph Ducasse, who had
been entrusted with a copy of the message his master handed to the
Sheriffs, to make sure it was published. It quickly was, and found a
ready market, for its author, though untitled, was a great aristocrat
with an earl for a father and the daughter of an earl for a mother;
he was the brother of one of the most famous beauties of her time,
the uncle of the reigning king's chief minister, the great-nephew of
that paragon and poet Sir Philip Sidney, and, to top it all, a former
colonel of Ironsides.

That dying paper of a single printed sheet was the first of his
works ever published. But many hundreds of pages were to follow,
which extended his stormy life to make him a hero who gave
backbone to the whig tradition and resistance to autocracy on both
sides of the Atlantic. His real life may have been overlaid by his
posthumous achievement, but it would be difficult to say that one
did not justify the other.

A Great Connection

THROUGHOUT a life devoted to opposing monarchy Algernon Sidney was deeply and proudly conscious of his high birth. 'Though I am not a peer,' he said towards the end of his life 'yet I am a chip of wood from which they are made.' Just how high his birth was, and how it influenced his career, can be measured by evoking a scene which we know occurred in 1587, thirty-six years before he was born, and almost a century before his death.

In that year Sir Philip Sidney, by common consent the paragon of his time, lay dying at Arnhem. Round his bed were his uncle Robert Dudley, Earl of Leicester, commander of the expedition; Robert Devereux, Earl of Essex, who was to marry Philip Sidney's widow; Henry Percy, later Earl of Northumberland, who married Devereux' sister and was Algernon's maternal grandfather; Algernon's other grandfather, Robert Sidney, the dying man's younger brother. Beside Philip's pillow was the dying man's wife Frances, daughter of the Queen's Secretary of State Francis Walsingham, and at his bedhead the modest figure of Philip's secretary, William Temple.

More than one of the survivors of this group lived long enough for Algernon to remember meeting them. Frances, after suffering two more widowhoods, was still living not far from his home when he was nine years old. So was his grandfather Northumberland.

All his life he was to see much of the Temples in their successive generations. But the most memorable of all was the dying man
at the centre of the scene at Arnhem, his great-uncle, the family
hero.

The exact date of Algernon's birth, curiously enough, is not
recorded, but on 15 January 1623 the Penshurst accounts show a
fee of £20 to Mrs Stephens, a midwife, for attendance on his mother
Dorothy, Lady Lisle, and this must be very near his birthday. The
accounts also show that a cradle and other requirements for what
was almost an annual event in the family had been ordered a
month before, and the birth seems to have been a difficult one. Mrs
Stephens' fee was large, and she stayed the unusually long period
of six weeks. The absence of any official records suggests informal
baptism of a child not expected to live, and the delay in Lady Lisle's
churching* until the following June that she took a long time to
recover from the birth of her second son.

When Algernon was born Dorothy Lisle was twenty-five and
had been six years married to Robert Lisle, heir to the earldom of
Leicester and the great house at Penshurst which three years later
became his. But earl though her husband might be, Dorothy, was a
Percy and belonged to a far older and more powerful nobility. Their
long line had suffered many casualties and political miscalculations,
but they had survived the Wars of the Roses and the ascendancy of
the Tudors still to reign almost feudally in the northwest, though
calmer times had induced them now to move their principal seat to
Petworth, in Sussex. In consequence Dorothy was far from being
an unequal partner in her marriage, whether household affairs or
politics were concerned. She had all the fire of the Percys, and
transmitted it to her second son, to whom she gave the peculiarly
Percy name of Algernon, then borne by her brother, the future tenth
Earl of Northumberland, who was the boy's godfather and was to
have a powerful influence on his career. To her first-born, a daughter,
she gave her own name, Dorothy. Her correspondence with her
husband shows a woman of forcible opinions, and on her deathbed

* Brigid Haydon in *Archaeologica Cantiana* lxxvi (1961) marshals the evidence of
Algernon's birth convincingly. In 1620 and 1621 Lady Lisle gave birth to children
with other names, and a little girl was baptized in 1624. Algernon's portrait at Penshurst,
which he commissioned himself, is dated 1663 and endorsed 'aetatis suae 41'; and the
label on his coffin records his death in December 1683 as 'in his sixty first year'. The
only evidence against January 1623 is his chance remark in a letter of 1661 that he is
'growing near forty'. Common enough among people of 38.

she asked his pardon for their many quarrels – an interview which he recorded in a touching memorandum.

The ascent of the Sidneys to grandeur had been more recent and more systematic than that of the Percys. They had made their great advance in the sixteenth century as courtiers and administrators, and above all by judicious marriages. Sir William Sidney had received the magnificent Penshurst estate, in the heart of England's richest county, as a reward for acting as tutor to King Edward VI. His son Henry, who firmly established the family's fortunes, was one of Elizabeth's greatest proconsuls, and married a Dudley which made him brother-in-law to the Queen's favourite. After serving as ambassador in France he had three terms governing Ireland – indeed for forty years one of his relations was ruling Ireland if he was not ruling it himself. So great were his proconsular capacities that for seventeen of those forty years he was entrusted with the government of Wales as well.

Sir Henry not only married a Dudley, and married his eldest son to a Walsingham: his tree spread to many other noble families – to the Montagus, Earls of Manchester; the Riches, Earls of Warwick; the Cecils, Earls of Salisbury; the Herberts, Earls of Pembroke. But by far his greatest family achievement was Philip, his eldest son. Though Philip died long before Algernon was born there can be no doubt that from childhood Philip was Algernon's model, and this was not only a matter of family hero-worship. Temperamentally and physically they resembled each other – the same pout of the lower lip, the same slight cleft in the chin, the same russet hair; and the same hot temper.

Sir Philip Sidney had been groomed to scale the political heights in the world of the elderly Queen – a story that might well, as his great-nephew's did, have ended on the scaffold – but in that there was nothing discreditable for a man of birth. So great a fame had he already reached when he was struck down by a Spanish bullet at the age of thirty-two, that he was accorded a state funeral at St Paul's – the first commoner ever to receive such an honour. On that day, it was remarked, mourning was worn in the streets of London as if for royalty.

This was not done out of respect for a great poet and a fallen soldier, but as a tribute to something for which Sidney had come preeminently to stand, both as a man of action and an intellectual: international Protestantism, which in one of his letters he describes as 'The Cause'. It included, but did not end with, the English rejection of Rome, for it extended to Germany, the Low Countries, and France. In the Netherlands it would soon be won, in France it would be lost – with consequences which dominated Algernon's lifetime.

As a young diplomat serving in Paris Philip had seen the Massacre of St Bartholemew which led to the deaths of thirty thousand Huguenots. The portrait of one Huguenot, Hubert Languet, whom he met during the massacre and helped to shelter, still hangs in an embrasure at Penshurst. A few months afterwards Languet became the young man's mentor, and in a remarkable correspondence Philip Sidney received instruction in the learning, political and moral theory, and international affairs of the Reformation world. No man could have been better qualified for this task of breeding an aristocratic pupil who was intended to rise high as a protestant statesman. He had been a disciple of Melancthon and known the earlier giants of reform; he was himself an active writer on political theory and, as a practising diplomat in the service of Saxony, had contacts all over Europe.[1] He was especially interested in the great intellectual problem of the age – political obligation and the rights of governments – and was probably the author of a work on the topic – *Vindiciae Contra Tyrannos* – which was later published in an English translation at the end of the Civil War, and much impressed Milton.[2] But he was also extremely well informed on current politics, and many of his letters to his pupil are filled with commentary and prediction based on reports of political meetings and military movements throughout Europe.

Philip commemorates Languet in the *Arcadia*:

> The song I sang old Lanquet had me taught,
> Lanquet, the shepherd best sweet Ister knewe,
> For clerkly rede, and hating what is naught,
> For faithfull heart, cleane hands, and mouth as trewe:
> With his sweete skill my skillesse youth he drewe,
> To have a feeling tast of him that sitts
> Beyond the heaven, far more beyond your witts.

When Algernon was growing up in Penshurst he would have been as much aware of his heroic great-uncle's tutor as of the great Sir Philip himself. He too would have read Languet's letters and have imbibed from them the doctrines of the Protestant international.

The proconsular Sir Henry Sidney would also have read Languet's letters for the useful information they contained, and certainly approved his son's choice of a tutor. He invited Languet to Penshurst, and after Philip's premature death continued to employ him for the next son, Robert, though with less success. Naturally Sir Henry was strict in his conformity to the established state of religious affairs in England, but his broader politico-religious sympathies were those represented by Languet. As Lord Lieutenant of Ireland he included on his staff a disciple of John Knox named Christopher Goodman, who had written a book called *How Supreme Powers Ought to be Obeyed by Their Subjects, and Whether They may by God's Law be Disobeyed*. Sir Henry even put forward Goodman's name for an Irish bishopric, but the Queen did not accept the recommendation, perhaps because of the book, perhaps because Goodman had publicly endorsed Knox's opinion that it was not proper for women to hold high political office. We also find Sir Henry attempting to raise economic standards in Ireland by settling skilled Huguenot refugees, 'wayeing how necessarie and expedient it is', he writes to Lord Treasurer Cecil, 'to have this countrie plentifullie peopled, and especiallie stored with mecanicall and handie craftsmen, whereof there is great want and scarcitie'.[3]

The Sidney tradition formed in the sixteenth century was one of puritanism and public service, deeply interested in politics both at home and abroad: very far from silken Arcadia and courtly hedonism. Philip Sidney himself was a difficult impetuous man who endlessly agitated for permission to fight for the Dutch rebels against Spain, and was given it only with reluctance – even Languet arguing with him that though the Dutch might be right in their struggle, the subject of another prince could not kill their enemies without sin. He had to be prevented almost by force from making a voyage of exploration to America, and gave great offence by writing to the Queen herself, in a letter he made public, objecting to her marrying the French prince, the Duc d'Alençon – something she had no intention of doing. Whether his great-nephew Algernon inherited these traits or deliberately adopted them does not matter. He had them.

Old Sir Henry did not long survive his brilliant and difficult son, and the new master of Penshurst was the second son, Robert: less distinguished, indeed, but one who did much to advance the family's status. Its marriage policy in earlier generations now began to fructify by inheritance, and Robert himself carried it further by marrying an heiress from South Wales called Barbara Gamage whose considerable property in Glamorganshire (it included coal mines) was added to the Sidney estates, and ultimately helped Robert, and in due course Algernon to a seat in Parliament. In 1597 he helped to endow the college at Cambridge which bears the family name, and in 1603 he was raised to the peerage in the coronation honours of James I. In due course, the male line of the Dudleys being extinct, Robert prevailed on King James to renew the Dudley titles in memory of his mother Mary Dudley, and so rose in successive steps to the viscountcy of Lisle and the earldom of Leicester, which he attained in 1618. Two years earlier he had gained the Garter, and married his eldest son into one of the greatest families in England – the Percys.

But he did not live long to enjoy his honours, for in 1626 he died and was succeeded by Algernon's father. This second Earl and second Robert of the family was a complicated, anxious man. By instinct he was bookish and retiring, and found it difficult to rec-oncile his intellectual interests with the public life he felt it his duty to lead. Old Sir Henry had been quite sure that education and study were no more than a means to an end, and when his son Philip was starting at school had told him he must be 'humble and obedient to your master, for unless you frame yourself to obey others, yea and feel what obedience is, you shall never be able to teach others to obey you'. One is sorry for the second earl, with his fiery wife, his numerous and difficult children, and his great position at a time in history when clear judgment and firm action were going to be indispensable for survival. The library at Penshurst was one of his great achievements and he was never happier than when he was in it.

In spite of these handicaps the Earl felt his first duty was the advancement of his family's greatness, and one of their continuing lacks was a house in London. They always had to stay with their Herbert relations, the earls of Pembroke, at their house in Baynard's Castle, Upper Thames Street, and there in fact Algernon was born.*

* The Herberts were among the most important Sidney connections, both socially and politically. The connection arose through Sir Philip Sidney's sister Mary, who had married the Earl of Pembroke, at whose country seat he spent his exile from court writing the *Arcadia*. The famous lines to her (Underneath this sable hearse ...) are disputed between Ben Jonson and William Browne. The first Sidney Earl of Leicester almost certainly owed his Welsh heiress and representation of Glamorgan to the immense interest of the Herberts in South Wales (see L. B. John, *The Parliamentary*

The Earl decided that his own contribution to the family grandeur would be a London mansion, and for this purpose he acquired a large plot in open country, not far from Westminster, which still preserves the name of Leicester Square, though the house he built there has long vanished.

This apparently brilliant investment was to prove the ruin of his family, both financially and domestically, and brooded over the Earl and his sons all their lives. Although the Sidneys were wealthy, with estates in six counties besides their native Kent, they were not nearly so rich as the great noble families like the Percys and the Herberts, whose social equals they now claimed to be. They had risen primarily by office, and old Sir Henry had watched every penny; but his son Robert had done little in the official world and his ascent in the social one under James I must undoubtedly have been expensive. The fact was that the Sidneys still needed the rewards of high office if they were to maintain their position.

Unfortunately, the Stuart Kings paid the rewards of civil and military office in arrears if they paid them at all, but the Earl hopefully did his duty by serving as an ambassador, first in Denmark and then in England's premier diplomatic post, Paris, although his retiring habits subtracted from his representative usefulness. At Copenhagen he spent much of his time compiling memoranda about Danish institutions and social life, but they were never transmitted home or published, since he wrote entirely for his own satisfaction – a habit he transmitted to his son. In Paris he spent much of his time in bookshops and talking to scholars, Grotius among them. As a linguist he had a considerable range, for he was fluent in Latin, French, Spanish and Italian, but he used his talent more for reading than for conversation, and his wife once complained that he loved his books more than he did her – and certainly more than getting on in the world. 'If either business or ceremony to such persons as may be useful to you', she once wrote to him, 'be the occasion of your seldom writing, I do dispense with the omission; but if your old inclination to reading be the cause, I do not forgive it.'[4]

Fellow-politicians were hesitant about the Earl's fitness for high office. Clarendon noted that he was well-read and addicted to mathematics but felt he was 'rather a speculative than a practical man, who expected greater certitude in the consultation of business

Representation of Glamorgan – unpublished Ph D Thesis of the University of Wales, 1934).

then the business of this world is capable of'.[5] Even Charles I, though himself far from decisive, was irritated by Leicester's alternating irresolution and obstinacy. Cromwell in his turn disliked and distrusted him. As time passed he became self-pitying and cantankerous, and smoked heavily: '3 lbs of tobacco for his Ldp' is a frequent entry in his steward's accounts. He was neither prudent and calculating, like his grandfather, nor ebullient and enterprising like his wife, and his private papers are filled with complaints about the injustices from which he suffered.

Two things especially preoccupied him: money, and his growing family. He often and gloomily reviewed his financial affairs and it must be admitted that his anxiety was justified. In the early 1630s he found that his income from property was only £4,000 a year, which by the standards of the times was substantial, but far from enough. From then onwards loans, mortgages and litigation cast gathering shadows on the Penshurst accounts, and the Earl's Will had to be repeatedly revised. He suspected his wife of making a profit on the household expenses, and made repeated complaints about her extravagance.

Algernon was the fourth surviving child of his family, with two elder sisters, Dorothy and Lucy, and an elder brother Philip, heir to both the estate and the name of the family hero. But many followed him, and in the end, out of the Countess's sixteen pregnancies, no fewer than eleven children grew to maturity; so that by 1640 the morning and evening prayers, at which the Earl required daily attendance by his whole household, must have been crowded. He contemplated his large family with depression – so many of them were girls who would have to be provided for. After Algernon came Ann, and then a third son bearing his own name Robert, and then five more daughters, Diana, Frances, Mary, Elizabeth and Isabella, with little Henry, a last unexpected arrival and the Countess's favourite, bringing up the rear. Marrying each of the seven girls would cost him a year's income for the settlement. Noble families never accepted less. Yet he did his duty by them, and between them two of the Sidney daughters were the ancestresses of five Prime Ministers.*

Most of Algernon's boyhood was spent in the Arcadia of

---

* From Dorothy descended the two Earls of Sunderland and Winston Churchill, and also the present Princess of Wales; from Lucy the Duke of Newcastle and his brother Henry Pelham.

Penshurst seeing this family grow, and gradually achieving a seniority in it. Successive owners since the medieval builders of the original hall had created a group of buildings in various styles which is now unique in England. The estate, which at this time covered four thousand acres, slopes gently up from the house to give an impression of peaceful remoteness, yet the village and its church are almost at the front door, the busy town of Tonbridge only a few miles away, and London itself, even in those days, was accessible in a few hours. So also was Calais, for Kent is England's finger pointing at the Continent.

Algernon had early experience of foreign travel. In 1632, when he was nine and his elder brother Philip was thirteen, the Earl took them to Denmark with him to introduce them to court life. The Thirty Years War was at its height, and the Earl demonstrated his sympathy with the Protestant cause by arranging for a Frankfurt publisher to mark his mission by printing the letters of Languet to Sir Philip Sidney.

The embassy lasted less than a year, and on his return to England the Earl made the first gestures towards the formal education of his sons by entering them at Gray's Inn. It was a common enough step, and in Algernon's case can hardly have been more than a formality, since he was only ten. But that he went away to school of some kind is shown by entries in the family accounts for 1634 describing what must be an outfit: 'a demi-carter hat with a silver band', provision for candles and medicine, and 'a bagg to put his books in'.[6]

Apart from this there is no record of Algernon's having attended any school or university; yet his command of Latin was not only sound but accomplished enough for him to take the place of official secretaries in drafting the final act of an international conference. He had a good knowledge of classical history, a passion for Tacitus, and a considerable range of modern languages. To some extent he must have been self-taught, but something he must have owed to Dr Henry Hammond, who became rector of Penshurst in 1633, at the age of twenty-eight, direct from a studentship at Christ Church, Oxford.

It is said that Hammond owed his appointment to a sermon which the Earl (who was of course the patron of Penshurst) heard him preach at court, but his connection with the Sidneys went back a good deal further. His wife was a Temple, daughter of that same

William Temple who had been Sir Philip Sidney's secretary and been present at his death-bed. After an uncomfortable implication in the Essex affair which followed, William Temple had established himself in Ireland where he acquired large holdings of land, and became a rather aggressive Provost of Trinity College Dublin. His son, the new rector of Penshurst's brother-in-law, was a gentleman of the bedchamber to Charles I and acted as the Earl's principal Whitehall correspondent and adviser. This Sir John Temple's name will figure in Algernon's later history, as will that of his son Sir William, Charles II's adviser on foreign affairs, and the patron of Swift, but most famous as the lover and husband of Dorothy Osborne.

The rector did not share the puritanical tendencies of the Sidneys and the Temples, and the Countess had reservations about his preaching, which she felt lacked spontaneity, for he insisted always on using notes. His Anglicanism was impeccable but he was far from being a mere scholarly conformist. When the moment came he showed himself a man of action and principle, quitted his benefice to wear a sword for the King, and went on to play a not unimportant part as spiritual and political adviser to Charles during the last phase of his life. It was from this decisive side of Hammond's character – so much on contrast with the Earl's – that Algernon perhaps drew most.

Soon after the Earl returned from Denmark with his two sons, the boys had their portrait painted at Penshurst. It is a far from happy picture. Philip, now sixteen and at Christ Church, looks a sullen, opinionated adolescent, and though Algernon, at twelve, with his flaming red hair similar to the lock of his great-uncle's which had been carefully preserved, seems more biddable, the expression on his face is very resolute. The mutual resentment of the brothers which was to last as long as Algernon lived was clearly implanted young. Philip was deeply conscious of his heirship, and though intelligent enough was self-centred, with little warmth or generosity in his character. Algernon was made to feel his position as younger brother keenly as a result, and the fact that until little Henry was added to the family he was mother's favourite probably did not help matters. She wrote enthusiastically to her husband about his progress. But in the mid 1630s the family's main pre-occupation was with the future of Dorothy, its first born, who was now eighteen. Her beauty had already aroused attention, and a reflective nature went with it. Few women of her time dealt better or more generously with the difficult years when they came. Her parents had refrained from throwing their treasure into court life at Whitehall, but that she should be married soon and well was an understood thing. Money would not be the first consideration. Social and political connection would be the deciding factors, and Dorothy, who had a mind of her own, was resolved not to be rushed. She had plenty of choice.

Edmund Waller, who has immortalized her in 'Go lovely rose' and the unfortunate alias 'Sacharissa' with its sugary overtone that so annoyed Dr Johnson,* made valiant efforts and was undoubtedly rich, as well as the nephew of John Hampden. But there was much against him which his excellent verses could not conquer. He was over thirty and a widower, and both the older Sidneys and Dorothy herself probably saw through him as wanting to buy his way into the aristocracy. Lady Leicester does not even mention his suitorship in her long letters to her husband and her sister the Countess of Carlisle. The family were right about Waller, for in due course he betrayed both the Parliament and the King. He toadied to Cromwell and sought preferment from Charles II, addressing excellent poems to both with as little success as he did to Dorothy. The badness of his character (there is no other word for it) is shown by the poisoned letter he sent when he was finally rejected, in which he congratulates Dorothy on her eventual marriage, wishes her a husband as good as he would have been, and hopes she will have early, numerous, and noisy children to be followed by a ripe old age that would give her time to reflect on the loss of her looks.

Dorothy's future was still unsettled in 1636 when the Earl was appointed ambassador in Paris. To accept this distinguished post he had to raise the huge sum of £10,000 by charging his estates, and leave the whole management of his domestic affairs, including Dorothy, to the Countess. Again he decided to take both his elder sons with him to enlarge their experience of diplomatic life.

Algernon thus spent four of his first sixteen years abroad as a privileged visitor to three of Europe's major capitals, for the embassy included an official visit to Rome and an audience with Pope Urban VIII. He saw at first hand the political and diplomatic worlds behind the scenes of the Thirty Years War which seemed so distant to most

---

* 'It suggests a spiritless mildness and dull good nature such as excites rather tenderness than esteem.' Johnson, *Lives of the Poets*.

Englishmen, yet was not without its influence on the mood of the English Parliament when it was at last again convened in 1640. Above all it gave him the training of a diplomat and commentator on foreign affairs, which was by no means commonplace, and it polished his languages in which he became as fluent as his father.

Left to rule Penshurst, and relieved of regular pregnancy by her husband's absence, the Countess threw herself into arranging his political future and Dorothy's marriage. She naturally consulted the Earl from time to time (sometimes in cipher) but her advisers also included her brother, the Earl of Northumberland, her sister, the widowed Countess of Carlisle (who was Strafford's mistress and a great friend of the Queen) and the family's ear at court, Sir John Temple.

Several more suitors were rejected, including a young Cavendish who turned out to have poor financial prospects and incipient signs of dissipation; but at last, in 1639, the matter was decided in favour of Lord Spencer, soon to be Earl of Sunderland. He was four years younger than Dorothy, who was now twenty-two, and the Spencers insisted on a very expensive settlement, but he shared Dorothy's qualities in being good-looking, honourable and brave. When the war broke out between the King and Parliament he remarked that he did not want to fight at all but, since fight he must, he was hanged if he would fight for the Parliament, and supposed he would fight for the King. This he accordingly did, and his death in a cavalry charge in 1643 brought an end to a brief but happy marriage.

On the political front the plan was that the Earl would move from the Paris embassy to fill an expected vacancy as Secretary of State. There were high hopes by both Lady Carlisle and Sir John Temple that Strafford, now the most powerful of Charles's ministers, would support the idea, as would the Earl's brother-in-law, Northumberland, who was Lord High Admiral. With their help the expected opposition of Archbishop Laud, who distrusted the churchmanship of both the Percys and the Sidneys, might be overcome. Lady Leicester wrote a personal appeal on behalf of her husband to the Queen, which was probably a mistake, for the Queen was extremely hostile to the Earl's promotion. But the decisive factor in the failure of the plan may well have been the King's dislike of appointing a minister to whom he was now deeply in debt. For three years the Earl had received nothing towards his salary and expenses in Paris, so the King owed him many thousands, of which he kept careful notes, to be used as a basis for reminders from time to time about this 'long and tedious business to the end that he may satisfie those to whom he is still indebted and free your Majesty of their and his further importunity'.[7] It is a small but striking illustration of the difficulties the King was now facing, which drove him in the following year to reassemble Parliament.

In an evil hour for himself the King decided to assign the vacant Secretaryship to Sir Henry Vane, a political climber who had risen to be Treasurer of the Navy under the Earl of Northumberland. This was hard for the Sidneys to bear, and the blow was the more cruel because they knew the Vanes well as neighbours in Kent. One of the Vane girls was a close friend of Dorothy, and was probably Waller's 'Amoret'.

In the spring of 1639 the Earl decided that the approaching marriage of his daughter and his own political position required his presence in England. He obtained leave of absence from the embassy, and after depositing his two sons at Penshurst, posted on to visit the King, who was at York making preparations to enforce episcopacy in Scotland. It was, in fact, the preliminary to the Civil War, and the army the King was assembling was the first seen on English soil for half a century.

The Earl was deeply alarmed about these developments, and told the King so. 'It was not God's will [he wrote afterwards] that the King should follow the advice I gave him to accommodate his differences with the Scots, and not to make war, where nothing was to be gained and much lost, which the world hath since found to be very true.'[8] The King did his best to be pleasant to the Earl, and paid him the compliment of making him a Privy Councillor, while at the same time ignoring his advice, evading his references to arrears of salary, and suggesting he should return to his post as soon as possible.

The return to Paris had to be deferred for Dorothy's wedding on 20 July, but the Earl was in a far from genial mood. The cost of the festivities, the marriage settlement, the builders' accounts for the as yet unfinished house in London, the need for yet more cash to sustain his embassy and service his existing loans, meant rapid and painful arrangement of more mortgages, and among these was one taken out by the appropriately named Edward Leech on Wolsingham, one of the Sidney properties in Norfolk.

This very much affected Algernon. For three generations Wolsingham had provided for the second son while Penshurst and the other entailed lands passed to the eldest. Algernon's father and grandfather – both second sons – had had it in their time before succeeding to Penshurst, and it had been clearly promised to him in his turn. In making the mortgage the Earl told his son about this shadow on his future, and undertook that if the mortgage was not redeemed he would be provided for in some other way. As soon as possible after the wedding the Earl left for Paris, but not before taking one other significant step. He arranged a cipher with his brother-in-law Northumberland to cover a secret correspondence about the dangerous political times they saw ahead. One would contribute about foreign affairs, and the other on domestic developments.[9]

This in its small way is a symptom of the mistrust and dissimulation which almost wantonly came to pervade the political world in which Algernon grew to manhood. Always endemic, it was to become epidemic, so as to make it almost impossible for historians to give the satisfactory account of the fabric and structure of politics of the mid century for which the modern mind craves; for nothing was quite what it seemed to be. Apparent alliances and groupings of opinion dissolve and reunite in fresh patterns, and almost everyone in politics knows he can depend only on himself. They move not so much in personal groupings as among the focuses of power which they so often identify in the cipher-keys or 'characters' of which they are so fond – 'Parliament', 'The Reformed Religion', 'The City', 'The Scots', 'The Army', 'The Roman Catholics' – and in this lies much of the psychology of conspiracy, the politics of the plot, which infected their public life. It was not just that plots flourished, or that people were especially credulous about their extent. Politics came to be seen as a plot, and belief in plots – even as distinct from their existence – as a necessity of carrying them on. As Lord Halifax was to put it, whether a plot were true or not, once it had gained hold on the public mind, one had to believe it.

When the Earl of Leicester set out in July 1639 to resume his duties he took a different selection of his family. The Countess went with him (as a result, her favourite little Henry was born in Paris) and so did the newly married couple, Dorothy and her husband. Since the

Earl thought it was now the turn of Robert, the third son, to have foreign experience, Philip and Algernon were left behind at Penshurst with the six girls and Mrs Cotton, the housekeeper. Philip was twenty-one, and by the standards of the time fully qualified to preside over his future inheritance as well as sit in Parliament, to which he was returned, no doubt by the Admiralty influence controlled by his father-in-law Northumberland, as M.P. for Yarmouth, Isle of Wight. Algernon was then just seventeen.

The next two years, which must have been so important in the formation of Algernon's outlook, are an almost total gap in the surviving record of his personal life. Towards their end, in the spring of 1641, he seems to have paid a visit to his parents in Paris, for he was shot at by an over-zealous butler who mistook him and a friend in the embassy garden in the dusk for intruders.[10]

He had inherited his father's passion for study and one suspects he spent much of his time in the Penshurst library, where he may have just possibly found a manuscript copy of a work defending absolute monarchy recently completed by a neighbouring squire, Sir Robert Filmer. But uppermost in the thoughts of both brothers was the part they and their family would play in the conflict that was now clearly breaking out.

The Earl of Northumberland did not think the Parliament convened in the spring of 1640 would last long. 'Such as have dependence on the Court', he wrote to his brother-in-law in March, 'are in divers places refused; and the most refractorie persons chosen.' In May he was beginning to make up his mind. 'It greeves my soule,' he wrote to Paris, 'to be involved in these councells [he was still Lord High Admiral]; and the sense I have of the miseries that are like to ensue is held by some to be disaffection in me; but I regard little what those persons say or think of me.'[11] Very soon he was to play an important part in ensuring that the navy would side with Parliament, a move with decisive results. His sister, Lady Carlisle, was beginning to give up her long-standing affair with Strafford and was soon to transfer her attentions to John Pym. Sir John Temple was equally despondent, and wrote about the same time to the Earl of Leicester:

I cannot without much regret think of the present condition of these times, and the weake constitution of this state to beare these shocks and violent concussions it is like to encounter withal. We had needs of able men to carrie it through; otherwise it may peradventure perish in our dayes et nous tous accabler en sa ruine.[12]

In the spring of 1641 the axe, laid aside for political purposes for more than a generation, was to be used again, but this time at the behest of Parliament, not in defence of the royal power; and by the death of Strafford the best chance the King ever had of recovering his position ended in a severe psychological defeat.

II

Background of Choice

THERE were many families of quality within easy riding distance of Penshurst, for the gentry of Kent were the most numerous and richest in the kingdom. They were also the most intellectual and enterprising, and there were many scholarly squires, and many with business interests in London. Some of them were concerned in the potentialities of America, especially Virginia. Two neighbouring families in particular were to have a lasting influence on Algernon's life: the Filmers of East Sutton, who came to represent all he detested, and the Vanes of Shipbourne, who provided him with the man he most admired of all men he knew in his life.

The Sidneys possessed many connections with the Filmers. The eldest daughter was a great friend of Dorothy's, and one of her brothers carried out some important errands for the Earl in 1640. The head of the family, Sir Robert, was not only a landowner and a magistrate but had a legal practice in London, mainly concerned with ecclesiastical cases. He had ginger hair, strong opinions, and an argumentative turn of mind, with ideas strongly favouring the established order. Studious, and even learned in an unsystematic way, Sir Robert devoted himself to finding a justification for his conservative beliefs, and thought he had found it in scripture, the law, but above all in the institution of the family. This last he felt to be his particular insight into the problem of obligation, and he embodied it in the book which was to lie unpublished for forty-two years, then emerging to fame and controversy in 1679 as *Patriarcha*.*

Filmer was not a disciplined thinker, and much fun has been made of him, but his contribution to political thought was original, in that unlike most earlier thinkers he absolutely denied the existence, or even the possibility, of natural rights, by pointing to the undoubted fact that far from being born free man comes into the world a helpless little being, totally dependent on those about him, especially his parents. From this he went on to argue (the inference is not logical) that there is a sense in which authority is always to be obeyed because that is the definition of authority, and if its commands cease to be obeyed because they are not regarded as right it is simply replaced by another source of legitimacy. But it is better (so Filmer thought) to attempt no such step as the replacement of existing authority. However wrong it may appear to be, it has the authority of the head of a family. These ideas were wrapped up in a ludicrous and easily demolished notion that Kings derived their authority by patriarchal descent from Noah. It did not need much research to point to the fact that monarchies (that of King David for instance) had at some stage in their history been founded on force, fraud, or popular choice, but Filmer's legal training made him a prisoner of the doctrine that kingship was in the nature of an estate descending like land by primogeniture in the male line, and strangely, though he had been born in the reign of Queen Elizabeth I, he never confronted the problem of how her sovereignty could be reconciled with his theory. Children, and even idiots, he maintained, provided they were eldest sons, could be the fathers of their peoples and ultimate authorities. If asked for further justification of this principle he pointed to the need for certainty in the source of power and its transmission.†

It was quite common for the intellectual gentry of Kent to

---

* For a full account of the textual history of *Patriarcha* see P. Laslett's edition (Blackwell, 1949) which describes the discovery of the MS *editio princeps* in 1939 and makes the necessary inference that more than one other MS copy must have been in existence.

† 'It is true, all kings be not the natural parents of their subjects, yet they all either are, or are to be reputed, as the next heirs of those progenitors who were at first the natural parents of the whole people, and in their right succeed to the exercise of the supreme jurisdiction. And such heirs are not only lords of their own children, but also of their brethren, and all others that were subject to their Fathers.' *Patriarcha* v.

publish their work or, if not, to circulate it in manuscript copies, and Filmer did both. With *Patriarcha*, he took the latter course. It appears to have been written about 1637, and he clearly considered it important, for several copies were made and one, in his own best legal hand, was bound handsomely with the royal arms embossed on both covers. It may have been intended as a presentation copy for the King himself.

It would be very extraordinary if awareness of *Patriarcha*'s composition, and probably a copy of the manuscript itself, did not reach so near and great a house as Penshurst very quickly. The Earl was after all chairman of the bench on which Filmer sat.

This at any rate offers a possible explanation for some otherwise puzzling facts: Algernon's minute knowledge of the *Patriarcha*, and his apparent ability to compose a voluminous reply to it within a fairly short time of its later appearance in print; and his reference (in 1683) to having worked on such a reply for many years past. All point to his having seen the text long before its publication in 1679. What is more, some of his quotations from Filmer vary considerably from that printed text.

Between 1638 and 1640, Algernon was outside the shadow of his own family patriarch, and for much of the time also of his elder brother, to whom Filmer taught he was all his life to be subject after their father's death, now that the small vestige of independence offered by the Norfolk estate had disappeared. The one other career open to a young man of his rank – the church – was closed to him by his father's parsimony in denying him a university education. It was a time for brooding and introspection. The patriarchal system argued with such fussy confidence by Filmer had not done at all well for him and in his ultimate reply to Filmer, *Discourses on Government*, one senses not only opposition to Filmer's ideas but detestation of all the man stood for.

Filmer's ideas were old fashioned even in his own time. Like the lawyer he was, he happily relies on precedents from the practice of kings and parliaments in the thirteenth, fourteenth and fifteenth centuries as valid for the seventeenth; quotes generously (often without acknowledgment) from Bodin's far abler work *La République*, which had been written more than sixty years before *Patriarcha*; and treats the sixteenth-century Jesuit Bellarmine almost as if he were a contemporary thinker. In fact the whole controversy centring on *Patriarcha* constitutes a warning against seeing ideas as

closely related to contemporary (or even recently preceding) literature or political structures. Filmer's ideas, formed when he was a
young man early in the seventeenth century, did not reach the
general public until its last two decades; and Algernon's reply to it
was not published until the very end of the seventeenth century,
having remained in manuscript almost as long as Filmer's book.

If one thinks of the history of political ideas as running more
or less hand in hand with chronological change this must seem
curious. But then society changed slowly, and England on the eve
of the Great Civil War was in many ways not very different from
the England of the Wars of the Roses. When magnates like Northumberland and Pembroke made their plans in 1639 for riding out
the impending storm they behaved much as their fifteenth-century
ancestors had done, and even when the war came its early battles
were fought in the same old way by local levies stiffened by hired
professionals and officered by gentry whose choice of side often had
very little to do with doctrine. The ancient law of treason, with its
barbarous penalties and peculiar quality of marking its victim for
doom as soon as he was accused, might have lain unused for decades
but now it was to claim hundreds of victims. The even more ruthless
procedure of attainder, which had not been employed for more than
a century and might have been thought of as obsolete, was still
there, to be used almost without hesitation to strike down Strafford.

The other neighbouring family, the Vanes, provided Algernon
with a hero and exemplar. Its head, Sir Henry Vane, had for many
years been following the ascending path which had been taken in
the sixteenth century by Algernon's great-grandfather, and just as
Sir William Sidney's fortunes had been founded as a courtier of a
Prince of Wales, so were Sir Henry Vane's. He was made Treasurer
to Charles, later Charles I, in 1617, and continued to have charge of
Charles's personal finances after his ascent to the throne. Other
offices and advantages followed, culminating in the secretaryship of
state which the Earl of Leicester had coveted, and a magnificent
property in Yorkshire, Raby Castle, which was to be Vane's Penshurst and (he hoped) provide a title for the peerage on which he
now relied. In 1640 he became the King's principal office-holder in
the House of Commons, where he sat as member for Wilton – a
constituency, incidentally, entirely controlled by the Earl of Pembroke.

The readiness with which this successful careerist was to turn on the monarchy he had so long served with such profit to himself is one of the most instructive indicators of the way the opposing forces in the coming struggle came to align themselves. It has been attributed partly to pique, and certainly Vane's victim, Strafford, made a serious mistake in deliberately stealing Vane's intended title of Lord Raby by preempting it as his own second title when he was raised to an earldom. One can infer from it that Strafford in his turn saw Vane as a danger to his plans, and that so long as he survived as a minister, a peerage for Vane under any title was unlikely to be forthcoming.

The eldest son of Sir Henry Vane was a far more outstanding man than his father, and during Algernon's two years of comparative isolation at Penshurst was the main reason for his visits to Shipbourne. Harry Vane (he had the same name as his father but the contraction by which he was usually known makes a convenient distinction) was ten years older than Algernon and had already achieved an extraordinary career. In 1639 he had just returned from America, where he had spent two remarkable years, for one of which he had been, at the age of twenty-three, the youngest governor Massachusetts has ever had. He owed the post entirely to his outstanding personality and the votes of the struggling dissident community of an infant colony.

Harry, unlike Algernon, was an eldest son, and the two had first met during the Earl's embassy to Denmark in 1633 when Algernon was only ten and Harry was an attaché in the Earl of Leicester's suite; so it seems likely that Algernon's admiration for Harry originated very early in his life.* But soon after returning from Denmark Harry had decided, very much against his father's wishes, that the career of courtly diplomacy was not for him, and embarked on his adventure in Massachusetts.

Political calculation, for which Harry became a byword among his detractors, cannot have played a part in this move. While still at school he had gone through a religious experience which left a permanent mark, and led him gradually to reject all forms of organized religion, and so become a 'Seeker', who believed that while

---

* The appointment of Harry Vane to the Earl's suite would have been entirely a personal favour by the Earl to his neighbour Sir Henry Vane. There is other evidence to show the closeness of the Sidney and Vane families. Margaret Vane, Harry's sister, and Lucy Sidney, Algernon's, were close companions, and both made marriages into the Pelham family, just across the county boundary in Sussex.

God was assuredly to be found, the finding of the way to him was for the individual alone. Yet he was far from being a solemn precisian, in either manner or style. His wit and vivacity struck everyone who met him.

By the time he returned to England he already had more direct experience of real politics than most English politicians. It is true that experience had been in a miniature state of a few thousand inhabitants, but it had included a war and uninhibited politico-sectarian disputes, which in the end had led to his overthrow. He was now preparing to launch himself on a larger political stage, and was once more reconciled with his father, through whose good offices he was nominated as M.P. for the important northern naval base of Hull in the forthcoming Parliament, and to the valuable office of Joint Treasurer of the Navy. He was knighted, and was married – all in 1640.

Those who knew him were always impressed by a kind of magnetic quality. He was not physically impressive – Algernon admits that his hero was far from being a tall man, and was 'rather inclining to fat' – but even Clarendon, who regarded Harry Vane as a most dangerous enemy, comments on his 'great natural parts, profound dissimulation, and very ready, sharp, and weighty expression'. Then Clarendon adds something he found difficult to put into words: 'He had an unusual aspect, which, though it might naturally proceed from his father and mother, neither of which were beautiful persons, yet made men think there was something in him of the Extraordinary.'

Algernon wrote a eulogy of Harry Vane in which one can see the effects of this magnetism.

> His countenance was grave and serene, with an air that was august and venerable; his conversation was diverting and easie, with a good deal of eloquence and wit, full of facetious and innocent mirth. He had the mildest disposition imaginable, his principles were honest and sincere, ready to do good to all mankind, grateful and obliging to those he esteem'd good, of an inviolable Fidelity, one whom nobody ever repented of trusting with the most important affairs.

Algernon regarded the elder Vane with complete contempt as one 'too long versed in the corrupt intrigues of an infamous court': but the younger as 'the glory and support of a reviving state'. He was overgenerous to his hero in claiming for him a complete absence of deviousness, and more than one of Vane's contemporaries, including Cromwell, came to regret the trust they placed in him: but the second tribute to him as the glory of the reviving state is amply deserved. Unlike most of the leaders of the great rebellion who have captured the historical memory he was essentially a civilian, and always renounced the role of a military chief. But as a parliamentarian and an administrator he has claims to real greatness and originality. Without his efforts and extraordinary personality it is very doubtful if the House of Commons would have emerged as the victor. He was, perhaps, the first great parliamentary politician in the modern sense, the first to see that the House of Commons, by itself, as an institution, could be made into a power-base for government. Though his approach to the many political problems of his life was often devious there was always at the core of it a drive towards a rational solution which is uncommon among the politicians of his time, whether fanatical or manoeuvring.

On 10 December 1640, when the Long Parliament had been sitting for about a month, Northumberland wrote to Leicester to say that he had again raised with the King the possibility of Leicester's becoming Secretary of State. He had done so with some diffidence because there was now an open difference of opinion between him and the King on the subject of Strafford, who was already under attack in Parliament, and he had not been surprised to find Charles unresponsive to his suggestion. His other significant piece of news was that Sir Henry Vane was 'thinking of changing his condition'. In fact he was planning to change sides, and the part he and his son played in the downfall of Strafford by their well-timed revelations of state secrets was decisive. Harry Vane in a few months established himself as one of the leading politicians in the House of Commons.

The elimination of Strafford in May 1641 led to an application from the Earl of Leicester for the vacant Lord Lieutenancy of Ireland and in June Algernon's father was appointed to the place which old Sir Henry Sidney had four times filled with such distinction. It took him some time to disentangle himself from his embassy in Paris and though he was briefly in England in May he did not arrive in England permanently until October, the very month Ireland burst into rebellion.

The reciprocal effects of English and Irish politics on one another have never been more profound than in the period which was now opening. Without the shadow of Strafford's Irish connection and the vision of him at the head of a savage Irish army sent to subjugate England, the attack on him could hardly have succeeded. Now the same stories began to be attached to the King himself, assisted by lurid reports of the horrors of the rebellion. The truth was bad enough, but the journalists improved on it with pathetic accounts of the refugees, and the threat to protestantism in both islands, which swept through the heightened popular consciousness of London. The new politicians in the Commons seized on the issue with loud demands for the instant despatch of an army to put down the rebellion, and when the King seemed to hesitate, it was rumoured that he favoured the rebels. Parliament must act, and if necessary act alone. Men were recruited, money was raised. Nothing could have propelled Parliament more powerfully in the direction of assuming sovereignty for itself.

The new Lord Lieutenant found himself not only faced by a dangerous rebellion in the kingdom he was supposed to govern, but caught in the centre of the developing conflict between King and Parliament. In this, one of the big technological advances since the fifteenth century played a major part, for the conflict now in progress, which resembles the Wars of the Roses in some respects, is a War of the Roses with newspapers. The new-born press that had come into existence with the disappearance of effective censorship and plenty to write about, turned Leicester into a prominent figure. There was a rumour that he was being poisoned by catholic agents. Lists of the regiments he was raising were printed. Certainly he did set about organizing an expeditionary force which included a regiment of infantry under an experienced professional officer, Lieutenant Colonel George Monk, who had till recently been serving in the King's operations against Scotland. The force sailed for Ireland before the end of the year.

Both Algernon and his brothers found themselves involved in these plans. That summer their uncle Northumberland had been trying to find the boys jobs, but hopes that Algernon would be given a commission in the Dutch army fell through when the Prince of Orange decided to confer it elsewhere. Now they were to be cavalry officers in the Irish expeditionary force, and Philip was to command the Lord Lieutenant's own regiment of horse, with Algernon and his next brother Robert as troop commanders. They set off with their regiment early in December 1641 and for the next eighteen months Algernon was to learn soldiering and politics in the miserable and treacherous world of the Irish rebellion. The second in command of his regiment was Sir Richard Grenville, one of the most odious commanders of the Civil War.

The Earl was also party, that winter, to the scheme hatched by Parliament and the City to pay for the war in Ireland. This plan, which was agreed to by the King and perhaps did more than any violence to poison Anglo-Irish relations, was based on the idea that the Irish themselves should pay for putting down their rebellion. The money advanced by the City for the expeditionary force was therefore secured on land belonging to Irish rebels which would be confiscated when the rebellion had been crushed. Later parliamentary thinking on finance was to be on the same lines, for when it came to war with the King (or rather his partisans, for the parliamentarians were always careful never to say the King was their actual opponent) the estates of those opposed to Parliament would be liable for the costs of both sides.

Lord Leicester spent the winter of 1641–42 in London, trying to balance the conflicting wishes of his two masters, either of whom, he now began to see, could independently decide to dismiss him. Important elements in this dilemma were firstly that the King still owed him a large sum for previous services and did not look as if he was in a position to pay either that or his salary as Lord Lieutenant; and secondly that Parliament had been careful to pass resolutions approving his appointment and coming close to guaranteeing his salary. His was an impossible task because the purpose of both King and Parliament was to use the Irish war in their conflict against one another, and nothing could be more hypocritical than the lengthy exchange of messages between them in which each asserted their determination to end the rebellion but made insinuations about the good faith of the other side.

Why Leicester should have ever taken the post of Lord Lieutenant at this dangerous time is difficult to explain. He was naturally a shy man; and as a practised diplomatist must have understood the basic conflict. Though he had some land in Ireland it was not an important asset. One can only guess that he was influenced by a tradition of public service, especially in Ireland, the glory of succeeding his grandfather as a viceroy, and his financial needs.

Even in easy times, he was quite unsuitable for such a role and both his quarrelling masters must have seen it, as must all his sons.

Yet he persisted. At one point in the exchanges about Ireland between King and Parliament that winter, the King thought he had played a trump card by declaring he intended to go to Ireland himself and reduce it to order. It was a step that would have eliminated the need for any viceroy, and for a moment the parliamentarians were shaken, but the bluff was called. Leicester's dilemma, he complained afterwards, made him so inattentive to his own finances that he had to leave them to the Countess, but if the King was not going to Ireland then he at least would.

His brother-in-law Northumberland saw matters more clearly, as Lord High Admiral. That spring of 1642 he made sure that in the conflict that was now breaking out the navy, which was the one permanent armed force England possessed, would not be available to the King. In summer the Civil War formally began. Most peers and about a third of the House of Commons sided with the King and abandoned Westminster, but Leicester's most powerful relations threw in their lot with the majority of the House of Commons which proclaimed the parliamentary cause.

Commitment

THE young Sidneys took some time to move their six hundred cavalry to Ireland, and did not disembark at Dublin until late December 1641 when the rebellion had been in progress for two months. They were greeted by at least one familiar face in the family's old dependent Sir John Temple, who was now Master of the Rolls in Ireland and a member of the Irish Privy Council responsible for the civilian side of government. Their immediate superior as Commander-in-Chief, the Earl of Ormonde, who had recently returned from a conference with the King, kept Philip, now Lord Lisle, with the bulk of his cavalrymen in Dublin for service against the rebels in the Pale, but Algernon, with his troop of 72 horse, was sent north to strengthen the fortresses of Drogheda and Dundalk. For several generations there had been no love lost between Ormonde's family, the Butlers, and the Sidneys.

Dublin watched events at Westminster as passionately as Westminster watched Ireland, but the pattern of reciprocity was not the same. The Irish rebellion itself had been touched off by the English domestic conflict over the fate of Strafford, under whose six years of government Ireland had prospered. He had set himself to foster economic development and although head of an Anglican establishment had been easy-going in matters of religion. Ireland, in his day, had been a well-administered colony where peace and order reigned, good relations with native rulers and local opinion were preserved, and attention was given to public works and agricultural improvement. Strafford had been a popular governor – not at all the iron tyrant denounced in England – but it was not so much his personal fate as the triumph it gave to the English parliamentary opposition that had caused the Catholic gentry of the Pale to rise, in the justifiable fear that the strengthened hand of Parliament would now fall heavily on Catholic Ireland.

So began, in the words of Bellings, the contemporary historian of the rebellion, this 'warr of many parts, carried on under the notions of soe many interests, perplexed with such diversity of rents and divisions, among those who seemed to be of a side, as will transmitt to posterity observations perhaps as usefull, although not soe memorable and full, as a warr manadged with more noise, greater power, and between Princes.'[1]

By the time the Sidney brothers arrived the rebellion had already assumed the complexity this so well describes, with neither rebels nor those supposed to suppress them acting with any semblance of unity, and all parties watching anxiously to see how developments in England would affect their positions. If the King was to gain the upper hand some rebels at any rate would support a government in his name; if Parliament, a section of the Dublin government would make common cause with the rebels. As the factions warred and manoeuvred against each other – 'Old' and 'New' English, native catholic gentry, local war lords, Scotch presbyterian settlers – the peasantry, finding nobody to stop them, paid off old scores and drove away the cattle. Philip and Algernon can be forgiven for not being quite sure whom they were supposed to be fighting and whence their orders were supposed to come.

They fully expected that orders would come from their father himself, and the Earl actually set out for his new government in January. He even got as far as Chester, but was recalled peremptorily by the King to avoid prejudicing the negotiations with Parliament (and possibly because the King had no desire to supersede Ormonde by an hereditary opponent of his family). Many, including probably the young Sidneys themselves, thought the recall of Leicester showed that the King was not carrying on these negotiations in good faith, and that when the moment came he would compromise with the Irish rebels. In view of what was soon to happen they were probably right. Leicester remained Lord Lieutenant, but virtually without influence, and the young Sidneys found themselves subordinate to the Earl of Ormonde.

Ormonde had been trained by Strafford as his right-hand man and natural successor, but for that very reason could not now possibly enter into the post he had so confidently expected. He can hardly have welcomed the Sidneys as representatives of the man who had been appointed instead, and probably had them in mind when he commented that 'the English lately sent over did not well agree with the old or new raised forces in Ireland'.[2] To his credit he put up with them, but this did not stop him, as the months passed, from by-passing their father and corresponding direct with the King, any more than it stopped them from relying more on their father's instructions than on his.

It was in the civilian element of the Dublin government that the Sidneys found their friends. The Irish Privy Council, on the whole, looked to Parliament as protectors of the protestant interest but, more particularly, of what was known as the 'New' English interest of official and business families who had settled from the mainland during the past hundred years or so. The Temples were such a family, and Sir John had an additional reason for disliking the Earl of Ormonde. Temple was a contractor for army supplies and the Commander-in-Chief strongly suspected him of profiteering. On this subject Temple corresponded at length with his old patron the Lord Lieutenant, who had quite enough reasons already to be irritated about the Earl of Ormonde, but was powerless to do anything about it.

Supplies (and pay) were the perpetual anxiety for all seventeenth-century armies, but in very few can they have been more pressing than in Ireland that autumn of 1642. The cavalry, in particular, were 'endureing all the extremetyes of want, not having so much money or credit as wherewith to shoe a horse'. There were noisy protests from the officers. 'Within these four dayes', the Lords Justices wrote to London, 'several captaines and officers came with considerable numbers to us ... and openly expressed the sense of their sufferings in so high termes, so passionately, and with so little estimacion of our authoritye, finding us unable to pay them, as we find manifestly that notwithstanding all our endeavours, it is now become utterly impossible to containe this army any longer from dispanding.'[3] Some commanders were reduced to turning their soldiers back into the farmhands they had so recently been, to raise crops of vegetables in commandeered fields. But neither King nor Parliament came forward with the money to finance the war which both professed to consider so important. The King had none. The money raised by Parliament to reconquer Ireland on the security of confiscated Irish land was now diverted to the preparations for war in England. It would not be much of an exaggeration to say that Ireland was now being asked to pay not only for the Irish civil war but in large measure for the English one as well.

Philip and Algernon corresponded regularly with their parents, the elder mostly with his father and the younger, significantly, with his mother. Much of what must have been an interesting if doleful series of letters has disappeared, and those from England would have told the two boys how the war was breaking out all over the country and men were making their own choices. Most of the important Sidney relations – not only Northumberland and Pembroke, but Manchester, Essex, Warwick, Salisbury and Holland – openly rallied to Parliament and the only significant exception was Dorothy's young husband Lord Spencer.

The Temple connection was split. The rector of Penshurst, after refusing to attend a committee which the House of Commons had set up for depriving scandalous ministers, left in disguise at the head of a troop of cavalry he had raised for the King. His nephew, later to gain fame as Charles I's gaoler at Carisbrooke, joined the Parliamentary forces, and his brother-in-law, the rev. Thomas Temple, who had a living in Bedfordshire, preached enthusiastically for the Parliamentary cause. At the end of May Parliament resolved that the King was waging war on his people. In July the first blows of the Civil War were struck near Manchester. And on 22 August 1642 the hoisting of the royal standard at Nottingham formally began the conflict.

For month after month the Sidney brothers dragged on a miserable existence without pay or prospects or even a chance of deciding where they stood, for their powerless father refused to come down on either side. There were no pitched battles – only raids, skirmishes and punitive expeditions in which villages harbouring (or supposed to be harbouring) rebels were destroyed. In August Algernon was quartered in Bishops Court, Leinster, then at Trim, then at Rathmines, by which time his original troop of 72 horse had shrunk to 30. He now also had an infantry company which was found to produce 23 officers and men on parade out of a nominal strength of 49. The rest were listed as absent, deserted or dead. In many parts of the island the writ of the Dublin government no longer ran, and inside the government tension increased as the two contestants in England competed more and more openly for exclusive control of Ireland. In November 1642 two representatives of Parliament, Reynolds and Goodwin, arrived in Dublin and after inviting themselves to seats on the Irish Privy Council began to try to bring the army under parliamentary control, with Algernon's elder brother Philip as its commander.* At about the same time Ormonde reported to the King that he regarded Lisle as an unreliable officer. Lisle, relying on his position as commander of the cavalry, claimed the right to act as Ormonde's deputy with the rank of Lieutenant-General. The wretched Earl of Leicester, ignored by all the principal parties, was kept abreast of events by long letters from Sir John Temple which interlarded his usual personal complaints about Ormonde.[4]

Early in the New Year the parliamentary emissaries departed, convinced that there was mischief somewhere, and so there was. In February 1643 the King, without telling his Lord Lieutenant, wrote to Ormonde instructing him to patch up an agreement with the rebels and (this part was in cipher) to bring back the English forces in Ireland to support the royal cause on the mainland. The first part of this message quickly became known, and the secret part was widely suspected.

Charles's action, though perfectly understandable in the circumstances, was never forgotten or forgiven by the Sidneys. It was covert, it was a betrayal (or so it seemed to them) of the Protestant Cause, and worst of all an insult to their family – both father and sons. It is true that the Earl hung on a bit longer to his ineffectual viceroyalty, but no Sidney thereafter trusted a Stuart.

While these orders were still on their way Ormonde decided on a serious spring campaign and an end to sporadic and destructive raiding. Algernon and Philip thus faced their first real battle, for all the available cavalry – some eight hundred of them – were assembled

---

* The parliamentary mission brought some money with it. Though quite inadequate to serve any serious purpose (only £20,000) it may be significant that in November and December modest sums were issued to help officers' messes ('drink money' at the rate of a shilling a day per officer for a week in each case). Lord Lisle signed for thirty-nine names, Algernon for twenty-eight.

to take part, with Philip in command. Altogether the government's army numbered about 3,000 men, rather smaller than the rebel force commanded by the Catholic Lord Preston which had appeared in the south east of Ireland. Lisle had hoped to command the field force, but Ormonde, no doubt realizing the challenge this might bring to his authority, took charge himself, so it was with a thoroughly disgruntled cavalry commander that they encountered the enemy on 19 March 1643 at a place called New Ross, some twenty miles north of Wexford.

Ormonde was victorious, but the battle reflected no credit on Philip Lisle, who galloped off the field at a critical stage in the fighting, carrying a number of his men with him and shouting, according to some eye-witnesses, for a guide to Dungannon. The troops had to be rallied by a wounded subordinate and Lisle was the recipient of some strong language from the regimental doctor about poltroonery. Whether it was loss of nerve or the worse offence of deliberately trying to lose the battle out of pique, Philip never quite lived it down.

Algernon was present at the action but there is no record of either his behaviour or his thoughts. It was not his character to betray, and his respect for his elder brother, which was never very great anyway, can hardly have increased. There was a military enquiry, of which Monk was a member, in which the wounded Major Norris testified to Philip Lisle's loss of nerve, and described how he himself had to rally the men and lead them back into action. The record of the enquiry, with the findings significantly torn off, survives in the De L'Isle papers.[5]

So long as the Earl clung to his meaningless Lord Lieutenancy his sons were expected to stay in Ireland, but serious strains on that feeble policy were now appearing as Ormonde's negotiations with the rebels began. In London furious parliamentarians denounced Ormonde as a traitor, and in Dublin the pro-parliamentary party trembled for their future under the threatened 'Pacification'. For the young Sidneys the alarming prospect was opening up (Ormonde's secret orders could not long be concealed) of being shipped back to England with their men to fight for the King, whether they liked it or not. They were, in fact, being driven to a choice.

On 18 June 1643 Algernon wrote to his mother seeking family permission to come home. After making the point that Ireland was now 'noe fit place for me to stay in', he insists on his need for a career. He is a younger son 'that hath no stock to rely upon. I have already suffered something in that kind.' But a civilian post, with its inevitable reliance on favour, he utterly rejects. 'I am not likely,' he writes proudly, 'to seeke after those employments which others receive with greedinesse.' In short he would have to choose a side and fight. 'Nothing but extreame necessities shall make me think of bearing arms in England, and yet it is the only way for those that have not estates, and, besides there is soe few that abstaine from warre for the same reason as I doe [this seems to be a covert hit at his father's neutralism] that I do not know that in many men's eyes it prove dishonourable to me.'[6]

This insistence on honour and reputation almost suggests Algernon did not then particularly care which side he fought on, and sensitiveness about his standing in society remained one of the strongest traits in his character. But although he gave no indication of his choice in the letter (which was just as well, because it fell into enemy hands) there can be little doubt that his choice was made. He wanted to come back to England before being sent there as part of Ormonde's army so that he could freely choose to fight for Parliament.

Nor did he wait for a reply. Before the end of June both brothers, accompanied by Sir Richard Grenville, left Ireland secretly and landed near Manchester, then controlled by Parliamentary forces who promptly arrested them, and they were held in custody for nearly three months. Any officers coming from Ireland at that moment were bound to arouse suspicions, and these were reinforced when Algernon was found to be carrying a letter addressed to the Cavalier commander in neighbouring Chester, Sir Orlando Bridgman. The local Parliamentarian commander, realizing that in Philip Lisle he had an M.P. among his prisoners and was therefore in breach of privilege, sent the party off to London under escort for the House itself to settle their future. What explanations were offered is not known, but the troublesome letter was smoothed away and Philip Lisle resumed his seat in Parliament while Algernon was left to reflect on his position. This was the only little ripple on his choice of Parliament, but it is just possible his story would have been different if he had landed from Ireland a little nearer Chester.

Ormonde moved rapidly in response to the King's orders and by the autumn of 1643 troops released by the Irish truce were disembarking at Minehead and Bristol to join the King's army.

English they might mainly be, but the cry was raised that they were no more than the vanguard of the savage Catholic army Parliament's propagandists always conjured up as ready to be launched against the mainland. As for Temple, who had stayed in Dublin, Ormonde lodged him in gaol as a profiteer.

Algernon spent that winter at Penshurst, where many influences must have converged on him to make him finally decide for Parliament. His mother favoured it; most of his near relations had already declared for it; the death of Hampden and the mortal illness of Pym had opened the heights of parliamentary politics and the organization of the war to Harry Vane, who was almost certainly a visitor to Penshurst in the autumn. Finally the Earl himself appeared at Penshurst in December, a humiliated and very angry man. The King had at last summoned up the resolution to dismiss him and give Ormonde the Lord Lieutenancy. He wrote a long and indignant letter to the Queen demanding an explanation, and although, even after this affront, he remained persistently neutral, his sons could no longer be embarrassed by having a father actually in attendance on the King at Oxford.

Algernon's engagement to the Parliamentary cause was not, then, a matter of sudden enthusiasm. Family pressures and family politics played their part, and so did his desire to make a name for himself; but it is impossible to doubt that his strongest motive – just as it was the strongest moving force in his character – was a sense of honour which (as often happens) came to be almost indistinguishable from conviction of the rectitude of the cause he had adopted. That had been reinforced by his interpretation of his experience in Ireland. There is little in his life to show that he shared the almost irrational horror of Irish Catholics that was felt by so many Englishmen of his time, and although he had seen dreadful things in Ireland he was in a position to take a balanced view of the atrocity stories that fed mainland prejudice. He was himself tolerant in matters of conscience and religion, which, as we shall see, extended even to the cardinals of Rome itself. But in his eyes the King had betrayed his trust in Ireland, which was to suppress the rebellion; and had done this secretly, by slow calculated steps, in order the better to wage war against his own people. From the winter of 1643–44 at the latest, Algernon became an enemy to any political system depending on the rule of a single man who was able to manipulate political factors secretly in his own mind before reaching decisions which then became binding on others.

The future of both brothers was settled in the early months of 1644. Philip's military career was to cease (the débâcle of New Ross was no doubt in mind here) but he would continue in Parliament as a supporter of its war and a guardian of the family's interests. Algernon was to take a commission in the Parliamentary army. Like the aristocrat he was he chose a personal motto, 'Sanctus Amor Patriae dat Animum' – 'sacred love of country gives one spirit'. These arrangements were duly confirmed by votes in the House of Commons on 10 May approving Algernon as a captain in his cousin the Earl of Manchester's regiment of horse, and awarding him the large sum of £400 for back pay. Philip got only formal thanks for his 'great and faithful services' – a political gesture against Ormonde rather than a recognition of his success.

Manchester's was one of the four cavalry regiments in the army raised by the Eastern Association, of which Manchester himself was general. Cromwell was his deputy and commander of the Eastern Association cavalry as a whole, which was already the best trained force on either side of what had so far been an amateurish and bumbling conflict. That May Cromwell's command was concentrated in the Midlands for training under his eye, when he received orders to march northwards.[7]

These orders show that although Algernon's commission as a captain had been approved only three days earlier, he was already a colonel commanding a regiment. He must in fact have joined well before being commissioned, and have impressed Cromwell as the kind of officer he wanted in the force which the enemy was soon to christen 'Ironsides'. Noble birth and good connections would not have helped him here, for Cromwell consistently despised gentleman amateurs, whether on his own side or the other.

The march northwards was part of a much larger strategic plan of which Harry Vane, now with the Parliamentary forces besieging York, was at the centre. Three parliamentary armies were to be concentrated in Yorkshire – those of the Eastern Association under Manchester, of the Yorkshire Association under Fairfax, and of the Scots under the Earl of Leven – with the objects of capturing York, opposing the enemy army that was advancing under Prince Rupert from the west to its relief, and then if possible sweeping Rupert out of Lancashire. If the plan succeeded Parliament would control all northern England and close at least some of the west coast ports to the dreaded Royalist reinforcements from Ireland. It might even open the way to a counter-attack across the Irish Sea. The resulting battle of Marston Moor was the biggest that has yet been fought on English soil.

Altogether more than 40,000 men were deployed by the two sides over a front of one and a half miles between the little villages of Long Marston and Tockwith. To Algernon, on the left of the Parliamentary army and facing eastwards at the head of a thousand well-trained men, everything he had seen of war till then must have seemed insignificant. The scale was six times what it had been at New Ross. Opposite him was the enemy's main cavalry force under Rupert himself. In the enemy centre, rather to Algernon's right, were infantry regiments which had recently arrived from Ireland: Algernon had fought alongside them only fifteen months ago.

The two armies that spoke the same language stared at each other all the summer afternoon without exchanging a shot, and most of the soldiers thought there would be no action that day. Then, suddenly, at half past seven with the setting sun behind him, Cromwell launched his four regiments at Rupert. Within a few minutes battle spread along the whole line. Algernon had the extraordinary experience of charging as part of an armoured force four thousand strong, whose weight and training drove the opposing cavalry from the field, but that was not all. Cromwell's troopers swept round the rear of the enemy to the rescue of their right wing which was shaking from a similar Royalist charge. This extraordinary initiative – unauthorized, so far as is known, by any of the three generals, seniors to him on the field – won the battle and made Cromwell's military reputation. The fighting went on till midnight when the last of the stubborn royalist Yorkshire infantrymen were cut down, driven from the field, or made prisoners.

Although about 4,000 royalists were killed casualties on the Parliamentary side were slight; but Algernon was among them. He was badly wounded, though whether in the initial impact with Rupert or later in Cromwell's famous manoeuvre is not known, and the injury, which was in the leg, left him with a limp. He was lucky to get out alive and described afterwards how he was rescued by a friendly trooper who refused to give his name. He had made his mark in the world, and as the chaplain to the Earl of Manchester's regiment put it in the newspapers, he had charged 'with great gallantry at the head of my lord's regiment of horse'.[9] He had shown he could fight for the opinions he had chosen and had recovered the family's good name from the discredit of New Ross. What was more, he was a genuine holder of the rank that in coming years was to count for much: Colonel.

The Essay on Love:
and Parliament

NONE of Sidney's works was published in his lifetime and it is difficult to decide when they were composed, but the earliest of them is undoubtedly the short piece known as the *Essay on Love*. It is the work of a young man, and may possibly belong to the period after Dorothy's wedding when he was left behind at Penshurst, but the likeliest time he would have had leisure and inclination to write it, would have been as a colonel of twenty-two recuperating from wounds received on the cavalry charge in which he had covered himself with glory. It is written with no thought of publication and its only purpose is to express his own thoughts and feelings: the dangerous habit he had inherited from his father.

Its sixteen pages, written at a time 'which I confess hath with more violence transported me than a man of understanding ought to be by any passion', gives us the only direct knowledge we have about his private feelings on the relationship between the sexes. Many more famous men have left less, but as something written from the heart it is a touching commentary on the life of colonel, parliamentarian, conspirator and martyr. Algernon never married, and the reason was neither misogyny or homosexuality. He was not an easy man, and he seemed shy and awkward to his contemporaries – particularly to women – but most men of his class did marry, and there is some evidence that he had affairs. The most likely explanation for his batchelordom is a conflict between pride of birth and bitter consciousness of poverty. From his earliest manhood he could see nothing to offer a wife except his sword and political adventure – and what family of his class would give their daughter and her dowry for that?

'Love', he begins, 'is the passion that hath passed all censures.' It can apply to anything in the world and every tendency of the people in it, but what he is concerned with is only one kind of love, the love 'to beauty, the height of which we call being in love': sexual passion.

He then (and it was unusual to put pen to paper about such a thing, even in private) decisively rejects homosexuality: 'That of man to man, if it go further than friendship (which little cares for beauty) I only take to be rooted in the most unnatural of vices, and therefore detestable; and, understanding nothing of it, I leave the discourse to those that do; and for that which I intend to mention, conclude it doth imply necessarily difference of sexes.'

Beauty was the test. 'Love is the most intensive desire of the soul to enjoy beauty; and where it is reciprocal is the most entire and exact union of hearts ... I can only conclude that whatsoever pleaseth the eye and fancy is beautiful; whatsoever we think beautiful we desire to enjoy, and that desire is love.'

Platonist as this may seem he was not writing an essay on aesthetics. The Puritan (if the term has any defining strength) and the colonel of Ironsides found a sexual instinct in him which he regarded as precious and saw his female partner as not only his equal but in many ways his superior. Human nature (here he consciously echoes St Paul) was partly 'celestial and angelical' and partly 'terrestrial, fleshly, bestial, which is his body', but his inference is not St Paul's.

A man's affections should spring equally from both his natures, and he should reject that which solely consists in the admiration of the soul, as that which he can very imperfectly judge of; and where the knowledge is imperfect the desire must needs be very cold ... A man, to love as a man, must have regard to both and can fix his heart neither absolutely on that which is too high to be understood, nor too low to be approved; a mixed creation must have mixed affections, and can love only where he finds a mind of such excellence as to delight his understanding, and a body of beauty to please his senses.

At this point one wonders whether Milton's essay on *The Doctrine and Discipline of Divorce*, which was published in 1644, had come his way. Milton, whose marriage to a physically attractive but unintellectual woman had ended in separation, argued for divorce on grounds of incompatibility, but only, it seems, on the initiative of the husband. Sidney took a different view of women from Milton:

> It is true that women have not those helps from study and education that men have, but in the natural powers of the mind they are in no way inferior. They exempt themselves from the trouble of those knotty sciences that serve only to deceive fools, which furnish the tongue with words, but tend nothing to the framing of the understanding; and instead of this they have a pleasantness of wit very much beyond men, and well-composedness of judgement, which if they did not deserve our love, would move our envy: and unto whatsoever they apply themselves, either learning, business, domestic or public government, shew themselves at least equal to our sex. I would gladly except military business, naturally disliking anything of violence among them; but even in that many of them have been excellent. But above all the softness, gentleness and sweetness that are in them doth justly move our love and admiration; whereas men's minds are as rugged as their faces, fit for boisterous action by the strength and hardness of their bodies, but incapable of giving pleasure.

He may well have been drawing his examples, consciously or unconsciously, from the women among whom he had been brought up – his mother the Countess and Dorothy, his beautiful and intelligent elder sister. There is a note of tolerance and respect in the passage which one would not expect from a man of his time, whichever faction he belonged to.

The *Essay* is not merely a juvenile philosophical reflection. It is autobiographical in that the writer says he is at that moment in love. It is a side of Algernon's life of which the glimpses are so few (there is only one other) that even the most fragmentary evidence must be used. But one can at least point to a candidate as the woman who earned much admiration for her whole sex.

Lucy Walter, or Walters, or Waters, or Barlow made her first appearance in London in the spring of 1644 as a refugee from the war in Wales. From accounts she gave later she had been born in 1630, which would make her only fourteen, but this, like her story of having been born of a well-connected family and brought up in Roch Castle on the wild coast of Pembrokeshire, cannot be relied on.* What is certain is that she was both beautiful and attractive. John Evelyn, who met her in Paris in the summer of 1649, thought her 'browne, beautiful, and bold' though he adds that he also found her 'insipid'. They were on their way to visit the exiled claimant to the English throne, Charles II, whose mistress *en titre* Lucy now was, as well as the mother of his first recognised child, only a few months old, James, later Duke of Monmouth

Lucy, as John Aubrey put it, 'could deny nobody', and the list of her lovers is a long one, so one doubts Evelyn's 'insipid'. Charles and his adviser Bennet (later Earl of Arlington, with whom she had an affair during Charles' temporary absence) were not the kind of men to be interested in a dull young woman, however good-looking. But she was certainly a woman who made the man's side of sex easy, and to the shy young Algernon it must have been a revelation.

The evidence is primarily in a remark recorded by a man who was no friend of Algernon's: James, Duke of York, the brother of Charles II and later his successor. He claims that Algernon himself told him he had 'given her – Lucy – fifty gold pieces, but having to join his regiment hastily had missed his bargain'.[1] There is only one occasion on which this could have happened – when Lucy was in London and Algernon had a regiment he had to hurry to join: and that was in the spring of 1644. There are reasons for questioning the genuineness of James's entry: when he wrote it he regarded Algernon as a deadly enemy; the whole episode of Lucy was discreditable, and her son, who had been made Duke of Monmouth by his enthusiastic father, had been the standard-bearer of those who sought to exclude James from the throne. Above all it is difficult to see when Algernon and James could have met on terms which would allow such a remark: in 1645, when James was a twelve-year old prisoner at Petworth and Algernon was at Chichester? At some point when they were both in the Netherlands? When, long afterwards, Algernon returned to England as a man under surveillance? Yet it seems unlikely that James would have simply invented it. The greater probability is that he had the substance from Algernon's brother Robert, who was an officer in the Dutch army while the royal brothers (and Lucy) were in exile there, and had many oppor-

---

* Even then Roch Castle had long been an uninhabited ruin. It was brought back to temporary use as a cavalier stronghold early in 1644 because of its defensive strength, but was nevertheless captured by the parliamentarians, and abandoned again.

tunities for talking to James. Lucy would be an easy subject of conversation for Robert Sidney, for he had been her lover himself immediately before she passed into the arms of Charles, and there was a strong rumour (which may well have been correct) that he, not Charles, was the father of the Duke of Monmouth.

But whatever its long-term consequences, and whether Algernon's passion in 1644 was an unfulfilled affair with Lucy or something quite different, its only fruit was *The Essay on Love*.*

The winter of Algernon's convalescence from his wound at Marston Moor was also the time of political and military decisions which led to the victory of Parliament and in the longer term its downfall from the unrestrained sovereignty it was assuming. Negotiations with the King collapsed, the old aristocratic generals were ousted from their commands in the Parliamentary forces, and a professional army directly responsible to Parliament, the New Model, was organized. For everyone the stakes were being raised.

For the Sidney family the times were particularly difficult. The Earl's finances were under more strain than ever. To the King's unpaid debt for the Paris embassy there was now added two years' unpaid salary and expenses as Lord Lieutenant. Rents from his far-flung estates, especially those in Wales, were difficult if not impossible to collect, and the mortgage instalments on Wolsingham, which Algernon still hoped to see redeemed, fell into arrears – in fact at Michaelmas 1645 the mortgagee, 'that unworthy and unfaithfull gentleman whom I thought my friend and so treated him', foreclosed. No wonder there was 'much ado and miserable wrangling' with the Countess about household expenses.

It was essential the family should realise a free asset by arranging for Philip to get married, and the necessary negotiations took place early in 1645, articles being signed on 25 May. The bride, Catherine Cecil, though only seventeen, was suitable from every point of view. She was not only a daughter of the Earl of Salisbury – who was a cousin and on the Parliamentary side – but she brought £6,100 with her. Perhaps the most important thing of all was that Salisbury's London estate, still commemorated by Cecil Court and the Salisbury

---

* Here I have discounted the unsupported suggestion in the Verney Papers (*Letters Illustrative of the Reign of William III* ed. G. P. R. James (1841) p 273) that Algernon had an illegitimate daughter who later married his secretary Ducasse. No direct evidence of such a daughter's existence has been found.

Tavern, marched conveniently on the eastern boundary of the Sidneys' Leicester House property, where the young couple were to live.

So far the Earl had been able to build on only part of the site, and the rest, even in 1645, was ripe for development, which the Earl, not yet having limited his freedom with an entail, was at liberty to carry out. Unfortunately it was all mortgaged.

The Earl brooded much over such problems and in his many wills and codicils was to make many different dispositions, taking account of marriages and deaths in his numerous family and the varying esteem in which he held individual members of it at different times: but the central fact always remained. Somehow Leicester House was going to have to provide for all his children except Dorothy and Philip – and in 1645 six of the girls were still unmarried: but one of the Cecil family's firmest points was that if their girl married Philip, Leicester Fields should descend to the couple's heirs. What could be more rational, seeing they were neighbours and Philip in his turn would be Earl of Leicester? So by the marriage articles there was a compromise. Leicester House itself was entailed to Philip on his father's death, but his inheritance of the land round it (which was charged with portions for the daughters and the payment of the Earl's numerous debts) would go to Philip only if he paid off the mortgage within a certain time. It was also to be security for small annuities (£150 a year each) to Algernon and little Henry. Robert, the middle brother, was already disliked by his father, and was left out. Just what happened if Philip did not pay off the mortgage was not made absolutely plain.

On 18 March 1645 Algernon's name was approved as colonel of one of the eleven cavalry regiments in the New Model Army, with daily pay of £2. One of his subordinates was a younger brother of Cromwell's closest collaborator and future son-in-law Henry Ireton, and his immediate superior was to be Cromwell himself. Early in April he received orders to join his regiment in the southern midlands where the Parliamentary Army was concentrating for the campaign which led to the decisive victory of Naseby. But he did not take part in the battle which made Parliament sovereign in England. In a letter to Fairfax, the Commander-in-Chief, he resigned from the Army, saying that his wounds, particularly that in his leg, were still not fully cured so he would not be able to do credit either to himself or the cause, and he had been offered the governorship of Chichester. Fairfax approved the appointment accordingly on 10 May.[2]

This was not such a backwater as it might seem at first sight for a capable young colonel with battle experience. There was still plenty of fighting in the southern counties even after Naseby, and the Chichester garrison was often called on for operational contingents. Not far to Algernon's north the royalist stronghold of Basing House still blocked the main road from London to the West Country. There was also a new problem – militant protest against the war itself by the bands of peasants, small farmers, and lesser gentry who were weary of being taxed, conscripted and plundered by both sides and demanded a settlement. These 'Clubmen' as they came to be called, were obnoxious to both parties (except so far as they could sometimes be used to embarrass the other) but especially to Parliament, since it was now winning, and less in a mood to compromise. Algernon received repeated orders from London to take severe action against the Clubmen, but seems largely to have confined himself to posting notices ordering them to disperse.[3]

The reasons for Algernon's presence in Chichester were as much political as military. Petworth, his uncle Northumberland's residence, was not far away, and besides providing him with friendly hospitality imposed an important responsibility on the commander of the nearest parliamentary garrison, for it was the place of custody for the King's four younger children. James, Elizabeth, Henry and Henrietta had fallen into Parliament's hands during the winter, and on the same day in March as the House of Lords had approved the officer corps of the New Model they had assigned the care of these little hostages (along with a substantial allowance for their upkeep) to the Earl and Countess of Northumberland. Later two of them were to move even further within the Sidney orbit, and find themselves at Penshurst.

Even nearer Chichester than Petworth was another family that was close to the Sidneys: the Pelhams. They were already one of the richest and most influential families in Sussex, and the kernel from which the greatest whig interest of the next century would grow. Sir Thomas Pelham, the head of the family, was M.P. for Sussex as his forebears had been since the days of Elizabeth I, and though now middle-aged had recently married (as his third wife) Harry Vane's sister Margaret. His heir, John, was engaged to Algernon's sister Lucy. And, as it happened, in the summer of 1645 there was a by-election for Chichester.

The House of Commons had allowed no by-elections for three years, and was now seriously depleted not only by normal casualties but by the mass expulsion of about a third of its membership at the beginning of the war. During the previous winter the House had anxiously debated this question of the need for 'recruitment', trying to balance claims to be a representative assembly against the risks that would threaten from elections while the war was still going on. The outcome was that elections were authorised in some places but not in others. Chichester was one of those reenfranchised, as was Cardiff, which had recently been cleared of royalists, so restoring the influence of that strongly parliamentarian family, the Herberts.*

For Cardiff Algernon was himself a candidate, and at Chichester one of the vacancies was proposed for that old friend of the Sidney family, Sir John Temple, who had recently been released from the Dublin gaol to which he had been consigned by Ormonde. In both cases one can see the workings of family influence over parliamentary seats which was to become such a marked feature of the next century. Temple was brought in by the Sidneys, the Pelhams and the Percys; Algernon by the Sidneys but, above all, by the Earl of Pembroke, who was also instrumental in bringing in the future republican leader, Edmund Ludlow, for Wiltshire. The details of both by-elections are mysterious. There is no record of other candidates or of a poll in either, which is perhaps not surprising, but the absence of any official return, or even of the dates on which either Algernon or Temple actually took their seats, is puzzling. Temple probably took his seat before the end of 1645, and Algernon certainly did early in 1646.

The Parliament in which Algernon now joined his brother had made good their claim to absolute sovereignty as a kind of collective King.† Indeed, when they came to make themselves a Great Seal

---

* The writ for Chichester was authorised on 3 September 1645, and one for Cardiff on 5 November of the same year. There was some unexplained trouble over the Cardiff writ because another one, in exactly the same terms, was issued on 21 January 1646, so Algernon cannot have taken his seat until after that. But it must have been fairly soon afterwards.

† The stages between 1642 and 1646 by which Parliament exercised the sovereignty formerly wielded by the King would be interesting to trace. But it was all based on the legal doctrine of privilege. That Parliament had privileges was undoubted. So was the doctrine that each House could define (and alone define) its privileges. Therefore

they substituted for the monarch's effigy a collective portrait of themselves. They both legislated and reached executive decisions, and the distinction between the two processes was wholly unclear. The future religious organization of the country, the appointment of army officers, the imposition of penalties, the movements of regiments, the regulation of public holidays, the choice of contractors, the approval of loans, the decisions about which judges should go on which circuits, the exact size of rewards to be given to messengers – all was decided by debate on a motion and if need be by vote, in a House which sat steadily on throughout the year with scarcely a break. Innumerable committees buttressed the system – some to prepare the House's business, others to execute its decisions. Below this there was indeed the military bureaucracy now solidified in the New Model: but on the civilian side there was singularly little. The secretariats of the different committees, with varying instructions, were in frequent collision, and overriding decisions could be changed instantaneously by a division in the House.

There was still a House of Lords, coequal in theory with the Commons, and exercising a good deal of power in practice. But it was a very odd assembly, neither representative nor comprehensively aristocratic, for it lacked all the bishops and a majority of the lay peers. It consisted of those grandees who had taken the side of the Commons, and the number present at its sittings rarely rose above twenty. Sometimes it was only five or six. Something like a quarter of the peers who attended regularly were closely related to Algernon.

Attendance in the Commons was supposed to be compulsory, as was voting if present, so the records of divisions are quite a good guide to attendance. At an important division numbers could rise towards three hundred, and most assembled more than one hundred members. Less than fifty was very rare.* Since, despite recent recruitment, the House was well below its original strength of just over five hundred and many members were on authorized or unauthorized absence, the turn-out was good, and whipping must have occurred.

Algernon entered the House of Commons when it was in the zenith of its sense of power, certain of victory and hardly glimpsing

---

anything a House chose to do could be said to be its privilege, and resistance to the House's decision was a breach of privilege punishable by the House at its absolute discretion.

*In 81 divisions between 1 April and 16 November 1647 the highest number voting was on 3 June (277) and the lowest on 14 May (59).

the difficulties that lay ahead. Many of its members thought that a tamed King could soon be brought to the compromise which would provide Parliament with the one thing it lacked, an obedient yet effective executive arm: a minority doubted it, feeling that matters had gone too far for such a compromise to be possible. It was with this grouping – the so-called Independents – that Algernon identified himself. Although he was to hold other commands and was known as Colonel Sidney for the rest of his life, a politician he now became, whose first experience was of an assembly that with all its faults and absurdities was on the crest of its confidence and reaching decisions on large matters and small in a stream of debate and vote.

He found himself caught up almost at once in a renewal of the obsession with Ireland which united all factions in the Commons, for now the war on the mainland was won the subjugation of the other island, whence alone the defeated King could hope for support, once more headed the agenda. No time could have been apter for the appearance of a young member who had fought in Ireland, or for the publication of the book describing the horrors of the rebellion there which the new member for Chichester, Sir John Temple, had composed in his Dublin prison. *The History of the Rebellion in Ireland*, published in 1646, not only caught contemporary imagination but set a conventional view for several generations, and the gradual exposure of its exaggerations and partiality has been very slow.

The bitter topic of Temple's book had already contributed much to the conflict between King and Parliament and so to the ruin of the King. Its next phase, now beginning, was to precipitate the collision between Parliament and its army, which was to lead to the destruction of Parliament in its turn. Though the opening passages of this new phase, in which the Sidneys were again leading figures, were in some ways ludicrous, it was part of the continuing tragic drama which – as much English as Irish – begins with the rising of 1641 and ends half a century later with the Treaty of Limerick.

Parliament had a Committee for the affairs of Ireland, and very soon both Algernon's brother Philip and Sir John Temple were members of it. There was general agreement that an expeditionary force should be found from the now largely unemployed New Model to reconquer Ireland, but the question of how it should be commanded produced difficulties. Parliament already had a commander in Ireland: Murrough O'Brien, Earl of Inchiquin, Lord

President of Munster, who was now waging a desultory but brutal war against Ormonde, the King's Lord Lieutenant. Despite his name (which Lord Leicester considered was in itself a disqualification from any office) O'Brien described himself as a Protestant. At one time he had fought for the King, and was to change sides again, to earn the nickname 'Murrough of the Burnings'. He was in fact a war lord, but he had his friends in the House of Commons at Westminster, and did not at all accept the idea of an English commander from the mainland being placed above him.

Nevertheless Parliament resolved to put both the civil and military government of Ireland in the hands of a Lord Lieutenant they would themselves appoint, and on 21 January 1646 decided without a division that this important post should go to Algernon's brother Philip. Opponents of the scheme added the rider that his term of office should be limited to one year from the date his commission was made out. Algernon was to be his deputy, with the rank of Lieutenant-General and the command of the cavalry.

Why was Lisle chosen? There were plenty of unemployed generals with better records than his to choose from, but very few of them were in Parliament, and most, even of those, were peers such as Essex and Manchester who had been discredited and removed from their commands during the previous winter. The compromising majority of the House of Commons – the so-called Presbyterians – was beginning to be nervous about the officers thrown up by the New Model: they were employees, and ought not to have a post appropriate to a master. On the other hand, from the point of view of the 'Independent' grouping in the House both Lisle and his brother Algernon normally voted with them and were acceptable. Lisle thus seemed a perfect choice, despite his inglorious battle record, and a Parliament which had overthrown the King now unanimously entrusted its favourite project to the representative of a noble family which had been a prop of the monarchy for several generations.

Parliament could decide quickly, but putting things into execution was another matter. The Committee for Irish Affairs rapidly came forward with their plan, but the day it was presented to the House (9 February 1646) was also marked by the appearance of Lord Inchiquin to be publicly thanked by Parliament for his exertions in Ireland. Naturally he and his allies took this opportunity to slow down progress and the whole subject was laid aside for two months, at the end of which (15 April) the two Houses formally approved Lisle's commission without removing Inchiquin, and time began to run.

Lisle and Algernon still had to obtain Parliamentary approval to raise troops, and this was not received until 15 June. Then things began to go even more seriously wrong. The troops of the New Model did not want to serve in Ireland, where conditions were notoriously bad and the pay unreliable. Colonel Jones, who was mustering the expeditionary force at St Albans, despairingly reported that most units were arriving under strength, the worst being 'Captain Coe, his troop, consisting of a captain, a lieutenant, two trumpeters and three soldiers; in all officers and soldiers to the number of seven'. Then came the news that not a man would march for the port of embarkation until he received every penny of his arrears, and this included Colonel Jones himself, who pointed out that with £4,700 back pay owing to him he did not feel he could afford service in Ireland. He tactfully drew attention to a confiscated Cavalier estate in Cheshire (his native county) which he thought would suit him very well if the Committee could see their way to transfer it to him.[4]

These were early portents in the issue which was to dominate the politics of the coming year, the demands of the Army Agitators, when the New Model suddenly begins to look extraordinarily like a Trade Union in relation to its masters, Parliament. After all it was the largest body of directly employed wage-earners in a single organization yet seen in England: and a work force already organized for militant action.

On 31 July came another blow, which was ultimately to prove fatal to the expedition. The House of Commons decided by a single vote not to send the six New Model regiments to Ireland after all and the normal majority lost control of the House. The 'Independent' leader Heselrige and the Army's spokesman, Cromwell, had at first pleaded for further delay and were beaten handsomely; but when, encouraged by this, supporters of the Sidneys pushed the main question of sending the regiments to the vote, they were defeated by what may well have been an ambush, for the numbers voting in the second division were much higher than in the first.

Philip and Algernon were now reduced to assembling an army from scratch, with four months of Philip's twelve-month term already gone. It says much for their resolution that they persisted, beating up men from idle garrisons, disbanded regiments, and parties of new recruits brought in by unemployed officers of dubious background. Colonel Jones was sweetened with the promise that he should be Deputy Governor of Dublin (Algernon was to be Governor) when it was reconquered from the King's forces. By September the budget was showing signs of strain – though not before the Earl of Leicester, who was taking a great interest in the expedition from his self-imposed exile at Penshurst, had slipped in a bill of £3,500 for his unpaid expenses as Lord Lieutenant four years earlier. Admittedly the Earl had never got there, but he had set out, and could point to a resolution of Parliament saying he should go. It was approved.[5]

The Earl's revived interest in politics led him, on 31 December 1646, to start a journal to which we owe many of the most vivid descriptions of the next six dramatic years, including Cromwell's famous remark about the mace. This is all the stranger because throughout the period the Earl rarely left Penshurst, and firmly declined the suggestions of fellow-peers that he should appear in the House of Lords. Clearly he despised them – 'Still the same moderate' is his curt comment on Pembroke when, on the abolition of the House of Lords, he arranged to get himself a seat in the Commons.[6]*

For these reasons the Earl depended almost entirely on others for his journal. Some entries are taken from news-sheets (about whose politics he enters growling comments), others from parliamentary papers, and eye-witness accounts which must (though he does not acknowledge them) be based on letters received from his relations and friends. Thus we probably owe to the Earl's elder daughter, Dorothy, the substance of the Leicester Diary's account of the abduction of the King by Cornet Joyce, which the Earl was recording within three days of its occurrence at Holmby House. Holmby is very near Dorothy's mansion of Althorp, and the King was a regular visitor there during his detention. Similarly it can hardly have been anyone but Algernon who provided the scene for which the Leicester Diary is most celebrated, Cromwell's coup d'état of April 1653, at which the Diary abruptly breaks off.

Naturally the Diary closely follows the adventures of Philip

---

* The Earl also records with satisfaction stories of the sexual peccadilloes of the Puritan clergy and other anecdotes. These were omitted by the editor of 1825 but are now accessible in the Historical MSS Commission volumes.

and Algernon in Ireland, for which they at last set out on 1 February 1647, with only two months of Philip's term of office still to run. Nor could he expect an extension, for by the time he embarked Parliament had resolved to separate civilian and military authority in Ireland without making a nomination to either. Undeterred, the brothers landed six miles from Cork on 21 February to reconquer Ireland and confront their nominal associate, Lord Inchiquin. They had a sizeable force of five thousand infantry, but unfortunately only 120 cavalry, having unwisely accepted Inchiquin's advice that grave shortage of fodder in Ireland would make it better to leave the rest behind.

In three weeks Lisle and Inchiquin were at one another's throats with Lisle insisting, in the indignant Lord President's words, that 'he was determined to agitate the business of the army without taking cognisance of me.'[7] Had not Parliament assured him he would not be interfered with? Had he not got commissions from Parliament, and, for good measure, from the King as well? What was more they were written on parchment, whereas the new Lord Lieutenant's was on paper.

By the day Lisle's commission was due to run out, which was 15 April, the Parliamentary generals had very nearly come to armed conflict with each other. That morning a file of Lisle's musketeers, ready for action, was drawn up outside Inchiquin's headquarters at Cork, and Algernon went in to parley. Inchiquin, who was watching the clock, simply blustered on and Algernon made a dignified withdrawal saying it was not for him to discuss the Lord Lieutenant's orders. Making the best haste he could to his brother's headquarters he found the senior officers assembled to hear formal publication of orders integrating the two armies under the Sidneys. Close behind him came Inchiquin himself, having shouldered his way through the file of musketeers and their smoking matches. Brandishing his commissions and drawing attention to the excellence of their parchment, he pointed out that his rival now had only half an hour of his term to run – a fact which had apparently been kept from several of the officers present – and that there would be trouble both in Ireland and Westminster for anyone who obeyed him after that. Algernon, who was presiding, again made a dignified withdrawal, and the other officers agreed to sit out time. When the clock struck midday most of them agreed to serve under Inchiquin.

The baffled Sidneys first contemplated force and then attempted negotiation, but both were useless against Inchiquin's insistence that he was now the only lawful Commander-in-Chief and they were mere private citizens. Reluctantly they packed their trunks and said they would leave, but the Lord President of Munster had not finished with them yet. When they asked the port authorities to load their luggage (it included the handsome plate intended for the Lord Lieutenant's table) they were told it could not be taken on board without the Commander-in-Chief's approval which, after requiring application in due form, Inchiquin graciously gave.

They sailed on 17 April, accompanied by the faithful Temple but leaving their army and supplies, which had been so patiently and expensively assembled, for their rival. Spring gales delayed them six days in the Irish Sea before they disembarked at Minehead and made their way as fast as they could to London, consoling themselves with the thought that at least Algernon was still the lawfully appointed Governor of Dublin. But their enemies had been before them even on this: supported by the intolerable old Sir Henry Vane the House had passed a resolution removing Algernon from his Governorship and appointing Colonel Michael Jones instead. When they got to Westminster they were not even allowed to deliver a report and the House was silent about any compensation for Lord Lisle.

Algernon was treated more kindly. The failure had not been his responsibility and he had behaved with dignity. On 7 May he was appointed Governor of Dover Castle, an important garrison conveniently near his family seat and consistent with pursuing his career at Westminster. So for the next four years he was provided for, but it is not surprising that even worse relations with his brother followed their second voyage together to Ireland.

The expedition's farcical side should not be allowed to obscure its political importance, as a significant episode in the drama which was now leading to a British Republic under the aegis of the Army, in which the reconquest of Ireland was an indispensible preliminary. That reconquest was not only the dearest and most unifying wish of those now in power, whatever their political opinions: it carried with it an immense investment of national sentiment, religious zeal, and speculative money, and without it no Parliamentary regime could really appear as a convincing successor to the Tudor and Stuart monarchs.

Yet the only force which could achieve the reconquest was the

New Model, as Cromwell knew, and was eventually to show, and the decision not to send it at the time of Lisle's expedition was the first evidence of the way the balance of power was tilting against the 'Presbyterian' majority in the Commons, and in favour of the Army as an independent political power. Holles, the 'Presbyterian' leader, had seen the position clearly, for his aim in proposing the use of the New Model in Ireland had a dual motive. They were the best soldiers available, but it would also be most desirable that these formidable and expensive men, having no battles in England left to fight, should be occupied in Ireland. If he could have mustered only a few more votes history would have taken a different course, and very probably the troopers would have been safely across the sea in the summer of 1647, not raiding Holmby House to take the King out of the hands of Parliament or, a little later, marching on London, claiming to be a more effective representative of the people than Parliament itself.

'The Great Business'

ALGERNON, M.P. for Cardiff, a colonel, and Governor of Dover Castle at the age of 24, now entered a period which English history has always found it difficult to digest, and illustrates with peculiar force the total and justified mistrust which infected the political world. If his path through these strange times has its slippery passages, he was always seeking and eventually finding the hard ground for which he was to be remembered.

'When ... Armys', he wrote long afterwards, 'were suffered to continue in the same hands longer than the law did direct, Soldiery came to be accounted a Trade, and those who had the worse designs against the Commonwealth, began to favour all manner of Licentiousness and Rapine, that they might gain the favour of the Legions, who became by that means unruly and seditious.'[1] As with many of his classical allusions he meant this for his own times, and particularly for the fourteen years between the triumph of Naseby and the Restoration, during which a professional army, acting by its own internal pressures, became an independent and often dominant force in politics. The phenomenon is common, and in some countries has established a tradition, which can almost be called constitutional, by which the armed forces are seen, or at any rate see themselves, as the ultimate guardians of the national interest with a legitimate right of intervention. It is remarkable that England, where this doctrine is now regarded with horror, should have been one of the first countries in modern history where it was asserted, and for a time was a reality. The most decisive result of the Restoration, perhaps, was its lasting repudiation.

To Algernon and his contemporaries 'the Army' meant something quite specific: the regiments raised and paid directly by Parliament as 'The New Model' from the winter of 1644 onwards. They were the men who triumphed at Naseby. Algernon had belonged to it and his words in his letter to Fairfax resigning his commission in 1645 are significant: although he held military commands for several years afterwards and was always known as 'Colonel', he 'resigned from the Army'. Service in the New Model set a man apart even from other soldiers, of whom there were many, and for him soldiering, in Algernon's word, increasingly became a 'Trade', and the resulting Trade Union entered into dispute with its employers, the Parliament.

The origins of that dispute lay in what would nowadays be called industrial redeployment. Victory in England and the urge to continue the war to a successful conclusion in Ireland had produced the obvious management decision to send some regiments to Ireland and disband the rest. To the majority in Parliament this disposed of the whole immense cost, for the Irish war was to be paid for by Ireland: but they measured neither the size of the problem nor the nature of industrial relations, and on the Army's side no infusion of political or religious ideology was needed to develop, in the early months of 1647, an apparatus of trade unionism complete with shop floor representatives (or 'Agitators'),* a negotiating forum (the Council of the Army) and a list of specific demands about severance pay, pensions for widows and the disabled, guaranteed terms of service for men retained, and statutory protection against lawsuits by civilians for damage done in the course of military operations. When these demands were resisted politicisation of the Army was the next stage, and its senior officers found themselves uncomfortably

---

* 'Agitator' as used in the seventeenth century meant an agent, and hence a deputy, shop steward, or representative. The more modern usage by Lenin and others for a person acting from outside to 'rouse consciousness' has replaced the older meaning, and has perhaps led to some misinterpretation of the period. The 'Agitators' of the Putney Debates were all elected.

squeezed between the pressure from their men and the obduracy of the employing Parliament.

The Army's transformation into a political force occurred between March 1647, when the original 'industrial' demands were presented unsuccessfully, and June 15 when the Army announced that it was 'not a mere mercenary army, hired to serve any arbitrary power of the state, but called forth and conjured by the several declarations of Parliament to the defence of their own and the people's just rights and liberties.' In this period of four months the crucial event was the debate in the Commons ending with the division of 25 May which decided that all men who refused to serve in Ireland should be discharged. The exceptionally high number of 251 members voted, and Algernon was one of the tellers for the minority.

This, the first record of his activity as a parliamentarian, shows that he sympathised with at any rate the 'industrial' demands of the soldiers. But when, at the end of July, the impatient Army marched on London to produce a crisis in which fifty-seven members seceded from the House for a time, placed themselves 'under the protection of the Army', and denounced their colleagues remaining in Westminster as no longer legitimate, Algernon was not among them, though his brother Philip undoubtedly was.*

The apparent paradox gives a bearing on Algernon's political position. As a former New Model officer and an aristocrat he would have responded to the appeals of the soldiers for fair treatment, and disliked their hamfisted handling by the parliamentary majority: but he was scandalised by an Army with political claims and the possibility of a Parliament living under its protection. He liked neither the calculating 'grandees' at the head of the Army nor the levelling junior officers and rankers with their demands for social change which even reached as far as an incomes policy with a maximum of £2,000 a year (which should be restricted to Dukes, Earls, and Viscounts). Worst of all was the impulse now given to the majority in Parliament to escape their dilemma by compromising with the King.

* There are four lists of the seceders of July 1647 of which the most authoritative is in Lords' Journals, which gives the names of those who signed the seceders' manifesto. Algernon's is included only in the fourth, which is the least reliable, and was compiled by Sir John Percival, who was one of the deadly Irish enemies of the Sidney family. It is quite likely that Algernon neither seceded nor attended at Westminster during this awkward period.

To him then, as throughout his subsequent life, the determining factor was his devotion to the new idea of Parliament as the sole legitimate source of authority. Republican in the strict sense he may not have been, but there can be no doubt about his opposition to King Charles, which went back to his miserable service in Ireland and a sense of personal betrayal by the King's serpentine policy. Under the monarchy's professions of paternalistic non-account-ability it was in its nature corrupt, capricious, and dishonest, creating for its support a class of parasites feeding on the public and justifying itself only by its usefulness to the monarch. Peerage and titles of honour were devalued to recruit it, and bishops, with their humble backgrounds, were bound to be servile careerists.

In this he was neither a theoretician nor a wayward, guilt-ridden member of the upper classes rejecting his traditions. His stance arose from a passionate detestation of monarchy:

> Princes are like birds of prey [he was later to write in *Court Maxims*]. Those endowed with noble spirits, like the eagle, preserve their own, seek their prey abroad, and teach their young ones the use of their beaks and talons. Others that are base and cowardly ... seek the easier prey. They must have blood. That of foreigners is not shed without danger: their own subjects may be murdered ...[2]

This was written in the wake of the death of his hero Harry Vane, but from the ruling idea he never varied. An institution that necessarily put some bad or incompetent characters in supreme power could not be sound. James I, with his 'filthy ways not fit to be mentioned', was an example which shows the depth of the disgust.

Such a man could not subscribe to the doctrine of Holles and the parliamentary majority that the 'malignant party' surrounding the King, and not the King himself, bore the guilt of the war. That, to Algernon, was cant which left the door open to bringing back the old evils: the 'malignants' were no more than an emanation of the monarchy whose supporters included men whom he respected, such as his own brother-in-law, who had taken up Charles's cause on principle. These feelings separated him not only from the par-liamentary majority but from his father and his elder brother – one a nervous neutral, and the other increasingly a worshipper of the Army's rising sun.

His mind therefore concentrated on Parliament as an idea which provided a legitimacy far superior to the asserted divine right of the

King, since it was the result of choice. Just how that choice was made did not interest him, for he was not a democrat in our sense of the word and methods of election, range of the franchise, equalization of constituencies – though all these were matters of passionate contemporary debate – find no mention in his writings. Some people, he was sure, were too stupid or base to be entrusted with votes, but if – as was the tradition in some constituencies – they had them, he did not object. As for the parliamentarians themselves they might – they should – differ on particular issues and opinions, but only as a kind of collective personality arguing with itself and then resolving on action. Parliament should not be an arena for contesting doctrines and allegiances, and those holding perverse and dangerous opinions should have no place in it. All should agree about the essentials, and be 'honest' and 'well-affected'. If these views sound simplistic they nevertheless live vigorously today in the idea of a 'one-party state'.

An aristocratic republican can hardly be a good party man, but can readily find himself a member of a like-minded coterie disagreeing on particular points while sharing intellectual sympathies.* During the late 1640's such a coterie – the so-called Commonwealthmen – begins to be distinguishable. They rejected the compromising majority and its chieftain Holles, and the increasingly militaristic minority with its great demagogue, Sir Arthur Heselrige. So far as they had a leading parliamentary light it was Harry Vane, but they often spoke and even voted against one another.

One can nevertheless associate certain characteristics with the Commonwealthman. His motives tend to be rationalistic rather than religious or instinctive loyalism, he was often of superior family and education, came from the south of England or the Midlands, and had frequently come into Parliament as the result of a by-election. To take three examples, Edmund Ludlow, Henry Marten, and Henry Neville were all the sons of knights based respectively in Wiltshire, Oxfordshire, and Berkshire, had been to university, and two of them, like Algernon himself, had in the parlance of that time been 'recruited' to fill parliamentary vacancies.

* The modern historian, when discussing party, is influenced by modern English political practice by which party is closely associated with voting behaviour: but in the seventeenth century it was by no means obligatory for the like-minded to vote in the same lobby on particular issues. Modern American political practice is far closer to that of Sidney's time.

Yet it would be difficult to imagine more diverse personalities. Ludlow's stolidness and solemnity were famous. At Oxford he had infuriated his tutor during a discussion on appearance and reality by insisting that a horn-shaped shadow really was a horn if it was thought to be one, until the tutor was reduced to shouting 'Then toot it, you idiot, toot it!' At the beginning of the war he and some other earnest friends had employed a professional sergeant to drill them, and he can almost claim to have invented the phrase 'the Public Service' which so often recurs in his utterances. 'My cornet' he writes, describing one of the engagements in which he was involved, 'was shot through the body, and into the thigh, and his horse in two places ... the bullet that went in at his belly was found in the chine of his back, with a piece of the wasteband of his breeches, which being cut out, he wonderfully recovered to be in some measure serviceable to the publick.'[3]

When he came into Parliament for Wiltshire in 1645 it was with the help of Algernon's great relation the Earl of Pembroke, and when he decided to get married a few years later he found a wife from the family of Stradling, in Algernon's constituency of Glamorgan. The Sidneys were related to the Stradlings and Algernon very probably had something to do with his placid friend's marriage.

If there is something of a protobenthamism in the humourless Ludlow. Henry Marten offers a quite different kind of radical personality, of which a later example is Wilkes. Nobody could have been less of a puritan than Marten, and his notorious womanising earned him the double distinction of being denounced as a 'whoremaster' by both Charles I and Cromwell. His religious principles were at best doubtful, and, some thought, absent. His irreverent wit was often aimed at the self-conscious pomposity of the House of Commons itself, as when he suggested giving statutory authority to the Great Seal to touch for the King's Evil, since a ponderous member had suggested the King should be stopped from doing it himself. His protests against the absurd overworking of Parliament have probably given us the saying that a quart cannot be got into a pint pot. His actual words were 'a pint pot cannot hold a pottle of liquor.' But he was far more than merely the jester of the House; his interventions at crucial moments were often decisive, and he was to be a leading regicide. This strange, witty man escaped death at the Restoration only through a joke made by a member of the House of Lords who observed that since sacrifices should be without blemish they could hardly offer up 'such a rotten old rascal'.

The serious-minded Algernon can hardly have approved of Marten, but they sometimes acted together, and on one such occasion bringing in Algernon's cousin Henry Neville, for Abingdon in 1649.* Though politically Marten's disciple, and sharing his gift for satire, Neville was happier with his pen than as a debater, and his destiny was as a political writer. He lived to form a kind of bridge between the heroic age of English republicanism and the crystallization of interests which eventually produced the Revolution settlement of 1688–89: and he was probably Algernon's literary heir.

There were perhaps twenty Commonwealthmen in all – men identified with neither the compromising 'Presbyterians', the religious enthusiasts, the social reformers, the military chieftains, the lawyers, or the business men who between them formed that strange Parliament. They were distinctive enough for Cromwell to invite them to dinner as a group during his political soundings of 1647–48 and infuriate them by his indifference to forms of government, maintaining that 'any of them might be good in themselves, or for us, as Providence might direct us.' At last, losing patience with the opinionated Ludlow, Cromwell followed the Oxford tutor's example and hurled a cushion at his head. Ludlow replied in kind, and the whole conference broke up in disorder.[4]

The one opinion the Commonwealthmen shared was dislike of pragmatism. They differed in their religious views, and were on the whole surprisingly tolerant in an intolerant age; they often differed on specific political issues. But reason, they considered, must govern public life: loyalty on the one hand and pragmatism on the other did not suffice. Political theory must govern practice, and in a world where the old certainties seemed to be dissolving it appeared to them that intellect could actually produce results.

The little group survived and even increased in importance during the seven years between the triumph of Parliament in 1646 and the Cromwellian coup d'état which swept away the Rump in April 1653. It is the period in which Parliamentary government in the most literal sense of the words became a reality in this country, and despite the smallness of their numbers the Commonwealthmen, with their almost mystic belief in the supremacy of Parliament as

* Algernon was teller for the majority on his election petition, which was allowed on a close division of 19 to 17 (CJ 11 Oct 1649).

both legislature and executive, helped to set its distinctive style. So attached did they become to their idea of the House of Commons that it began to seem to some of them (though not to Henry Marten) that there need never be another general election, and the principle of popular choice might be sufficiently honoured by the election of fresh 'well-affected and honest' members when vacancies occurred through death, resignation, or possibly expulsion for unsuitability. In any event, for those who thought on these lines, the House would always have a veto on a new member, and some Commonwealthmen toyed with the idea of maintaining the old House in existence to review the choices of the constituencies before letting a new House take its place.

To those who thought with this logic the great events of 1648–49 and even the dramatic end of Charles I were not seen as interruptions of principle in the doctrine of parliamentary continuity which they had discovered. The English republic in terms of practical reality begins at Naseby in 1645,* or, at latest, with Pride's Purge, for which Ludlow and Marten helped to provide the list of unacceptable members.

For Algernon the revolutionary years of 1647–49 imposed peculiar and paradoxical strains. Faced with three foci of power – the Parliament, the King, and the Army – he was a devotee of the first, an avowed enemy of the second, and increasingly nervous of the third. He had shown his sympathy for the soldiers in May 1647, but the Army's occupation of London two months later was an open defiance of the parliamentary cause for which he had fought, so he could not place himself among the parliamentarians who put themselves under military protection. But it was equally distasteful to him that those who stayed in session at Westminster voted a definite overture to the King, and it was this, not the irregular behaviour of the seceders, that was declared void when the rift in Parliament was cobbled up. That summer the Army's distrust of the Sidneys was demonstrated by the arrival at Penshurst of Major Gibbons 'and his whole troupe' from Ireton's regiment of horse to camp in the park for several months.

Yet the Army itself was divided. The growing politicization of the middle and lower ranks demonstrated in The Agreement of the

* Sidney, in his *Character of Sir Henry Vane* describes how Vane was called from his bed at midnight to hear the news of Naseby, 'by which he saw his party establish'd but himself likewise made secure, and an immortal glory obtain'd for him.'

People and its demands for parliamentary reform caused senior officers to begin thinking, like the parliamentarians before them, of an accommodation with the King, and Charles in his turn to see the possibility of yet returning to power. The pressure on him was the greater because he now began to see that he was playing not only for his crown but for his life. In the Army's Putney Debates, in the church there in October 1647, the argument had begun to come from the ranks that since, by the ordeal of battle, God had declared against the King, his life was forfeit to man.

In November 1647 Charles slipped out of the hands of the Army to acquire a sort of semi-independence in the Isle of Wight as the ward of the Parliamentary governor, Colonel Robert Hammond, and hatch the celebrated scheme for the renewal of hostilities with Scottish support which is known as 'The Engagement'. The so-called 'Second Civil War' which followed, and would be better described as a royalist rebellion, came surprisingly near success, finally ruined Charles, and healed the rift which had appeared between the senior officers in the Army and the men in the ranks.

The fresh upsurge of bloodshed and bitterness made the position of Algernon even more precarious than it was already. Colonel Hammond, who was widely suspected of conniving at Charles's plot, might indeed be a cousin of Cromwell and the son-in-law of Hampden but he was also closely connected with the Penshurst family as the brother-in-law of their political adherent Sir John Temple, and the brother of the Royalist ex-rector of Penshurst, Henry Hammond who was now with Charles in the Isle of Wight. Worse still for Algernon was the implication of his maternal aunt, Lucy, Countess of Carlisle, in the rising, and the fact that her current lover, the Earl of Holland, had at her instance been designated to command the Royalist forces in England.

Algernon's native county of Kent, which had so far escaped military operations, was one of the main theatres of the new conflict, and his own military command, Dover Castle, was besieged by the Royalists. Major Gibbons and his troops at Penshurst departed for action, but their places on the lawns were soon taken by a much less mannerly detachment from the Parliamentarian forces commanded by the fire-eating Sir Michael Livesey, for whose rudeness and vandalism the Earl of Leicester was later to obtain an apology. But Algernon himself did not take part in the defence of the fortress he commanded. He left it to his deputy, Major Boys, and did not return to Dover until July, when the siege had been raised and the fighting was all but over.

Family considerations already mentioned may well have come in, but there were probably political ones also to explain this uncharacteristic ambiguity. The 'Second Civil War', though it was launched in the name of the King, was far from being a mere renewal of the old struggle. The nature of the regime against which it was fought was beginning to look more military than Parliamentarian. The Kentish fighting was touched off not by proclamations and manifestos but by local protests against the interference of military committees, such as the arrest of some young men for playing the prohibited game of football. There was an element in the whole episode which recalls the movement of the 'Clubmen', against which Algernon had been so inactive when he was in Chichester two years earlier; and whatever the rebel leaders may have had in their thoughts, some of them claimed to be fighting not for absolute monarchy but for 'a free parliament'.[5]

There is thus a good deal of circumstantial evidence to explain what seems to have been a deliberate decision on Algernon's part not to be involved in the war of 1648 in spite of its being – or perhaps because it was – so near his own home. But there is another, direct, piece of evidence which suggests that he may have had some sympathy with the rebels. This is a letter he wrote in the autumn of 1648[6] to William Aylesbury, brother-in-law to the exiled Prince of Wales's chief of staff, the Earl of Clarendon. Aylesbury was an old acquaintance who had worked for Algernon's father during the time of his Paris embassy, but the subject is curious, since it concerns an enquiry from Aylesbury about the possibility of rehabilitating the Duke of Buckingham, who had been one of the most prominent anti-Parliamentarian chieftains in the movement of 1648. Algernon is careful to say there is nothing he can do personally for Buckingham, but strikes an oddly encouraging note by suggesting the atmosphere is now quite good for Buckingham to make an official submission in the hope of getting off lightly. 'Now that all men are inclined to peace with the King and his party much more gentleness is to be expected now than at another time.'

This is so different a judgment from the one commonly taken of the months immediately following the suppression of the renewed Royalist outbreak that it demands explanation. Yet it was correct

so far as Westminster was concerned. The Army was indeed infuriated by the need to fight yet again, but in Parliament for a few weeks
there was an illusion of peace and settlement in the air while a
parliamentary delegation, headed by Holles the leader of the compromisers and Harry Vane the leader of the minority which had till
then been against a settlement, once more opened negotiations with
the King in a reaction against the Army's growing power. The
Army had presented its political demands to the House of Commons
on 20 November as *The Remonstrance of the Army*, and the most
spectacular was the trial and elimination of that 'Man of Blood', the
King. On 30 November the Army began its second march on
London. Next day the parliamentary delegation reported to the
House of Commons on their negotiations with the King.

The only escape for Parliament would have been to dissociate
themselves from the King and all further negotiations with him,
and this is what Vane, with the support of the Commonwealthmen,
urged in his report on the King's proposals. His view, as he told
the House, was that they were not put forward in good faith – a
view we now know to have been correct – and should be rejected.
The debate occupied three parliamentary days, the last of which
started on Monday morning and did not end until Tuesday afternoon. Those for rejection fought to get the substantive question
before the House and their compromising opponents raised procedural points to stop them, in the calculation that once the House
voted, rejection would be inevitable. Part of the time had to be
spent on discussing the news, which arrived during the debate, that
the King had been removed from Hammond's dubious supervision
by the Army, and appointing a drafting committee to write a letter
to Hammond telling him to stand firm in his charge.* The average
attendance over the thirty-six hours is said to have been 250 – a
remarkably full House.

Algernon was continuously present at this marathon to rescue
Parliament, and played a significant part. A first attempt to get a
vote on the main issue was made on the first day of the debate,
and defeated. Next day, when the Army actually entered London,
Algernon was one of the tellers for a second attempt, in partnership
with the much more moderate Richard Knightley, who may have
begun to understand the dangers of prevarication. On Tuesday

* Sir John Temple was put on the Committee, perhaps in the hope that he would
exert his avuncular authority. In a few days it was to cost him his seat.

morning a third attempt was made, and again frustrated. This time two Commonwealthmen, Ludlow and Nicholas Love, were the tellers for the minority.*

By Tuesday afternoon attendance was beginning to drop through sheer weariness and at least twenty-five members had gone home to bed, when the compromisers in a sudden sally moved that 'The Answer of the King to the Propositions of both Houses are ground for this House to proceed upon for the Settlement of the Peace of the Kingdom', and carried it by 129 to 83. It opened the way to negotiations with a view to a Restoration. That night a small committee of Army officers and sympathetic M.P.s (Ludlow was among them) spent a second night out of bed making a list of compromisers on which the Army's pickets, under the command of Colonel Pride, would act when the House met next morning at eight.

Large numbers of troops were deployed to prevent interference as Colonel Pride, prompted by a friendly M.P., identified the members on his list and courteously took them into custody. The fact that the colonel had started his career as a drayman must have rankled, and even those who were allowed past to take their places never accepted that the Purge had the authority of the House.†

Algernon and his brother Philip thus survived in a House reduced to 200 members, consoling themselves for the affront with

---

* S. R. Gardiner (*Great Civil War* iii 573) represents this vote as a tactical move by the opponents of the King's proposals to get them adopted, and so justify intervention by the Army, and suggests that the slightly reworded form of the question it was sought to move was the work of 'some earnest lover of peace' whom he does not identify. Such an elaborate supposition seems unnecessary. The question on this occasion was to be 'Whether the King's Answers to the Propositions of both Houses be satisfactory' which is hardly distinguishable from the two earlier motions on which the House had refused to vote – 'Whether the King's Answer is or is not satisfactory'. The difference is much more likely to be attributable to a desire not to get the motion ruled out of order as something the House had already refused to vote on, or possibly to sheer exhaustion.

† A way round the problem was found by the device of making the right to sit conditional on forswearing the fatal vote that negotiations with the King should continue. But it was never clear exactly who was entitled to sit in the Rump (Worden p. 387), which is remarkable in a body which soon claimed absolute sovereignty. Pride is thought to have had only about 100 names on his list, but at least as many decided not to risk attendance when they knew what was happening, so the House lost more than half the members qualified to sit.

the thought that what had happened was better than the other possibilities of recent weeks – negotiations with the King or (as some Army officers had suggested) a dissolution with fresh elections or a secession of Army sympathizers claiming to be a rival Parliament. Philip was now whole-heartedly for the Army, but Algernon is unlikely to have been so compliant, and it is also unlikely that he was present at the sittings of early December (made, at that point, in secrecy) which decided the House of Commons alone was sovereign in the name of the people, and laid the groundwork of the republic which the Army demanded. Harry Vane was certainly not there, for he foresaw the next step and was determined to have nothing to do with it.

Despite Parliament's fine phrases, the decisions were now being taken by the Council of Officers, which began planning the King's trial on 20 December. The House of Commons did not appoint its own committee for the purpose until three days later, and Philip was on it. Algernon was not. During a great part of that extraordinary Christmas season he was mainly occupied in getting some private business settled for his parents by another parliamentary committee; the rest he spent at Penshurst.

On 6 January the Commons set up the court to try the King. It was to consist of one hundred and thirty-six commissioners, of whom more than a hundred were M.P.s – about half the number who had survived the Purge. Most of the others were Army officers, and the inclusion of so many M.P.s clearly shows the intention of the organisers to implicate the Parliament as closely as they could in 'The Great Business' which now had to be done. None was asked beforehand so one can believe Algernon when he said he was surprised at seeing his name on the list when he returned from his Christmas holiday at Penshurst.

When, more than eleven years later, he tried to recall his connection with the trial in detail, he was naturally anxious to dissociate himself from it, though he could never bring himself to say that guilt attached to those who took part. In fact he had more to do with it than he ever admitted. His own account, in a letter to his father,[7] is that as soon as he found himself named he went to the Commission which was already sitting in the Painted Chamber at Westminster, listened for a time, and then intervened to say that in his opinion the King could not be tried by any court, and no man by this one; drawing from Cromwell the ruthless and celebrated reply – 'I tell you we will cut off his head with the crown upon it'. He then left, and did not attend again.

Part of this can be accepted, but not all. The reason for believing his protest is that it was in almost the same terms as the one made just before Christmas in the House of Lords by his uncle Northumberland, and there can be no doubt that Algernon genuinely believed that such a court could not be set up by the House of Commons alone. Nor does Cromwell's remark sound invented, especially as there were plenty of witnesses to it. But he did not leave after only one meeting. He attended at least two, perhaps three. The attendance book shows it.

We know from a letter to his father on 10 January 1649[8] that he was then in London, and he must have known he was a Commissioner. The Commission met on that day for a procedural discussion, and although he does not mention attending the meeting he could have done so. The carefully kept attendance book shows he did attend two further meetings on the 15th and 19th when the indictment was finally agreed and it was decided to proceed to the open trial. They were working against time, for the prudent House of Commons, as was always its way when faced with dangerous business, had set a limit of 6 February for the whole operation to be completed, and there must have been many who were secretly hoping the Army would be cheated by mere delay. This important time limit goes far towards explaining Charles's own tactics at the trial and the forcing of the pace by the court.

Although Algernon can thus be convicted of lacking frankness about his record in 'The Great Business', the truth is in some ways more impressive than his own version. His protest must have been as late as 19 January, for he certainly did not attend the open trial at any of its sessions; so he seems to have stayed as long as he could to argue for constitutionalism as a kind of forlorn hope, before the reply he claims to have made to Cromwell on leaving the room: 'I cannot stop you, but I will keep myself clean from having any hand in this business.'

A little prim, perhaps, but one must remember that many of those nominated to the Commission, including Harry Vane, never attended at all, and thus contributed in their way to the certainty of the outcome. And there can be little doubt that at the meetings Algernon said a great deal more than he recorded, for he mentions also[9] that he urged an alternative 'not very fit for a letter', which was almost certainly a political rather than a judicial solution: deposition by Act of Parliament and statutory abolition of the monarchy. But for Cromwell and the senior officers, concerned above all for the discipline of the Army, this was no longer a choice.*

Algernon Sidney, then, was not a regicide, though often accused of being so.† But 'The Great Business' undoubtedly left a lasting impression on him. Charles fought every inch of the way, and when all else seemed to have failed, theatrically offered to produce completely new terms to be presented by Parliament. But even that was not his last bid for survival. That was martyrdom.

He had thought about it and prepared for it from the moment he realised he might have to die a public death; what he feared most was the secret violence so often dealt out to discarded kings, and which he might have expected from a rival monarch. But these enemies would seek a traditional public death for him so as to assert their own legitimacy and satisfy the men in the ranks by hewing Agag in pieces before the altar of the Lord.

For this, a brave end and a chance of explanation, and even a measure of respect, was part of the ritual. Marvell detected Charles's approach as is shown in the theatrical metaphor which extends through two stanzas of the *Horatian Ode to Cromwell* (my italics):

> ... That thence the Royal *actor* borne
> The *tragic scaffold* might *adorn*,
> While round the armed bands

* It is nevertheless interesting that even in the Army there were some officers who were troubled about 'cutting off the head with the crown upon it'. Major Francis White wrote to the Commander-in-Chief, Fairfax, almost echoing Algernon by saying that 'though killing the King might be a just thing' he could not see 'how it may justly be done'. Algernon deliberately refused to describe his alternative since he was writing in 1660, after the Restoration, which he accepted, though reluctantly, as lawful, since sanctioned by Parliament. The matter is very fully discussed in Blencowe 281–83, where Sir James Mackintosh, after reviewing the various possibilities, suggests the one I have adopted.

† When considered closely, definition of the regicides is not easy. Does it, for instance mean being present at, and silently assenting to the sentence, or signing the death warrant? Only 44 persons did both, and only 28 of them were M.P.s – including seven who were also senior Army officers. Only three prominent civilian politicians were among them – Ludlow, Marten and Scot. Even on the morning of the execution the three colonels in charge were trying to protect themselves. One refused to sign the final order to the executioner, and another refused to be present.

Did *clap their bloody hands.*
He nothing common did or mean
Upon that *memorable scene* ...

But Charles intended more than a traditionally dignified end. He designed a political presence after his death which would be free from all his living errors and deviousness and prolong the struggle of his line. Defiance, argument, offers to compromise, might fail and that was why the closing words of his notes for the last interview he gave (three short-hand writers were present, and at least one journalist – a Leveller) were 'I am the martyr of the people'. The effect was slightly spoiled because the earnest Bishop Juxon chose that moment to remind him he had so far said nothing about the Church of England, and he hastily added that of course he died a devout Anglican, but martyrdom was the final idea he wished to leave.

That political presence after death was not to depend on a final utterance, for he knew also that the day after his death his spiritual biography would assert his martyrdom. He had seen the manuscript and the book was already in type. *Eikon Basilike* (the title was in Greek characters, it was said, to puzzle the Army's bookshop inspectors) became the best-seller of 1649, and the disputes about its authorship and exact provenance matter little in comparison with the fact that its subject knew of it and its message.

During the open trial Algernon spent a prudent week at Penshurst and although he came back to London the day before the execution he probably did not witness it. Very few Parliamentarians chose to do so – not even those who had been active members of the court – though the Earl of Pembroke watched incognito from a private window and may have been the source of the account which the Earl of Leicester copied into his diary.

The Parliamentarians, including Algernon and his brother, were needed a few hundred yards away where the House of Commons, almost as the axe fell, were passing a resolution abolishing both the monarchy and the House of Lords, leaving them the sole sovereigns. Matters had proceeded with the precision for which the New Model was famous, but the margin had been narrow: only six days remained of the time allotted by Parliament, and Cromwell himself had been at the House the previous evening canvassing additional signatures for the death warrant.

Algernon was later to defend the execution as a justified act of state, and never recorded the personal impressions it made on him. But it is difficult not to believe that one of them was the realization that in martyrdom – political martyrdom – the King had discovered a new and potent weapon. There had been many religious martyrs in English history, and many great politicians who had died on the scaffold; but these laymen, though they had earned respect at their ends, had been seen as men who had played high and lost.* It was not so with Charles, and it was not to be so with Algernon.

---

* Sir Thomas More may be claimed as an exception; but great though he was, and good as was his end, it can hardly be said that his death was deliberately symbolic, as a martyr's must be.

Troubles of a Noble Family

THROUGHOUT Algernon's active life two forces acted on his spiky emotional character to make him curl and uncurl, shake his spines and sulk by turns, like the porcupine which adorned his family crest: his passion for the cause to which he had given himself, and a sense of loyalty to his family and its interests that often in practice conflicted with what he saw as his duty. It was a conflict he found it particularly difficult to resolve because, unlike such great contemporaries as Cromwell and Vane, who understood well how to conceal their thoughts, Algernon was given either to passionate outbursts of excessive frankness or resentful silence. He never learned to be a successful intriguer, but was in the end to gain the prize of true consistency in a generation when attachment to principle was loudly praised but little valued.

The conflicting demands of family and politics were especially severe during the wintry months Algernon spent with his brother Philip after the King's execution. It is hard to imagine a more dismal household. Besides Philip and Algernon their aunt, Lady Carlisle, was there awaiting the decision of the victors on her lover the Earl of Holland, who was now on trial with the other captured leaders of the 'Second Civil War'; so was Algernon's elder sister Dorothy, the Cavalier Lord Sunderland's window, with her elder son and heir 'the swete little boy Harry Spencer', as his grandfather called him, who was dangerously ill. The Countess of Leicester joined the sad party in February to comfort her sister and daughter. They were not only melancholy but dangerous company for the parliamentary brothers.

Nevertheless they did their utmost for Holland when his petition for mercy came before the House, and it was rejected by only one vote. He and his fellow-leaders went to the block on 6 March in what was now becoming a reign of terror. On 14 March little Harry Spencer died. And next day Major-General Harrison arrived at Leicester House with a warrant for the arrest of Lady Carlisle, whom he lodged in the Tower, where she stayed for the next eighteen months.

Despite the addition of these family embarrassments to the disapproval Algernon had already earned for his stand over the King's trial, he participated zealously in the work of laying the foundations of the infant republic. He was a member (unlike Philip) of the committee preparing the bills formally abolishing both the monarchy and the House of Lords; and of another committee, in its way just as important, to review the very fabric of power, the local magistracy. He was in the House when the old great seal was ceremonially smashed and the pieces presented to Henry Marten, who had presided over the committee that had designed the new one bearing a collective portrait of the Commons. He became, and always remained, a believer that the Rump, the purged unicameral Parliament, was the best government England had ever had.

With revolutionary gestures over, a more cautious and protective mood began to creep through the sovereign House as it approached the question of new institutions. Members began by passing a resolution that they had no intention of changing any of the country's fundamental laws and statutes, which after all, their triumphant struggle had been waged to defend against the encroachments of the King. As for executive authority, they decided in principle to exercise it themselves, through a new Council of State which should be as like as possible to the parliamentary committee to whom the detailed management of the war had been entrusted. Its forty-one members would be elected annually by the House itself, and most of them would have to be M.P.s which, considering the active membership of the Rump was now down to about eighty, made it almost a miniature of the House itself. It would not have a permanent chairman, but would elect one for each meeting, would have elaborate, restrictive terms of reference, and be regularly accountable. It would even meet at Derby House, where the old war committee had met.*

The real difficulties began to emerge with the 'engagement' or oath of loyalty by which, in that age of mistrust, the members of the Council of State would be bound to the new regime. It was clear the formula adopted would not end there – it would soon be extended to other M.P.s, office-holders and magistrates, and perhaps even as a condition of the rights of citizenship. The formula proposed by Cromwell's son-in-law Ireton on 14 February was framed to commit anyone taking it to specific approval of the King's trial and execution.

In the debate that followed Algernon was Ireton's chief adversary, and showed a degree of self-control that was unusual for him. There was uproar when he said the engagement proposed 'would prove a snare to many an honest man, but every knave would slip through it!' and Lord Grey of Groby, who had been one of the most enthusiastic regicides, shouted that such words were a personal insult to him and all who had sat on the court; but Algernon, who had chosen his words with care, sat silent in his place, refusing to be drawn further. Rather to his surprise he was rescued by another regicide, the eccentric intellectual Marten, who pointed out that Algernon had not said those taking the engagement would necessarily be knaves, but that knaves would take it while others, though not knaves, might have scruples. So it was referred back for further consideration and a few days later the Army leaders came back with a wording which omitted retrospective approval of the trial.[1]

The episode marks a further stage in Algernon's consistent opposition to the claims of the Army and the rise of Cromwell, and it was reciprocated by them. Unlike Philip, who was now actively cultivating Cromwell and was rewarded by election to a seat on the Council of State in four successive years, Algernon was denied one until the very last months of the Rump's regime; and when in 1650 Ludlow suggested to Cromwell that Algernon should be given the

---

*Much of this doctrinaire austerity soon disappeared. A President came to be designated at the beginning of each year, and the Council soon decided to set up in Whitehall Palace, now vacant, in spite of its objectionable associations. It was much more commodious, especially for the Council's inevitably growing staff. But there were many complaints about the lavish expenditure on furniture and hangings.

post of deputy to Ireton in Ireland, Cromwell significantly remarked that he had undesirable connections.[2]

The enmity of the Army was not limited to stopping Algernon's advancement. In the autumn of 1649 a sequence of events began which was intended to destroy him, and led to a confrontation between Parliament and the Army. Soon after the end of the 'Second Civil War' the locally recruited garrison of Dover Castle, of which Algernon remained governor by resolution of Parliament, had been strengthened by a contingent of regular troops from Major-General Harrison's regiment, commanded by a certain Captain Henry Cannon, who in his day had been an Agitator and a participant in the Army's Putney Debates in 1647. Very soon Captain Cannon and his officers, perhaps encouraged by Major-General Harrison, began an investigation of their absent governor, and although the surviving official references do not – probably deliberately – tell us the precise allegations, they can be guessed: neglect of duty during the fighting of 1648, or possibly worse – correspondence with the enemy. By the spring of 1650 a case was being mounted before a court martial which the Council of State asked the Commander-in-Chief to expedite.

When Major-General Harrison arrested Lady Carlisle in March 1649 the Earl of Leicester decided to break his long absence from London and arrived at Leicester House two days after his sister-in-law had been taken to the Tower. He stayed three months, during which he gloomily recorded in his diary various events in the collapse of the old order such as the appearance in the Commons of two of his former colleagues in the abolished House of Lords, and a banquet at the Grocer's Hall with Fairfax and Cromwell flanking the Speaker as guests of honour. From his description the Earl must have been there, so presumably was invited, but he was clearly shocked by what he considered the vulgar splendour of the occasion, and especially by the handsome presentations that were made after dinner to men he regarded as dangerous, overrated adventurers.

He had a good deal more to do, however, than observe events and give such support as he could to his wife, sister-in-law, and daughter. He was also involved in a strange negotiation which must have included the Army chiefs, the leaders of the House of Commons, and his wife's brother, the Earl of Northumberland, who was also now in London. The result was important for the Sidney family, but its exact significance is not easy to understand.

The issue was the future of the two sad little relics of the dead King's family, Henry and Elizabeth, who had for some years been in Parliamentary custody with the Earl of Northumberland as their guardian. Now eight and thirteen, they had been brought to London to say farewell to their father and Northumberland, despite the handsome allowance he got for them, wished to rid himself of the responsibility, for reasons that can be guessed. The children were not an active political danger like their grown-up brothers now in exile, but they were pathetic reminders of their fallen family, and it was far from inconceivable that some faction might make a bid for legitimacy by means of a regency for a child monarch. It would, too, be most embarrassing for their guardian if either of them died. The obvious solution was simply to send them to their mother the Queen in Paris; but in the bitter spring of 1649 that would have seemed too like a concession. The House had considered it, but could not bring itself to agree. The disagreeable job of custody was then offered elsewhere, but declined. Now it was offered to the Earl of Leicester.

Or rather to the Countess, for she, not her husband, was to be the statutory custodian. Perhaps her cautious husband preferred it so, perhaps a woman was regarded as a more suitable custodian of two young children, and certainly she was a sounder parliamentarian than her husband. Whatever the reasons, they must have been very strong to outweigh the fact that the new custodian of Parliament's little prisoners was the fond sister of another, much more culpable prisoner of Parliament. The Earl's acquiescence is puzzling. He had always been so careful to avoid involvement with the new regime, which at heart he detested. Perhaps he was influenced by the handsome allowance Parliament offered, but if so he was to be disappointed. The Countess insisted on keeping it herself and would not even give him credit for it in the housekeeping accounts.

One suspects an element of hostage-taking, on the Government side, and when the final release of the royal children was agreed a year later Lady Carlisle was also released; but another calculation could also have entered the minds of those concerned. It was in the unspoken interest of them all to remove these embarrassing children from the political scene, and there could be no better starting point for the continent than Penshurst. That it was so convenient for

Dover, would have been noted by Captain Cannon in his feud against Algernon, and by his superior, Major General Harrison.

The military investigation at Dover rumbled on against manifest divisions of opinion in the Council of State. In October 1650 it recorded that 'the whole matter has been before the Council of War and Colonel Sidney adjudged to be a fit person to be continued in his trust.'[3] But Cannon did not give up. He was thoroughly entrenched at Dover (which Algernon rarely visited), had been appointed Deputy Governor, and had taken over the armoury. He was reporting directly to Harrison about fresh discoveries but when asked by the Council of State to say what they were, refused to put them on paper. The matter became public, petitions were got up, and further investigations ordered. At last, in January 1651, Algernon took the courageous step of personally raising the matter in the House by demanding protection of a Member from court martial and thus precipitating a conflict of principle between Parliament and the Army.

The House ordered all proceedings to stop while a committee went into the affair, and a messenger was sent to Dover with a letter ordering Cannon, in the name of Parliament, to abstain from all further action. In a week he reported that he had found Cannon and his fellow-officers busy breaking into a strong-box which they thought contained evidence. He had offered Parliament's letter, but they had refused to accept it, saying they would receive nothing except what was transmitted to them by their military superiors. The indignant House ordered that Cannon should at once appear before them. But the crisis was avoided. Behind the scenes a bargain seems to have been struck. Cannon was recalled to his regiment and ceased to be Deputy Governor. Algernon resigned his command.[4]

The matter dropped, but it cast a further shadow over Algernon's political progress. At the outset of the republic he had been at the centre of things, a member of important and hardworking committees to which (in May 1649) had been added the most important of all, consisting of eight members under Harry Vane's chairmanship and which required attendance twice a week, to consider a more rational distribution of seats at a future general election.* He was also involved in the committee for achieving

---

* They reported on 9 January 1650 and produced a quite democratic scheme. Seats were distributed on the basis of estimated population to counties, and all municipal

one of Vane's favourite projects, the integration of Scotland with England.

But from early 1650 his attendance at Westminster was less frequent and he was much more at Penshurst, though the atmosphere there cannot have been any more cheerful than it was at Leicester House.

Round its table, besides the Earl and Countess and the two little royalties (Parliament had directed that they should receive no special privileges), there were still five surviving unmarried sisters: Ann, Diana, Frances, Elizabeth, and Algernon's favourite Isabella, who was now sixteen. Ann had an attachment for a penniless clergyman, which was to end in an elopement. Then there was little Henry Sidney, at eleven the youngest of the family; and the Earl's nephew and ward, Viscount Strangford.

Philip, Viscount Strangford, can best be described as a juvenile delinquent. He came of an extremely rich commercial family with whom the Sidneys had several intermarriages, and had lost both his parents by the time he was only ten. The family name was Smythe, and their fortunes had been founded by Philip's grandfather, who had been controller of customs for the Port of London under Elizabeth and James I.

The Earl had taken over the guardianship of his nephew for reasons not wholly disinterested, since the boy's large landed assets provided a useful addition to his own cash flow, and he had not expected that even in his teens Philip would be perfectly capable of spending as much and more. He perhaps brought a ray of cheerfulness among the younger members of that gloomy household, and Algernon, to begin with at any rate, rather liked him – and even lent him money. Isabella liked him too, but the Countess detested him and charged her husband for him in the housekeeping accounts on the ground that since the Earl received the boy's income he should pay for his keep.

Almost everything the Earl now did had an aspect of family finance. When a daughter died he made arrangements to claw her potential settlement back into capital. When he was required to take the engagement of loyalty to the new regime he at first demurred, but was persuaded by his eldest son who pointed out that failure to do so would mean he would no longer have the right to be heard

seats (London excepted) were to be abolished. Algernon's influence can be detected in the recommendation that Kent should have more seats than any other county.

in any of his numerous legal actions. Even so he increasingly disliked his heir, and had a particular disapproval of the young man's cultivation of Cromwell, so Philip was allowed only £800 a year, of which £200 was conditional on the survival of his wife. To Algernon he allowed £2000, which at this time, along with his official salary for Dover, made him comfortably off.

But the Earl now had to bear another cross which had only a little to do with money. It concerned the new rector of Penshurst who, on the abolition of patronage, had been appointed without consulting the Earl, by a Parliamentary committee. The reverend John Maudit was to be a grievous burden. He was the very pattern of a careerist puritan cleric. Son of an Exeter shopkeeper, he had gone up to the Oxford college bearing his native city's name when he was fifteen and graduated M.A. in the year the Civil War broke out. Oxford might then have been the Cavalier capital but he did well, and was made a fellow of his college immediately he became M.A. By 1648, when the hand of the victorious Parliament was beginning to fall heavily on Oxford, he was Sub-Rector, and the instinct for survival persuaded the university to make him Senior Proctor in 1649. His term of office was marked by purges of Cavalier sympathizers in the colleges and the conferment of an honorary degree on the Parliamentarian Commander-in-Chief, Fairfax, at which Maudit preached a sermon reminding the honorand of his responsibilities:

> You are in places of eminency, who are generalls and captaines of the armie, unbelief in you is more dangerous than in others, God will not spare you, if you give him not glorie before the people. Remember how God dealt with Moses at the Rock, when his Faith somewhat fayled, because he gave not glorie to God by believeing, at that time therefore the Lord cut him short of Canaan, this was the reason why Moses was not permitted more than a sight of the Godly land, neither shall you live to see the peace of Sion, and the fulfilling of the promise made to the Church in these latter days, if you will not believe.

When this was published as *The Christian Soudier's Great Engine, or the Mysteries and Mighty Workings of Faith* it was dedicated not to Fairfax but to Cromwell, and its preacher was rewarded first with a studentship of Christ Church, a regimental chaplaincy, a living at Abingdon and finally with the rectory of Penshurst where, on his arrival, he proclaimed his intention of 'endeavouring in much faithfulness a holy reformation'. He received no encouragement from the Earl who, noticing that the parish boundary ran through the middle of Penshurst Place, transferred his allegiance to the church in the next parish and took care that deaths and other events requiring clerical attendance in the house took place in rooms outside Mr Maudit's jurisdiction. Very soon there was open war between Penshurst Place and the rectory at its gates.

During 1650 while Algernon was struggling against the intrigues of Cannon, things went from bad to worse at Penshurst. The house was full of invalids. The elder of the two royalties, Princess Elizabeth, was clearly dying when she left on her journey to France and her mother, which Parliament had at last authorised but which was never completed. Her namesake Elizabeth Sidney was far from well, and also died that summer, and another of Algernon's sisters, Frances, was to follow her only a year later. The funerals were conducted by the reverend Mr Antrobus, incumbent of the next parish. Mr Maudit decided not to follow the practice of his predecessor in letting his glebe land to the Penshurst estate, but to farm it himself. The Earl objected, and 'Godly expostulations' on one side met aristocratic fury on the other. The Earl decided to create a rabbit warren on the border of Maudit's land.

But for Algernon the family development which had the most pernicious and lasting effect was the blossoming of Isabella's passion for Lord Strangford, the Earl's ward and nephew. She was barely seventeen. Little as either the Earl or the Countess liked the idea, marriage, the Countess decided in the spring of 1650, was the only thing. The Earl held out for a time, not so much because he thought Isabella was too young and he disliked Strangford anyway, but because he would lose the guardianship income and no doubt be asked for an account of it. But married they were in August 1650, with Mr Antrobus again officiating. Isabella, of course, had to have her £3000 and that alone, apart from the loss of cash flow from Strangford's estate, meant further manipulation of the Earl's finances, particularly as regarded Leicester House. Strangford left for London and set up in Covent Garden as a man of fashion.

It is strange that so austere a man as Algernon should have sided with the young couple on this matter, and one element in it was certainly his affection for Isabella, though at this stage he seems quite to have liked Strangford also. He not only lent Strangford money – and he was not the kind of man who repays loans – but agreed, since he was still a minor, though no longer a ward, to be his trustee in a legal action against a guardian who had preceded Lord Leicester for money Strangford considered was due to him.

He was to regret this decision for the rest of his life. It was to involve him in endless litigation, poison his family relationships, and impair his political career. Soon after launching his action against his first guardian Strangford demanded that Algernon should act as his trustee against the second one, Lord Leicester himself, over the guardianship accounts. Algernon naturally refused to sue his own father on behalf of someone else. Nevertheless he became more and more deeply involved, throughout the 1650s, in managing Strangford's affairs, and was constantly at Sterry, Strangford's house near Dover. Strangford was unpleasant and Isabella tearful. Bluster was mixed with promises to extract more loans from Algernon personally for several years afterwards. He tried to reform Strangford, and eventually packed him and Isabella off to France while he struggled, almost full-time, with their affairs – more, by now, in the hope of getting his own money back than anything else.[5] Algernon was never a rich man and after the loss of his post at Dover he was in perpetual financial trouble, though he was not extravagant. Horses were his main weakness, and at one stage he seems to have had a stable he was rather proud of. But there is evidence that he parted with capital assets from time to time. In 1648 he sold some East India stock to his brother Philip, and in 1652 some ground rents he had inherited.

His ultimate loss of faith in Isabella nearly broke his heart, and the absence of his usual self-consciousness in a letter to his father in 1660 renders it one of the most pathetic documents he has left:

> I confesse it was a folly; if my affection to hir, which was so hard to root out of my hart be not an excuse, I have none ... She desired me to come to hir chamber, acknowledged hir fault, begged pardon with so many expressions of repentance, affection and promises of amendment, as ever I heard from any tongue ... in short, I could not resist her praiers and teares, but received and helped hir as formerly, by which meanes, shee gained the power of doing me all this mischiefe under the name of her husband; for which I am mistaken if shee be not ere long sufficiently punished; though I should in no way resent it. . . .[6]

It is a strange mixture of affection, pride, resentment, with, in the background, a growing need to recover from the financial mess some kind of security for himself.

The British Republic

FROM the autumn of 1649 until well into 1651 Algernon was a good deal at Westminster, canvassing to the limit of his precarious reputation for the release of his imprisoned aunt and as a member of Harry Vane's Committee on a Future Representative, which was discussing how a new general election could safely be held consistent with the revolution now accomplished; but he was not leading a full political life. Only in 1651 did he began to attend the House regularly. In November of that year, though not a candidate for the Council of State, he was scrutineer at its election.

One of the signals that a member of the Sidney family was appearing on the political stage was a publication about the family hero, Sir Philip. The printing of his correspondence with Languet had coincided with the Earl of Leicester's embassy to Denmark, and his biography by his great friend Fulke Greville, which had lain unpublished in Warwick Castle for more than fifty years, made its appearance in 1652. This could hardly have been without the collaboration and approval of the Sidney family, especially as the male line of the Grevilles was at that time represented by minors.*

During Algernon's eighteen months or so of semi-retirement

* For the importance of the Greville connection in Algernon's history see pp 262–63.

the old landmarks of the political landscape were obliterated as if by a tidal wave and, after Cromwell's victory against Charles II and his Scottish army at Worcester in September 1651, the only significant centres of power left in the three kingdoms were the House of Commons, the Army and, in a measure, the City of London. The colours of the Commonwealth were firmly planted in Ireland, and after Worcester Scotland disintegrated as a separate power; one by one the Scottish counties decided to join England. The Republic triumphed from one extremity of the British Isles to the other. Early in October Jersey surrendered to Blake, and in February 1652 Colonel Overton occupied the Orkneys.

An even greater dream than the unity of the British Isles had come and gone in that short time. In the autumn of 1650 the Rump invited the Dutch to join not merely an alliance but 'a confederation perpetual' or even 'a full and perfect union', founded on Protestant Republicanism, which would be a new power in Northwestern Europe. Nearly forty years later the dream was to return – even in part to be achieved – but in its grandiose and more generous form it necessarily foundered. Economic competitiveness proved stronger than common principles, and by the summer of 1651 the Rump had passed to the other extreme by enacting its one piece of legislation that endured: the Navigation Act, aimed primarily against Dutch shipping, which lasted for two hundred years. When Algernon resumed his parliamentary career the two Protestant republics were on the brink of war.*

The Rump Parliament has often been thought of as a mere puppet of the victorious Army, but that is far from being how it thought of itself. Some of its members were indeed senior army officers and others – Algernon's elder brother Philip was among them – were being drawn into the embryonic court forming round Cromwell, but neither of these groups possessed the talisman of legitimacy which the most active parliamentarians treasured. They, and they alone, were its custodians in whose favour all other rivals had been destroyed. Those who had participated in exercising it

---

* Earlier biographers have sent Algernon to Holland while the negotiations for a union of the two republics were in train, but although the idea is attractive it is based on references which plainly relate to his younger brother Robert, who was a lieutenant-colonel in the Dutch service, and remained so until 1659. As a member of the entourage of Charles and his brother James in exile he was a useful channel of information for the Penshurst family about the royalist court and the Netherlands generally.

never ceased to be proud of recalling those triumphant days. The Dutch War that was now about to begin was to be their particular pride, for its success owed little to the Army, and a great deal to the parliamentarian who was now the Army's chief opponent, Harry Vane.

To what extent Vane's influence, or Algernon's own decision, brought about his sudden return to active politics it is impossible to say; but the amount of energy he displayed is remarkable. In the six months from November 1651 he was a teller in no fewer than sixteen divisions on a bewildering variety of topics: the sale of royal estates, the drainage of Lincolnshire Fens, Irish land, official appointments, lists of 'delinquents' who were to pay fines for opposing the Commonwealth.

It is clear that in all this he was no friend of the Army. Personally he had every reason not to be, and now it was becoming manifest that the Army threatened the whole concept of constitutional legitimacy for which the Rump stood; and beyond the Army, though pervading it also, were the clamorous disorderly sects with their revolutionary millenarian programmes and their claims that the muscle of society, the law, should be subject to popular change. Prominent among them was Algernon's personal enemy, the Fifth Monarchy Man, General Harrison. Algernon was a non-conformist in religion, and had nothing but contempt for bishops, but fanaticism disgusted him.

In rebuilding his political career, he did not identify himself with any particular group, not even the 'like-minded' Commonwealthmen, and one suspects that often he was himself the author of the questions in which he appears as a teller. Out of the sixteen he was in a minority on no fewer than eleven. But if there is an overall theme in his interventions it is one of moderation. When lists of 'delinquents' were before the House his interventions on particular names are for omitting or reducing the penalty proposed. One of his few successes was on a Bill to sell off the royal estates, in which the opposing teller was Harry Marten, and Windsor Castle was thus saved from going to auction. While Algernon remained a republican, he was now doing his best to ensure that the fabric of aristocracy should survive.

In the autumn of 1651 the tension between constitutionalism, whose sole representative the Rump now was, and the discordant demands for God-guided social change, began to be apparent in the controversy about what permanent arrangements for a representative assembly could and should be made. Algernon himself, as a member of Vane's committee, was an expert on it. There seems at first sight so much common ground between the disputants that the passionate and lasting disagreement which shattered the very basis of the republic needs more explanation than it has, until recently, received. Surely it must have been obvious to everyone that the Rump, even accepting its claim to legitimacy, was necessarily a temporary arrangement; and that its most pressing duty, which it alone could perform, was to establish the rules for a regular parliamentary regime? Many historians, therefore, have abandoned the controversy altogether by supposing that it was not a genuine one: and that either the Army, in its impatience for supreme power, would have ultimately seized on any issue to sweep its puppet aside; or the Rump's real aim was a kind of perpetual Parliament to which there would never again be a general election. Seats would simply be filled as vacancies arose, with the existing membership keeping a close watch to see that nobody unsuitable was admitted. A system perilously like co-option.

Some Rumpers did toy with this comfortable idea, just as some Army officers saw no value in the alleged legitimacy of parliamentarians. It is possible Algernon was among the former group, and may have been among the forty-seven members who voted against Cromwell's motion in November 1651 that the Rump should fix a date for its dissolution and in the meantime work out plans for a continuous parliamentary regime. It passed by a majority of only two, and the date fixed was 3 November 1654. 'So they have three yeares yet' was the Earl of Leicester's caustic entry in his diary when the news reached Penshurst.

Underlying what the Army saw as the Rump's prevarication and dilatoriness there was a genuine difficulty, arising from the idea of sovereignty itself. For the seventeenth-century constitutionalist sovereignty was seamless and could not cease without bringing an end to the state itself: hence the doctrine that one king succeeded another without the intermission of a moment. Now there was no king, and the House of Commons as at present constituted was the sovereign. How could it cease until another equally legitimate House of Commons had been brought into being? There could not be a void in sovereignty each time a new parliament was elected. This may seem unduly ideological. But one must remember that Parliament had already abolished all other institutions by which continuity could be preserved, and insisted on exercising executive powers itself.

This difficulty was linked with a more practical one. Neither the Rump nor the Army thought in terms of what we would call multi-party democracy. Both agreed that if the Revolution was to be preserved there must be some control by existing authority over both the right to vote and the right to be elected. The idea that those who had fought for the King in the war should have any voice in elections, let alone the chance of a seat in Parliament, was wholly unacceptable. Some, especially in the Army, went further, arguing that only people who showed genuine and positive support for the new republic should have any voice – thus excluding 'presbyterians' and 'neuters' as well as 'malignants' and 'delinquents'. Some existing authority, in fact, must be there to police the elections and sift the new assembly.

For eighteen months the House considered its 'Bill for a New Representative' with increasing urgency while the Army grew more impatient and suspicious; and Algernon succeeded in making his mark. In the autumn of 1652 his hard work began to be rewarded and his old hero, Sir Harry Vane, after suffering temporary eclipse, was once again a dominating figure at Westminster. Though Vane had never advocated the war into which Britain and Holland had drifted that summer, he was very much a war minister, and by September was presiding over a massive naval programme. One guesses that the renewed ascendency of Vane was decisive in carrying Algernon to success in the elections to the Council of State which took place early in November, and were the last the Rump was to hold. He received forty-five votes, much the same as his enemy General Harrison, who just scraped home. Many members voted who had not been seen in the House for a long time – always a sign of a coming struggle.

At this critical point in Algernon's political fortunes something occurred which profoundly affected his family and his political situation, and even his outlook. That August of 1652 his brother Philip's wife Catherine died of puerperal fever after giving birth to a daughter, and once again Mr Antrobus had to officiate at a Penshurst funeral. The Earl and Countess helpfully offered to give a home to Philip's two motherless children, but the arrangements for Philip's allowance of £800 a year were observed to the letter: it was to be reduced to £600 if his wife did not survive him, and reduced it was. Philip was beside himself with fury, and the quarrel that followed 'had such effects', in Algernon's words, 'as are not fit to be related.'[1] He adds, however, that they had been placed on record by the Earl himself, and in words which even an editor nearly two hundred years later thought it right to omit: On 16 December 1652, 'The Lord Lisle most unnecessarily and causelessly, undutifully and impiously, deffyed and affronted me, and not only so but assaulted and struck me in my own house at Penshurst.'[2] Father and son had to be physically dragged apart by the Countess and her younger son Robert, who was on a visit from the Netherlands.

The Earl was to live another quarter of a century, but he never forgave Philip, and Algernon became – for a time at any rate – the favourite son even though he could never be the heir. His political star was rising, and he had overcome, so far as was humanly possible, the iron laws of primogeniture. Penshurst and the title, of course, he could never have unless he survived Philip, but never again would he have to chafe and gird under Philip's authority, and his ambitions grew ever stronger.

Once on the Council of State he threw himself zealously into foreign affairs. The experience of protocol he had gained in his youth in Copenhagen and Paris turned out to be valuable and he was immensely hardworking. Though the Council of State was a large body containing many veteran politicians, such men had many other calls on their time, and their attendance at the Council, which met several times a week, was surprisingly patchy. A young London-based member such as Algernon, if he was willing to work, had ample opportunities, and within a few months he was as near to being the Republic's foreign minister as could be achieved without such a post formally existing, and became the normal spokesman for Council on external relations.*

As a result he was on his feet in the House almost every week during the winter of 1652–53, and in regular contact with diplomatic representatives as well as the Council's secretariat, of which Milton was the head. There was plenty for the Republic's overseas expert to do. At first the monarchies of the Continent had held it at arm's

---

* The procedure of the Council was to make one of its members responsible for following up and reporting to the House on each Council decision as it was made. Algernon was almost invariably given this responsibility where foreign affairs were concerned.

length, but its triumphs had begun to bring it recognition. Spain and Portugal had opened diplomatic relations and even France was moving towards them. Now the Commonwealth navy had appeared in the Mediterranean, and Tuscany and Venice were beginning to take notice of colonels who could float as well as march.

It was Algernon's happiest time, and though neither he nor Harry Vane, who now dominated the Council, had wanted the Dutch War, they worked together enthusiastically to win it. When Algernon came later to write his eulogy of Vane he dwelt particularly on the thirty-eight frigates (he wrongly claims Vane invented the term) which his hero got launched and commissioned. But if working closely with Vane was one source of happiness, the highest and most lasting was the sense that the strange institutions with which the Republic had endowed itself were working successfully, and monarchy could no longer be defended even as a necessary evil. As for the soldiers who made it possible, he would undoubtedly have shared the view so clearly expressed by Heselrige: 'The Army are our children. They come from us'.

The children were becoming more and more refractory. At the beginning of 1653 the Army brought the House firmly to the question of settling the representative system on a regular basis, and the date of dissolution before which legislation had to be passed was brought forward by twelve months to November of that very year. There was already a scheme on hand – based on the one Algernon and Vane had produced – and with both Army and Parliament demanding action on what were apparently similar lines the approaching collision between them has to be seen in terms of political attitudes.

The true issue was not whether the Rump should be dissolved, or even the details of the electoral system that should produce its successor, but the question of whether the Parliament or the Army should have the main voice in deciding that successor's composition.

In the scenes which followed Cromwell played a central role, but it is hard to believe – though Algernon certainly did – that he created the situation. In seizing and exploiting an opportunity, in deciding what had to be done and then doing it, he had no equal, but his political opinions were those of a conventional man. In the summer of 1652, for instance, he divided the House in support of applying a judicial precedent established by the now abolished House of Lords, and was opposed by Algernon Sidney and Henry Marten in alliance arguing that the validity of such precedents had vanished with the House that created them. On the issue of the 'New Representative' he tried until the very last moment to prevent the fatal collision between the House and the Army which was now impending. He might not follow the intellectuals of the House in their high-flown ideas about legitimacy, and rather despised the Brahminical pomposity with which they surrounded their status; but he saw clearly that legitimacy of some sort was a condition of what he valued above all, order; and the revolutionary cry from one of the officers at an army conference that 'it would be time enough to decide what should be placed in the room of the Rump when it had been abolished', did not meet with his approval.

But the Army was now a political structure in its own right, and its ideas had to be taken into account; and it had to be paid, even if the thought of a political void in which armed sectarians reconstructed society on millenarian lines horrified Cromwell as much as it did most members of Parliament. Algernon's old enemy, General Harrison, had no such reservations. The Army had won the Civil War, conquered Scotland, and decisively conquered Ireland. Now it should conquer England. If it did not, it would be told, as in the days of 1647–48, that it was no longer needed.

The picture as seen by the military revolutionaries was of the existing House reproducing itself: not necessarily prolonging its own life, though some feared that, but installing arrangements which would so control the membership of its successor that the Army's millenarian dream would be frustrated. When 19 April 1653 was reached, with only six months of the existing House left, the provision in the Bill on this crucial point was that the election should be held while the old House was still in existence. It would merely adjourn, could reassemble at any time, and certainly would do so to review the election results and ensure a suitable successor.

This was not good enough for the Army. The old House must die before the new one could succeed. That evening a conference was held and a compromise proposed by Cromwell seemed to be accepted both by the parliamentarians present (Algernon and Vane were among them) and the senior officers of the Army. The House would cease to exist before the election, but would leave behind forty nominated 'guardians' who would be the legitimate government until the new House assembled, and have the delicate task of reviewing the election results before that was allowed to happen.

There are three explanations for what happened next day: bad faith on one side or the other, or pure misunderstanding. Early that morning Cromwell received news that the House was proceeding with the Bill, and gained (or said he had gained) the impression that the compromise of the previous evening had been discarded. He decided, as he had in the case of the King, to cut off the head with the crown upon it.

Accompanied by Harrison and a body of troops he went down to the House and entered it, leaving the soldiers outside. The benches were full for the resumed debate on the Future Representative. Algernon was present, and the celebrated account of the scene that followed in his father's diary must come from his own report, and is probably in his words. For a time Cromwell sat quietly in his place, with Harrison beside him, listening.* Then he rose and began to speak –

> first ... to the commendation of the Parliament, for theyre paynes and care for the public good; but afterwards he changed his style, told them of theyr injustice, delays of justice, self-interest and other faults; then he sayd, Perhaps you thinke this is not Parlementary language, I confesse it is not, neither are you to expect any such from me, then he putt on his hat, went out of his place, and walked up and down the stage or floor in the middest of the House, with his hat on his head, and chid them soundly, looking sometimes and pointing particularly upon some persons ...[3].

The language was strong, but it was all calculated, for the style was familiar to him. It was that of a senior officer dressing down a slack body of troops. The theatrical denunciation of individuals by name – 'There sits a drunkard', 'a juggler without common honesty' – is characteristic and so is the general anathema, again and again repeated, 'you are no Parliament, I say you are no Parliament.' Call yourselves soldiers? The purpose of the performance was plainly the destruction of Parliament's precious talisman of legitimacy yet at the same time preserving, so far as he could, the idea that legitimacy would indeed reside in a true Parliament.

* This is interesting as an indicator of the underlying reasons for the intervention. It is generally assumed that the decision to dissolve the Rump by force was made by Cromwell before he set out, but (allowing always for the fact that we do not know what, exactly, was in the Bill that morning) this is not necessarily so, and before rising to his feet Cromwell waited until the motion for the Bill to pass was put. It is at least possible that it still included the objectionable clause, and did not incorporate the compromise Cromwell thought had been agreed. For a close discussion see Worden, *The Rump Parliament* 332–341.

Then, turning to Harrison, he told him to bring in the soldiers. By the time he returned with them a number of members had already left. Harrison then approached the Speaker, tugged his gown and handed him down from his chair, but as the House emptied Algernon still sat grimly in his place to the Speaker's right. Harrison asked him to leave 'but he sayd he would not go out, and sate still' until in response to Cromwell's 'Put him out' Harrison and Colonel Worsley put their hands on his shoulders as if to use force. He walked slowly to the door, staying long enough to hear Cromwell's last insults to Harry Vane and to the mace, Parliament's symbol of authority. Cromwell then took the unpassed Bill from the Clerk's table, put it in his pocket, and left, locking the door behind him and posting a guard outside.*

Whether Cromwell was right or not in making the accusation that Vane had 'juggled' with him will never be known. Vane always denied it, and so did Algernon. But for Algernon it was a crippling blow. Just as his political career at last seemed to be prospering the whole ground on which he stood was swept away. His enemy Harrison and his rival Philip had triumphed, and of Cromwell he must have felt as the Earl of Leicester had felt about Philip. He had been 'unnecessarily and causelessly, undutifully and impiously deffyed and affronted ... and not only so but assaulted and struck in his own House.'

---

* All these gestures were symbolic of the intention to destroy the claim of legitimacy. The last was especially important, since the idea that the House could lawfully meet nowhere but in that Chamber where 'they had their yeas and nays' had become part of parliamentary mystique. It arose first out of Charles I's unsuccessful attempt to establish a House of Commons at Oxford consisting of his own expelled supporters. The 'Seceders' of 1647 denied the validity of the proceedings which continued at Westminster, but did not dare claim to be a House themselves, even though the Speaker was among them. When, in 1659, first the Rump and then the members excluded by Pride's Purge were restored, a great parade was made of the fact that they re-entered sacred ground. Charles II's proposal to hold the second Exclusion Parliament outside London was regarded by many as unconstitutional. When the third Exclusion Parliament was held at Oxford there was a strong movement not to attend.

VIII

Caesarism

BUT, bless me [wrote Dorothy Osborne to her lover William Temple, when she heard of the great scene at Westminster], what will become of us all now? Is not this a strange turn? What does my Lord Lisle? ... If I had been so wise as to have taken hold of the offer was made to me by Henry Cromwell [Cromwell's son] I might have been in a fair way of preferment, for sure, they will be greater now than ever. Is it true that Algernon Sidney was so unwilling to leave the House, that the General was fain to take the pains to turn him out himself? Well, 'tis a pleasant world this. If Mr Pym were alive again I wonder what he would think of these proceedings, and whether this would appear as great a breach of the Privilege of Parliament as the demanding of the five members?[1]

Dorothy and his old school friend Temple might joke about it, but Algernon was not only politically but emotionally driven into the shadows to brood on the nobility of the Commonwealth for which he had struggled. The stroke was harder to bear because the Republic had been something he had seen in action, in which he felt destined to play a part until low-born Praetorians destroyed it. It opened, at last, the career he felt he deserved. He was only thirty, was to live as many years again, and twice more was to emerge into the broad daylight of public view: once when the Republic showed signs of reviving after the death of the hated Oliver, once in the last scenes of opposition to Charles II and final martyrdom. But apart from these occasions, in both of which he registered major political achievement, we have only a sequence of strange variegated glimpses of this disappointed but uncrushable man whose consolation was now study and, increasingly, conspiracy.*

For fifteen months after the dissolution of the Rump we have no news of him, and even then we only know he was living in a house off St Martin's Lane and was in touch with a Mr Kellerby about the sale of timber, possibly from the Strangford estates[2]. Much of the intervening time he no doubt spent at Penshurst, for he was no longer welcome in Leicester House, where his elder brother had established himself as a rising Commonwealth courtier, and member of the so-called 'Barebones' Parliament nominated by Cromwell the previous summer, but quickly dissolved. Its saintly members elected Philip to its short-lived Council of State. The whole thing was considered by strict constitutionalists like Algernon as an outrage.

When Algernon received his letter from Kellerby in June 1654, he was already on the move from St Martin's Lane, for in July he suddenly appears at the Hague where, on the thirty-first of that month, the Grand Pensionary of Holland, Jan de Witt, made a note 'Saak van Sidney' – the business of Sidney. That business was important, and although we do not know who Algernon was acting for, we do know what it concerned.

The title of Grand Pensionary suggests a comfortably rotund burgher but de Witt was in fact two years younger than Algernon – only twenty-eight – and already one of the most conspicuous statesmen in Europe. Algernon must have met him when he visited England in 1647, and seen in the young Dutchman exactly what he himself longed to be. De Witt had even excelled his elder brother Cornelius who patiently played second fiddle to Jan until the bitter end. His political skill and capacity for hard work were extraordinary, his manner eager and attractive, and despite his Calvinism his success with women was notorious. He was not of high birth, like Algernon, and perhaps the young colonel had rather looked down on him when he first met him six years earlier, but he had a

---

* The materials are more abundant than these words might suggest, for we have some seventy letters written by Algernon after 1653, many of them both long and interesting. The most important of them, however, concern his embassy in Copenhagen in 1659–60, and his last months of trial and imprisonment. The letters from Rome, where he spent nearly a year in 1660–61, are also numerous and remarkable, but for very long periods – especially from 1663 to 1677 – he left little trace, though more has now been recovered.

coat of arms going back to the thirteenth century, and now he was in control of the foreign policy of one of the most important powers in Europe.

Strictly speaking he was the chief official of only one – though the wealthiest – of the seven United Provinces, where each Province had its own constitution, its own assembly, and its own finances. The United Netherlands was very much a congeries of communities united only in form by the assembly of delegates which made up Their High Mightinesses the States of the United Provinces and, narrowly mandated by their provinces, behaved more like a conference of diplomats than a national assembly.

In the United Provinces the Constitution designated no 'single person' at the head of affairs, but until 1651 that vacuum had been filled by the pervasive influence of the House of Orange, the greatest landowner in the country and the symbol of its struggle for independence. Two years after the end of monarchy in England the republicans of the Netherlands had bottled up the power of the House of Orange. Its current representative was a child – the future William III of England, and nephew to the exiled Charles II. This connection between Orange and Stuart gave common cause to republicans on both sides of the North Sea. For their part the House of Orange, though excluded from open power, gave help and money to the exiled heir of Charles I and the country swarmed with Cavalier exiles. In 1650 some of them had murdered the English Commonwealth's ambassador.

When Algernon arrived in the Hague in July 1654 the two republics were moving towards peace with one another after the hostilities in which Vane and Algernon himself had played such an enthusiastic part to bring England out with advantage. A treaty had just been signed in Westminster which seemed to settle all the issues, yet left one point outstanding, which Cromwell insisted on but de Witt opposed. Cromwell demanded a secret guarantee that no member of the House of Orange would ever be permitted to hold office in any of the seven provinces. De Witt would personally have been happy enough to agree but knew that such a limitation on their powers was something which the provinces would never unanimously accept. He initiated a secret assembly of the States of Holland alone. Even there he found a strong minority against the proposal, but it was carried and on the strength of it he instructed the Dutch ambassador in London to give the guarantee.

Algernon's arrival coincided with the disclosure that these secret and unconstitutional instructions had been given. The country was in an uproar. The supreme assembly of the United Provinces demanded that the instructions should be laid before them; but de Witt frustrated them by arranging that the London embassy should close with Cromwell before copies of their instructions could be produced in Holland. He then set to work composing a powerful (and very long) defence of his action which was published later in the summer, and was a complete success. De Witt's tortuous conduct of these negotiations is generally considered a triumph of diplomacy. Algernon's mission was concerned with it.

Late in July, when the excitement was at its highest, Algernon had a long conversation with de Witt on which both men reported separately to the Dutch ambassador in London, Van Beverning. Algernon's letter was the briefer, and a copy found its way to Thurloe, Cromwell's chief of intelligence, who had arrangements for intercepting all Algernon's correspondence. It warned Beverning that 'unless those in favour of the [Anglo-Dutch] treaty in Holland did not take more care they will run the hazard to repent themselves ere long.'[3] De Witt's letter is equally cryptic. The result of his talk to Sidney, he tells Van Beverning, is advice that the Calvinist Dutch clergy should be encouraged to preach as energetically as possible on the theme that Cromwell was a true friend to the Protestant Reformed Religion, intended an understanding with the 'English Presbyterians', planned a firm church settlement in England, and was opposed to sectaries and visionaries.[4]

Algernon stayed some months longer at the Hague and continued to write letters to England which were faithfully intercepted by Cromwell's secret service. Early in August he reported to his father on the success of de Witt's defensive document and how 'The States of Holland go on vigorously with their designs, and 'tis thought they will suddenly silence the other grumbling provinces ... Many rant here; others disavow what is done, but what more they will do I cannot tell.'[5] He stayed till September, but by that time the excitement had died down and his letters home report no more than passing events.

What was he up to in the Netherlands, advising its leading statesman to organize a propaganda campaign from Dutch pulpits to reassure the burghers that Cromwell, the odious usurper and destroyer of the English Parliament, was a respectable moderate statesman? One would almost think he was now the emissary of the man who hardly more than a year before had personally ruined his career. It seems impossible that it should have been so, yet there is another small piece of evidence which could support it – at any rate superficially. In that very year, 1654, Milton published a political pamphlet, intended for the learned world, since it was in Latin, and designed to support the new regime headed by Cromwell.[6] It came out in May, just before Algernon's visit to the Netherlands began, and must have been subject to official influence, for Milton had continued in his post of Secretary to the Council of State after the coup d'état.

In it he parades the new heroes of the republic, military and civilian, with Cromwell coming first. Harrison, significantly, is missing, having had his sting drawn, and among the civilians the lawyer Whitelocke, whom Cromwell had so passionately denounced, is included, but not Vane. There is also the ambiguous utterance that 'the illustrious name of Sidney has always been on our side'. It could refer to both Philip and Algernon, and would be true of Philip. It can be read as a small olive branch to the constitutionalists, and suggests that even if the Cromwellians did not arrange Algernon's visit, they were aware of it.

Some of the constitutionalists agreed to sit in the assembly known as Cromwell's Second Parliament, which met in the summer of 1654, but Algernon was not among them, and there is no evidence that he wished to be, or was asked. From that fatal 20 April onwards he never mentioned Cromwell – and he mentioned him often – except as a tyrant and usurper. It would be necessary to go against all we know of his character to suppose he changed his colours so quickly and completely, as to become a Cromwellian diplomatic agent.

The probable explanation is that he was the agent of the constitutionalist opposition to Cromwell, with the mission of assuring de Witt that on this issue of excluding the House of Orange the opposition were at one with the Protector. In confirmation of this is the fact that he did not report to the Protector or to Thurloe. What we know of his mission from his side is in letters which were intercepted by Cromwell's intelligence service. It is unusual (though admittedly not unknown) to intercept the reports of one's own agents.

Indeed Algernon may not have been above making a little

mischief for Cromwell as well as helping to promote the treaty which republicans of every shade in England wanted. By urging de Witt to show Cromwell as a potential compromiser, 'opposed to sectaries and visionaries', the trust between the Protector and such men as Harrison would be still further impaired.[7]

The uneasy dictatorship of Cromwell endured for another four years after Algernon's return from Holland, and he spent most of them away from London. Apart from one single episode, he played no further political role, and Philip would hardly tolerate his brother at Leicester House. As a result Algernon had plenty of time in which to use his father's large library to do some of the extensive but eclectic reading of history that later went into *Discourses Concerning Government*, and develop into the studious, almost solemn figure he later became, marking him among his contemporaries as the best informed layman they had ever met. 'He studied the history of government in all its branches', Burnet was to write, 'beyond any man I ever knew.' One must always remember that despite his high birth Algernon was self-taught, and never acquired the discipline and conciseness of a formally educated scholar.

But it was not an untroubled retirement. Penshurst was no refuge from the misery and labour created by Isabella and her husband Strangford, who had now repudiated the Earl's guardianship and was bombarding him with litigious complaints about the guardianship accounts. More than once Algernon, in response to the pleas of his favourite sister, paid bills for Strangford, and spent long periods at their house at Sterry, near Dover. Indeed he became more and more deeply involved in Strangford's tangled affairs.* There also he was spotted as a frequent visitor by Thurloe's intelligence agents, who had identified Sterry House as a possible staging post for Cavalier couriers on their way to and from the Continent. Altogether the Strangford connection was the most unfortunate of his life.[8]

---

* He even packed the Strangfords off to France for a time and managed their estates himself. Dr Jonathan Scott in his *Algernon Sidney and the English Republic* (Cambridge University Press 1988) has gone deeply into the surviving legal records and argues that Sidney, in his desperate struggle for financial independence, planned to divert Strangford's property to his own possession, and so came very near being a fraudulent trustee. Strangford certainly made such accusations, and fraudulent trusteeship was common in the seventeenth century. Algernon was certainly trying to get his own money back, and probably more (see p. 145 *post*), but looking at the evidence as a whole I doubt if he set out systematically to defraud the Strangfords.

Nor were these the only family miseries of this time. Algernon's sister Ann eloped with her clergyman, and the Earl's response to her plea for forgiveness (and a little money), signed with hopeful pathos 'your sorrowing and repentant daughter Ann', met the stinging response that she had 'lost a good home, got one she was ashamed of, and had so far forgotten herself as a result that she signed herself plain Ann like a Queen'. He cancelled her dowry, but it is some comfort that he later forgave her to the extent of providing for her in his will.

The Earl was growing more and more morose. The trouble with Mr Maudit now developed into a battle with serious political implications. Maudit, in pursuit of his 'Godly Reformation', had the mediaeval carved ceiling bosses in the church sawn off. The Earl refused to pay tithe, and in reply to Maudit's applications pointed out that discussions in Parliament and among theologians had thrown doubt on whether such payments were in accordance with God's law. This insulting assumption of self-interested Quakerism was the last straw, and one Sunday in 1655 Maudit used his pulpit to denounce the Earl publicly as 'a wicked man, a cruel oppressor, and an enemy to Reformation'. Undeterred, the Earl sued him, not for simple slander but for *scandalum magnatum*, or insulting a peer of the realm. When the case came on at Maidstone Maudit pleaded in vain that the House of Lords had been abolished by Parliament. That might indeed be so, ruled the judge, or it might not: it was unnecessary to decide the point. Parliament had certainly not abolished Lords as such, so the gross offence of slandering them still existed and the Earl should be awarded £500 damages. The infuriated Maudit poured out his troubles in a pamphlet.*

It is hardly surprising that by 1658 things had grown so bad that the Earl and Countess were on the verge of separation. 'I have bin and am thinking,' he wrote to his wife's brother Northumberland, 'of a retrait for myself that your sister may live somewhere secure from my passions and more to her contentment.'[9]

Against this melancholy background Algernon made one more

---

* *A Defence of the Minister of Penshurst in the Case between him and the Earl of Leicester.* The Earl never got payment of his damages (though he always regarded them as a debt due to his estate and left them in his will to his third son Robert) but the case seriously damaged Maudit. His ruin was completed by the Restoration, as a result of which he was deprived of his living and spent the rest of his life ministering to a small dissenting congregation at Ottery St Mary in his native Devonshire, which he combined with keeping the Golden Lion at Exeter. He died in 1674.

excursion into politics as a member of the continuing constitutionalist protest against the Protectorate. In the summer of 1656 it showed a flicker of activity after the elections to Cromwell's so-called Third Parliament. The incidents were sporadic, but one suspects connected. One of them was Henry Neville's candidature for Berkshire, which was unsuccessful, and followed by an action against the returning officer for malpractice. It was turned into a *cause célèbre* by the patronage of several staunch republican chieftains, including Heselrige, Ludlow, and Scot. At the same time Harry Vane was lodged in prison by the authorities, and Algernon made a demonstration which can truly be described as dramatic.

He put on a play at Leicester House. Just what the play was is not known, but it must have been the first ever to be mounted in what is now the heart of theatreland, and tradition says it was *Julius Caesar*, with Algernon himself as Brutus. It seems to have been open to the public, and undoubtedly gave great offence to Cromwell, as we know from an indignant letter Philip Lisle wrote to the Earl:

> In my humble opinion the business of your Lordship's House hath past somewhat unluckily; and that it had been better used to do a seasonable courtesy to my Lord Protector, than to have such a play acted in it of publick affront to him, which doth much entertayne the towne. I have been in some places where they told me they were exceedingly pleased with the gallant relation of the chief actor in it . . . laying all other matters aside, this, which hath appeared most eminently on this occasion, is very extraordinary, that a *younger son* should so domineer in the house, that not only in this matter which I have spoken of I am uncertain whether I can have the liberty to look into it or no . . .[10]

In spite of his doubts he thought it his duty to offer Cromwell an apology on behalf of the family, and received a very curt reply.

On 3 September 1658 the great Protector died, leaving unsolved the problem of legitimacy and the conflicting claims of the constitutionalists and the military idealists. Yet it did seem in the next few months, during which Richard Cromwell presided over the political world, as if some progress was being made towards compromise. The organizers of Richard Cromwell's Parliament dropped all the experimental systems of the recent past and fell back on the old constituencies and the old electoral qualifications which had brought the Long Parliament into existence in 1640.

Some even of the most stubborn constitutionalists were won over by this gesture, and decided at a meeting held at Harry Vane's house in Hampstead that they would not only stand for election but would take their seats in what they still insisted on puritanically calling 'an assembly', provided they 'were fairly chosen and no unjust or dishonourable thing was required of them'. Though Algernon is not mentioned by name as having been at this meeting, and did not in fact seek election to Richard Cromwell's Parliament, he is unlikely to have been absent from such a gathering of old like-minded colleagues. But the new system could not last. The old constitutionalists opposed the seating of any members from Scotland or Ireland on the ground that they were Army nominees – which was true; and they protested against the setting up of a second chamber, which breached one of their most fundamental principles. In April 1659 the predominant faction in the Army decided to create a constitutional vacuum by abolishing the Parliament and deposing Richard Cromwell.

There followed twelve months in which it appears with hindsight as if the drama whose development had taken twelve years – from 1641 to 1653 – was being played backwards with astonishing speed. First the coup d'état of 1653 was reversed by the reassembling of the parliamentarians who had survived Pride's Purge; then in the autumn Pride's Purge itself was reversed by the readmission of the secluded 'Presbyterians'; in the spring of 1660 new elections on the old franchise produced a Parliament surprisingly like the House of 1640 before the expulsions organized by Pym and Hampden; the old hereditary House of Lords (minus for the time being the bishops) reappeared; and to complete the cycle a second Charles returned to Whitehall.

So, in symmetry, it may seem, but for those who lived through it there can have been no such sense of inevitable reaction. The road to the Restoration – and with it the final ruin of Algernon's hopes – may have begun in April 1659, but until nearly the last stage a new military dictatorship under one or other of the competing warlords must have seemed much more probable. For the Army's nature had changed. It was no longer the army of the Putney Debates, earnestly seeking the way to use its strength, but a collection of units whose primary loyalty was usually to a particular commander. Soldiering had indeed, in Algernon's words, 'become a trade'.

The idea of resssembling the Rump seems to have been Vane's, and some weeks in April were spent by that mysterious but influential clergyman, Dr John Owen, carrying out research into the survivorship of the old House, and making appropriate soundings. By the end of the month there was a meeting – again at Vane's house in Hampstead – between leaders of the Army and the constitutionalists, as a result of which former parliamentarians were formally approached and pressures put on the reluctant Speaker Lenthall once more to make himself the symbol of representative government. One can understand his misgivings. Twice he had confronted despots, then he had become a totem, and finally he had had to canvass the man who turned him out of the chair to give him a seat in the new upper house. Now he was forced back into the chair from which Harrison had dragged him. By early May there were sixteen former Rumpers ready to return, and by the 7th, with thirty, the organizers thought the sacred quorum of forty would be reached. There cannot have been many more than this when, on 16 May, they elected twenty-one of their number to be a Council of State along with ten others, mostly army officers. Algernon was one of the twenty-one, who, somewhat reinforced, marched into the empty House a few days later and declared themselves to be the House of Commons.

Thus suddenly restored to the centre of politics, Algernon wasted no time in taking up his old battle for the supremacy of civilian authority over the Army. As usual the issue of principle was masked by an apparent technicality – should Army officers receive their commissions from the Speaker or from the House itself? If from the House there could be (and probably would be) a debate and division on every individual case. Algernon raised the matter at the earliest possible opportunity – June 6 – urging the absolute right of the House. Harry Vane and even Ludlow were alarmed by the thought of irritating the Army so soon, and at the prospect that the candle of parliamentarianism which had just been relit should be snuffed out at once by the offended colonels. But Algernon, supported by Neville and Heselrige, carried the day.[11]

This vindication of the rights of the House of Commons was the last time Algernon's voice was heard there, and the last vote recorded of him. Even when he spoke he knew that the republic had other work for him, no less important in its way but distant from the centre of affairs to which he had so recently returned. In the middle of June he was appointed the Commonwealth's ambassador to Denmark and Sweden, and its representative at the international conference then struggling with a crisis which was on the point of involving all the nations of northwestern Europe in war. In the next few weeks he was briefed and equipped with elaborate ciphers, and early in July he sailed for Copenhagen in one of the republic's newest frigates, the *Langport*. He was only thirty-six and no doubt expected that he could soon return to his seat in Parliament with an enhanced reputation, to fulfil his ambitions; but it was to be a much longer farewell than that: he was not to see his country again for eighteen years, when youth and even middle age would have passed.

Before setting out, he seems to have had his portrait painted in miniature; it shows an almost supercilious reserve concealing an inner intensity. In the next two years he was to exhibit them in a new context, serving a country's rather than a party's interest, and to be one of the chief influences in saving Europe from war. Travelling almost in unison, but by land across Germany from the exiled court of Charles II in the Low Countries, was a renegade Parliamentary naval officer, Captain Thomas Whetstone, with a mission which permanently damaged Algernon's expectations of political greatness.

'The Ugly North'

THE balance of power in the Northern Kingdoms had greatly changed since Algernon had visited them as a boy twenty-six years earlier. At that time the dominant power had been the Crown of Denmark, whose possessions included not only the modern country of that name, but the present kingdom of Norway and what is now the southern coast of Sweden. As a result the Danish King had complete control of the narrow international waterway leading to and from the Baltic which was vital to the countries of Western Europe, with their world-wide maritime enterprise and its demands for timber and tar. Control of the Sound, where the narrows met the North Sea, had made the Danes and their King rich, for they levied a toll on every cargo that passed through in either direction.

But the emerging power of Sweden and ten years of war between the two Scandinavian kingdoms had broken Danish control of the Sound and, by the Treaty of Roskilde in 1658, its Northern coast had been transferred to Sweden. This had been welcomed by all the Western powers as offering an end to the extortionate tolls collected by the Danes. But their satisfaction was shortlived, for only a few months after the Treaty of Roskilde the King of Sweden, Charles X, renewed the war and soon brought Frederick III of Denmark to his knees. It looked as if the Western maritime powers would again have to deal with the same ruler on both sides of the Sound, but this time it would be Sweden. France, Britain and the Netherlands had therefore found common ground in an agreement signed at the Hague in May 1659 to impose peace between the warring monarchs on the basis of the Roskilde Treaty which shared control of the Sound between them. All three sent special missions to Denmark for this purpose, and in the case of the English and Dutch, the greater part of their navies.

Underneath this apparent concord in the cause of peace the three powers and their emissaries had their differences of approach. The Dutch favoured the Danes, the English the Swedes. Only the French were impartial between the two belligerents, but it was an impartiality dictated by *realpolitik*. The French envoy, the Chevalier du Terlon, was concerned to see that neither of his peace-making colleagues drove an advantageous bargain with one or other of the belligerents. It was therefore highly probable, given the immense concentration of Dutch, English, Danish, and Swedish naval and military force round the Sound, that the intervention for peace would end in a general war.

On 18 July the *Langport* cast anchor off Elsinore after a bright summer voyage somewhat delayed by easterly winds, bringing the English envoys to the scene of their mission. For Parliament, following its usual cautious habits, had given Algernon colleagues. Two of them accompanied him on his voyage: the other was already on the scene. One was Sir Robert Honeywood, whose claim to his place lay in being Harry Vane's brother-in-law. He had taken no part in politics or in the Civil War, had never sat in Parliament, and was now nearly sixty, but recent events had made him a non-parliamentary member of the Council of State. The second was Thomas Boon, M.P. for the maritime constituency of Dartmouth and a loyal but obscure back-bencher in the Rump. The remaining commissioner was Admiral Sir Edward Montagu, commanding the English fleet in the Sound, who welcomed his colleagues on board his flagship, the *Naseby*. The welcome was no doubt the more splendid because Algernon and Montagu were related, though distantly. In attendance on Montagu was his youthful secretary, Samuel Pepys, and it is a pity he had not yet begun his diary.

Algernon had been warned about Montagu by Thurloe before setting out, and told that if the Admiral showed any sign of disaffection he should be put under arrest. Ever since the beginning of the Civil War Montagu had been steady in the Parliamentary cause, but now his loyalty to the republic was doubtful. As a Cavalier agent signing himself 'Herbert' had secretly written to Clarendon, the exiled King's chief adviser, 'When Montagu doth come home he will either lay by himself, or be laid by by the Parliament. This is the most favourable occasion that ever was to tempt him.' From this arose the journey of the Cavalier emissary Captain Whetstone, who must have arrived at Copenhagen almost at the same time as the Commonwealth Commissioners.[1]

As Pepys was gradually to discover with distress, Admiral Montagu had no religious ideals, but he had a principle, which was settled government. 'I had rather the nation were settled', he said later shortly before the Restoration, 'though I and my whole family should suffer by it.'[2] The second half of this remark was cant, for Montagu fully intended he and his family should prosper, but he did not seek office for himself. His aim, which it was to take a long time to achieve, was stability. The navy which he commanded had been a major, perhaps decisive, factor in the defeat of Charles I. Less than a year after Algernon's arrival at Elsinore, it would carry Charles II back to his throne, and Admiral Montagu would bear the sword of state before the King at his coronation just as he had borne it before the Lord Protector Oliver at his installation. It would not be a gross exaggeration to say that the seeds of the Restoration first sprouted at Elsinore.

Thoughts of this kind had probably begun to cross Montagu's mind even before he sailed with his fleet from England, but his mind was made up in the Sound. His conversion to the King's cause, he later told Pepys, 'commenced from his being in the Sound, when he found what usage he was likely to have from the Commonwealth.'[3] It is difficult to believe that Algernon's uncompromising rectitude as a representative of the Commonwealth did not contribute to this decision, and Montagu often afterwards referred to him as 'my mortal enemy'. English politics shadowed the relationships of the Commissioners.

To all this tension the cautious habits of the English Parliament had added one further string. For forty days beginning with Algernon's arrival in Denmark he, in collaboration with his fellow-commissioners, was to have total control of the Fleet assembled there. But it had already been on station for several months and was in urgent need of rest and refit; at the end of the time laid down, which would be 27 August, it should sail for home leaving only a squadron of fifteen ships behind, which would be far outnumbered by the Dutch and their friends the Danes.

Montagu did not fail to impress these facts on his guests as soon as they were on board his flagship. He showed them around his fleet, dwelling on the need for a refit and the longing of every man from the admiral downwards to be home again after spending so long at sea. Crews, he pointed out, had been thinned by death and sickness, and there were no replacements. It was only too clear to Algernon that England's weight in the negotiations had to be exercised quickly, or it would be gone.

Even apart from these troubles the situation was far more precarious than he had expected when setting out. On land the Swedes and Danes confronted each other in arms at the approaches to Copenhagen, and at sea the Danes were getting ready to ferry over reinforcements provided by their German ally Brandenburg. A Swedish squadron was hovering in the Sound to stop them, and the Dutch were saying that if there was a collision they would support their friends the Danes.

Never, in his whole career, did Algernon show more successful command of an explosive situation. He neither postured nor sulked. Almost as soon as he was ashore he threatened to send Montagu's fleet to sea if the Dutch insisted on protecting the Danes. Protocol, the favourite resort of the Dutch, was swept aside by his insistence on meeting them anywhere they liked. Honeywood and Boon, and even Montagu, he treated as subordinates, and the fleet as being entirely under his control. As a result the Dutch withdrew, the Danes and Swedes stayed where they were, and the representatives of the three powers were once again in a position to resume the task of bringing the warring kings back into negotiation.

What he did not know of, as yet, was the existence of Whetstone's mission. The Cavalier agent had arrived in Denmark only a week or so after Algernon himself, and immediately put himself in Montagu's way, first at a public dinner, where he professed not to recognize the admiral (who, however, recognized him), and then during a sight-seeing trip which the commissioners made to Copenhagen. This time he introduced himself to Montagu and arranged to meet an intermediary designated by the admiral. Two secret meetings followed, at which the King's letter to Montagu was delivered and answered, and Whetstone left for Lübeck in a ship thoughtfully provided by the Dutch, made his way across Germany, and reported to Clarendon that 'upon any appearance of disorders in England' the King 'might expect a good account' of Montagu, who would write further when he got home.*

Algernon has left vivid portraits of the two kings he was trying to force into agreement during the short time he would have force at his disposal. He had a poor opinion of the Danish king, Frederick III – 'a heavy, sleepy man who does not understand business and is easily governed by his advisers and his wife.' Frederick adopted the infuriating tactic of agreeing to everything the mediators proposed (subject of course to the approval of his various German allies) and plaintively suggesting that if his opponent did not agree too the mediators should brand him as the 'refuser' and act against him accordingly. Perhaps he was more cunning than Algernon gave him credit for; in the following year he carried out a coup d'état which made him an absolute ruler.

Charles X of Sweden was well qualified for the role of 'refuser' – in fact he was rather like Algernon, and they came to have great respect and even affection for one another. But their first encounter was unfortunate. Charles, wrote Algernon, was 'soe violently transported with ambition and choller upon every slight occasion that he doth frequently omitt things that are most for his advantage, and doth often cast himself into thoes extremityes which would have ruined him.' When negotiations had been resumed, and the mediators presented the proposals agreed among themselves and accepted by the Danes, Algernon briskly told the King of Sweden he must accept or he would be forced to do so. The French ambassador was much shocked – 'un peu fort' was how he reported Algernon's style. The King took a step backwards, tapped his sword, said it was not for republics to dictate to monarchs, denounced the Dutch

---

* The story of Whetstone's mission can be pieced together from the Clarendon Papers iii, 493, 565, 570 and 703; Pepys 15 May and 7 Nov 1660; and BL Add. MS 28,094 which shows that the whole scheme originated with Sir Samuel Morland, an undersecretary in Thurloe's office, but also a Cavalier agent. The importance of this is that Clarendon would have been fully informed about Algernon's instructions, including those empowering him to suspend Montagu if he showed signs of disloyalty. If this was disclosed by Whetstone to Montagu, as it probably was, it would explain his remark that it was learning what he had to expect from a Commonwealth that clinched his decision. The intermediary between Whetstone and the Admiral was confusingly also called Edward Montagu – a cousin of the admiral and a convinced royalist.

as partial to the other side, and declared force would be met with force.

Yet the negotiations were kept alive, and although on 10 August Algernon wrote a long despatch to London describing what he had done and seeking further instructions, he was very much on his own.[4] A letter took a fortnight to reach London and even the most prompt instructions in return would take a month. But there could be no such, for in early August a dangerous Cavalier rising (the very one Clarendon had been planning when he sent Whetstone to suborn Montagu) took place under Sir George Booth, and was quickly followed by yet another coup d'état by Parliament's general, Lambert, who hurled the Rump once again into limbo. So Algernon battled on, drafting documents overnight in French and even Latin, interviewing kings, officials and allies, struggling by himself to carry out his instructions to bring peace to the North on terms acceptable to England.

All the Commissioners, including Montagu, had signed the despatch of 10 August, which reported that the main body of the fleet could not be sustained in the Sound beyond 22 August, but that the support of English diplomacy would still require the retention of a strong squadron. For the next fortnight there were agonized discussions among the Commissioners about how this could be managed. Montagu had privately, as a result of his conversations with Whetstone, decided to leave as little behind as possible, and dwelt on every possible argument against doing anything else: the choice of ships to stay on station would be invidious, and might even lead to mutiny; redistributing stores and ammunition would be necessary and could not be done in the time. Force was only needed if we were going to act against the Swedes, which would be against our interests and playing into the hands of the Dutch. But Algernon stuck to his guns, saying that 'if he should give his opinion for sending away the whole fleet he should deserve to lose his head, and that if his own father commanded the fleet, yet if he could in any ways in the world hinder the sailing of it, though by making the sailors mutiny against him, he would do it.'[5] The senior officers of the fleet were consulted and supported Montagu. The Dutch were consulted – would they, if the English fleet was reduced, reduce their own to the same extent? Alas they had no instructions to do any such thing. 'Colonel Sidney, while we discoursed, leaned in the window by himself in a discontented manner, and afterwards expressed himself against what we had asked.' So wrote Montagu. At last, the Commissioners agreed to take a formal vote on 21 August, on whether the whole fleet should be ordered home at once.

They met at seven in the morning of that day in Honeywood's room, and a sailing order was drafted. Algernon at once proposed an amendment retaining fiteeen ships, which the other three commissioners, after long discussion, rejected. Montagu promptly signed the order, followed by Honeywood. But when it came to the turn of the third Commissioner, Boon, he upset everything, as the most obscure member of a committee often does, by raising a fundamental question and wondering whether in fact they had any power to depart from their instructions. Montagu and Honeywood had to agree that strictly they had not, and Montagu furiously tore the order in half. But he carefully put the pieces in his pocket, for it carried one signature besides his own. Next day, after a stormy interview with the Dutch, at which he told them he intended to take his whole fleet home unless they reduced their own to fifteen ships – something he knew well they would refuse – he went on board, held a council of war with his officers, and sailed, leaving only one frigate and a ketch behind. There were still five days of the parliamentary limit to run. On the voyage home Montagu composed a long justification of his conduct, but it contained no references to Captain Whetstone. The arrival of the fleet in England was probably the decisive factor in ending the Republic, and it did not go to sea again until May 1660 when, with Montagu once more in command, it ferried the King home in triumph.

It would have been entirely understandable if Algernon had now thrown up his mission in fury and despair to follow Montagu back to England, especially as he now knew (because when Montagu had gone his Dutch colleagues thoughtfully told him) about Whetstone and his mission. He was, after all, a leading republican member of Parliament, and it was clear that his friends and principles in the revived Rump would need all the support they could get in Westminster. His ally Ludlow, almost at this very time, was making up his mind to throw up his responsibilities in Ireland and return to London for just these reasons, and Algernon had better grounds even than Ludlow. From his place in Westminster he could have denounced the treachery of the admiral who had laid the English negotiations in ruins. He had been relying on the whole fleet for another five days and on effective naval support after that to bring the defiant Charles X to the conference table that had now been prepared with such difficulty.* He had even gone so far with the King of Sweden as to tell him to his face that unless he was prepared to treat on the basis of the terms handed him by Algernon he would forfeit English friendship. Now all hope of a balanced settlement seemed at an end and the Dutch, with Denmark in their pocket and ample naval support, would have it all their own way.

There was yet another and more personal reason for going home. He had left his mother, to whom he had always been close, seriously ill, almost certainly from cancer. In fact she died (though Algernon did not yet know this) on 22 August, the very day Montagu sailed.

But the worst of his troubles was the crumbling of the regime at home, which placed him in the extraordinary position of an ambassador on a crucial mission who is suddenly deprived, not only of the military power on which he is depending, but of political authority. Occasionally his letters throw out hints that he might return: on 12 September he asks Whitehall 'to consider how long we may in this place be serviceable to the Commonwealth'[6], and in November when it was decided that one of the three remaining Commissioners should return he appears to have volunteered, but gave way when everyone else suggested the colourless Mr Boon. Nothing shows more clearly his obstinate sense of aristocratic honour and self-righteousness, yet nothing puts those unattractive qualities in a more sympathetic light of genuine nobility and personal disinterest. So far as his own interests were concerned the decision to stay on was imprudent to the point of foolhardiness. It permanently wrecked his career, and in his more sober moments he must have realized it would. His reward was that against all the odds he succeeded in his mission of bringing peace to the 'ugly North' as he called it, and achieving a settlement between Sweden and Denmark which has endured to this day. Indeed his achievement exceeded this.

The natural result of Montagu's departure was the collapse of negotiations and the renewal of hostilities. The adjacent tents into

---

* It was almost certainly Montagu's knowledge that this was so which precipitated his decision to sail before the forty days were up. It is interesting that the Cavalier headquarters in Holland appears to have known exactly how long the fleet was authorized to stay in the Sound when Whetstone's mission was planned. No doubt the information came from the spy in Thurloe's office.

which the opposing kings had been shepherded were struck, and the Danes were openly reinforced with the support of the Dutch. In his gloomy despatches Algernon's only comfort is the support he was still getting from the Chevalier du Terlon who was also now instructed to lean in favour of the Swedes. Rather pathetically Algernon begged the home government, even now, to send some naval support for the English position, but none was forthcoming. By the time that despatch reached London a military regime under Lambert was in process of taking control and on 12 October the Rump was once more suspended.

At this point, in the midst of complex negotiations, cheated by his colleagues, deserted by his fleet, and with the very government he represented tottering, Algernon made the ringing declaration of political faith by which his name was long celebrated. The occasion was an official visit to Copenhagen University during which he was invited, as a distinguished guest, to sign the Album or visitor's book and add a suitable motto, preferably in a learned language. To the astonishment of everyone this ambassador accredited to two Kings wrote:

> Philippus Sidney:
> Manus haec inimica tyrannis
> Ense petit placidam sub libertate quietem.

It is said that du Terlon was so shocked at this reflection on monarchy that, perhaps intending to do Algernon a favour, he arranged to have the page taken out. Certainly news quickly spread, and was reported all over Europe. More than any other single act of his life it ruined Algernon's career as a politician and made him a radical hero for a century and a half. Much ink has been spilt over the origins of these lines which in their admirable neatness recall Lucan, one of Algernon's favourite poets, but no classical source has been found for them* so it has generally been concluded that he composed them himself. It may be so; but the words 'Philippus Sidney' which precede the verse surely had a purpose, and, one suspects, a clue. They may have been no more than a reminder – even so, significant – of the hero in whose shoes he felt himself to stand, but it seems far more likely that even if the lines do not still

* I owe this assurance to Professor Robert Browning FBA, emeritus Professor of Classics and Ancient History at the University of London, who kindly carried out a search.

survive among the great Sir Philip's writing, they are in fact his, and had fixed themselves in his great-nephew's mind.

The gesture may have been rash, but it was also deliberate, in that it conveyed two distinct political messages. By the first line, asserting his opposition to monarchy, he proclaimed his loyalty to the British republic which he knew was now threatened. By the second, with its reference to the peace and liberty the sword is intended to bring, he affirmed his current task as a mediator. The 'placidam quietem' was not some generalized social happiness attributable to the disappearance of tyranny, but agreement to return to the terms of the Peace of Roskilde. That was the task to which, amid all his disadvantages, he continued to devote his energies.

Charles X had established his headquarters at Nycoping, in the south of Denmark, and there Algernon spent several weeks in October trying to extract concessions that would allow the negotiations to start again. He made some progress, perhaps because the two fiery men were beginning to have some respect for each other; there can be no doubt of Algernon's increasing admiration of the Vasa king who, like him, regarded difficulty as something to be despised by a man of honour. Algernon might have lost his fleet, but Charles's army was hardly in a condition to fight, and at last they agreed that Sweden would resume negotiations provided they were aimed at a general settlement which would bind Denmark's German and Polish allies.

When Algernon returned to Copenhagen early in November he found a delayed letter from Penshurst reporting his mother's death. If it was a blow – and it was certainly not an unexpected one – there is no emotional outburst in the reply he wrote to his father on 5 November. Stoicism and tenderness combine to produce some of the best sentences he ever wrote:

> I confess, persons in such tempers are most fit to dye, but they are also most wanted here; and we, that for a while are left in the world, are most apt, and perhaps with reason, to regret the loss of those we most want. It may be, light and humane passions are most suitably employed upon humane and worldly things, wherein we have some sensible concernment; thoughts, absolutely abstracted from ourselves are more suitable unto that steddinesse of mind that is much spoken of, little sought, and never found, than that which is seen among men.[7]

He knew that only a year or two before his mother's death there had been suggestions that she and the Earl should live apart, and after those few words and a rather superficial offer to come home if required, he plunges into a long and detailed account of the diplomatic situation in Scandinavia, ending with the suggestion that if his father is not interested in it he can always throw the letter in the fire.

Algernon later complained that his diplomatic colleagues were better informed through their own networks about what was happening in England than he was; and certainly during the confusion of that autumn Whitehall can have found little time to send instructions to its ambassador in the Sound. Nevertheless he had more information from home through friends and political colleagues than he chose to admit, and he wrote to them in return with presents of wine and fish, some of which (since the Earl, who did not receive any, got to hear of it) may even have gone to Isabella and her troublesome husband. He was in touch with the lawyer-politician Bulstrode Whitelocke who wrote to him in September just before Lambert's coup d'état, and when he replied to Whitelocke on 13 November from Elsinore he had a good deal of recent English political news of the most alarming kind.

Lambert and his officers, having as they thought ousted the Rump and occupied London, settled down to the discussion of further constitutional experiments. But the embers of parliamentary legitimacy had not been quite stamped out. A fragment of the Rump's Council of State led by Heselrige and Scot, authorized Monk, the Commander-in-Chief in Scotland, to take command of all the Commonwealth forces.* Monk began to move into England, and Lambert marched northwards to oppose him. A third Civil War seemed on the point of breaking out. Most of this news seems to have been known to Algernon early in November.

It was just the situation Admiral Montagu had foreseen when he assured Charles II through Whetstone that he would come out for the King 'upon any appearance of disorders in England', and

---

* This technical detail is not unimportant as evidence of contemporary political thinking. The sanctity of Parliament was thought of as attaching also to its Councils of State. Cromwell had been careful, in April 1653, to go on from the House of Commons to the Council of State and make sure it was well and truly dissolved too. And during the trials of the 'Rye House Conspirators' of 1683 hints were dropped that its leadership thought of themselves as a 'Council of State'. Indeed they may have done so, for most of them had been members of one or other of the Houses in the third Exclusion Parliament, whose sudden dissolution it would have been so easy to claim was unconstitutional.

Algernon too saw the danger that threatened the republic. Even his admiration for parliamentary purity seems to have faltered, and in writing to Whitelocke he condemns as ill-judged the decision to pit Monk against Lambert. 'I hope', he wrote, 'that you have ordered matters so as to keep the Army united.'[8] Vane and Ludlow too were working desperately for a compromise. Renewed Civil War was now too high a price to pay for the ideals of parliamentary sovereignty over the Army.

The matter was not decided by the politicians but by the soldiers themselves, and in a paradoxical way. In the Great Civil War Englishman had fought Englishman with great resolution, but the soldiers of 1659 had served together far too long to do that. Whenever one regiment confronted another in the confused winter of 1659–60, whether it was at Westminster in October, Portsmouth in December, or Northumberland in January, the pattern was the same. There would be a parley, possibly followed by votes in which both sides decided to support one of the two opposing commanders. So when Monk's advance pickets approached those of Lambert, both fired their pistols into the ground and exchanged jokes, and gradually Lambert's army melted away. Monk marched on unopposed to London, once more to install the Rump. Very soon the survivors of the compromisers excluded eleven years earlier by Pride's Purge reassembled with a demand that they too should be readmitted. Once more Speaker Lenthall was trundled out as the totem of parliamentary sovereignty, and once more debates began about when the twenty-year-old Parliament should dissolve itself and how its successor should be elected. For a moment Heselrige's pure republicanism dominated the House, Scot replaced the profound bureaucrat Thurloe as chief of the intelligence service, and Vane found himself suspended from the House for his compromising pains. A tide of public hatred and contempt began to wash round the fragmentary Parliament which, as Ludlow wrote sadly in retrospective exile, 'in the five years time that they governed without interruption had raised the glory of the nation wherein it had been buried by the negligence and corruption of the preceding governments, and had rendered the English name formidable to all Europe.'[9] They are words which Algernon, as the Rump's ambassador, would have proudly proclaimed. Monk, the inscrutable soldier of fortune, but still formally Parliament's servant, was feasted so often by City Companies that he had to issue a statement declining any further invitations. On 21 February he decided that the compromisers excluded by Pride's Purge should be allowed to take their seats once more.

Algernon spent most of that eventful winter at the Swedish court and despite his disapproval of monarchy, and as he came to know Charles X better, he began to feel he was the ideal leader of a nation – industrious, brave, public-spirited, incorruptible, self-sacrificing. Charles, now formally denounced by the Dutch and the Danes as 'the refuser' of mediation, had his back to the wall, and Algernon was accused afterwards of supporting him too strongly: but apart from the personal sympathy he clearly felt, he was almost certainly right from the point of view of the English interest and by early February he had made considerable progress towards a balanced settlement.

But Charles, though only thirty-seven, was an exhausted man, and on 22 February 1660, working almost to the last, he died. Algernon was with him only a few hours before the end, and wrote soon afterwards that

> the constancy and serenity of his mind, shewed in all the time of his sicknesse and the certain approaches of death, deserve not less praise if they are well considered. He would not so much as give himself the ease of a bed in the violence of his fever, saying, he did not live or reign for himself, but for his people.

Still at his desk the King insisted on putting his affairs in order even down to the last detail 'not forgetting either messages of compliment or civility to some that had obliged him, ordering several sums of money, even small ones, to be paid ... nothing could make him omitte the dutie which he thought he owed.'[10]

The King's death brought peace nearer, but it also tilted its terms against Sweden since Charles was succeeded by a regency, and Algernon typically considered this made his continued presence in Scandinavia even more necessary. Writing to his father on the day Charles X died, he admits he had always wanted to stay to see peace concluded, and 'now I am more unwilling to leave it undetermined; the chief inducement then was the interest of England; I can now add to that consideration, by all the rules of humanity and charity, to endeavour the protection of an infant and a very virtuous mother.'[11]

In his quixotic way he felt the mantle of the dead hero had fallen on him, and that he now had to do his best not only for

England but for Charles's widow and child. But time in London was now ticking away ineluctably towards the Restoration and the installation of a Charles very different from the one Algernon so much admired.

The negotiations which followed the death of Charles X were long and stormy, and Algernon frequently lost his temper with the Dutch who, as he complained to Whitehall, seemed to think 'we, having no force here, should in all things receive the law from their ministers, as if we served a state that had not a ship in the world, or was plunged into such difficulties and disorders, that we could never hope to see it recovered from them. We were of another opinion.'[12]

Later when there were complaints about his brusqueness, he characteristically answered that such tactics were not to be met 'by serious and set discourses: scattered words, slighting expressions and the like did my business' – of maintaining his place at the conference table. Given his situation and his natural perceptiveness one can understand the high line he took, especially when the Dutch, to impose delay, cavilled about the purity of the Latin in which he had prepared a draft of the treaty. But his 'slighting expressions' were remembered, and they included some unwise things.

He always denied having referred to Charles II as a bandit; but proudly admitted that, when asked by someone if it was true he had no part in the guilt of Charles I's death, he had replied 'Guilty! Why it was the justest and bravest action that ever was done in England or anywhere else!' A Dutch diplomat who happened to be near noted the remark and it duly received publicity, which did him great disservice in England.*

The stress of his extraordinary situation as an ambassador whom everyone knew would soon be disowned by his country began to induce an element of paranoia. Whilst in a small boat with his French colleague, a shot from a land battery suddenly fell near their craft. Algernon was convinced it was an attempt on his life, and was far from satisfied with the official explanation that the gunners had been engaged in target practice for the amusement of the Queen of Denmark, who might even, it was blandly added, have fired one of the guns herself. He made an effort to pass it off by

* Algernon later justified this outburst as not only proper but necessary in an ambassador of the republic, and explained that in private conversation with the King of Sweden he had made clear his reservations about the trial of Charles I.

replying that anything – even a cannon-ball – was a great favour from her Majesty, but when told the Queen had not seen any boat in the channel he fired up. Her Majesty, he said, had fine eyes, and presumably excellent vision as well. His gift for making enemies never deserted him.[13]

In April 1660 the Dutch overreached themselves in their hostility to Sweden and were again denounced by the Swedes as no longer fit to be mediators. The road to a settlement was suddenly opened to Algernon and his French colleagues on their own. 'As animals that are long in their mothers' wombs', Algernon later wrote to his father, 'are ordinarily long-lived, this treaty of peace, that hath been long in perfecting and finishing, will be of a proportionate continuance.'[14] The prediction was correct, for Sweden and Denmark have kept their frontiers since the day the treaty Algernon had laboured so hard for was signed on 27 May 1660. There were memorable celebrations at Copenhagen – naval salutes, fireworks, a *feu de joie* from the two armies, and much eating and drinking, from which du Terlon records that he and his colleagues returned 'très fatigués'. Only a week later the same kinds of scenes were reproduced in London for the re-entry of Charles II.

Algernon had sacrificed his future to his mission. On the very day the treaty was signed Admiral Montagu was made a Knight of the Garter on the quarter deck of his flagship by the restored Charles II. It had been the *Naseby* when Algernon had last seen it, but now it had been thoughtfully rechristened the *Royal Charles*.

Even to the Copenhagen triumph a drop of acid was added. Du Terlon claimed the right to sign the conclusive Latin text of the treaty first, by virtue of his seniority of appointment – even though the Latin drafting had been largely Algernon's work. Algernon's suggested compromise that they should sign side by side he could not accept, but perhaps, if there should be an English text, he would be willing to sign that second. But after considering it he found that too was impossible. Over a quiet lunch he told Algernon that if they had been negotiating with each other an English text would have been in order – but they were mediators, not principals, and a signed text in either of their languages would be altogether inappropriate. He went on in his *Mémoires* to claim the entire credit at the expense of a colleague who had sacrificed so much to the treaty.

Algernon now had to face his personal future. He had succeeded in his mission, and his party had collapsed. At one time he had thought of offering his services to Sweden, but the death of Charles X had put an end to that prospect. If the republic survived, he wrote to Whitelocke, he would be ready to serve further. 'If it returns to monarchy I desire nothing but liberty to retire, finding myself a very unfit stone for such a building.'[15]

That in the end was to be his position, but before returning to it he went through many agonies. Early in May the dying republic told him to stay at his post until he received further orders from their successors, and he wrote a proud but at the same time cautious letter to his father:

> I serve England, and will with as much care and diligence as I can, endeavour to advance its interests, and follow the orders of those that govern it. I reserve the determination of other points to councels upon the place. [But, he continued,] If I do not receive new orders I shall return speedily home, and shall then follow that way, which your Lordship shall direct, and my best friends advise, as far as I can, without breaking the rules of honour or conscience, which I am sure will never be expected from me, by your Lordship, nor those whose opinions I consider.[16]

It might have been more tactfully expressed, but it was clear that he did not intend either to cringe or apologize. The Earl was willing to do as much cringing as was needed. The Restoration must have been a relief to him. It meant the end of Mr Maudit and a new acceptable rector; and a seat in the restored House of Lords which he could occupy when he chose. He took the earliest opportunity to wait on Charles II, who received him affably, listened to his congratulations and professions of loyalty, and made him a Privy Councillor once more. The Earl was so encouraged that he again put in his quarter-of-a-century-old bill for the balance of his overdue expenses as Charles I's ambassador in Paris. It was paid. But he did not raise the question of Algernon's future. As for Philip, he was as quick as any to make his peace with the new regime, and despite his former attachment to Cromwell made sure of a full pardon, signed and sealed, covering all charges that could be brought against him. It was not obtained without concessions, for he had to yield up to the King a positive treasure-house of antiques and works of art he had acquired at bargain prices in auctions of royal property under the republic. They included three Raphaels, a Titian, a Giulio Romano, and a Correggio.

Algernon's report on the signature of the new treaty was addressed to the new King. He also wrote to his uncle the Earl of

Northumberland in a very melancholy strain before setting out on a round of farewell visits. After 'the destruction of the party for which many years I had followed and the desertion of some of my friends, who I had obliged in every manner, I was troubled to finde your Lordship lesse carefull to give me some reliefe, than I had hoped you would have bin.' He may, he adds, have been unwise in the choice of some of his friends, 'but for what concerns the party I should lye if I said I had found any [fault] . . . my fortune hath bin more than ordinary ill.'[17]

Algernon's attitude to the Restoration is a very important clue to both his character and his political thought. He could not welcome it, for it destroyed all he had fought for, but he acknowledged its constitutionality for it had been done by a Parliament he regarded as lawful. One cannot understand his relationship to Charles II without realizing that he saw him as a parliamentary king, whose birth alone gave him no right to his position. This was the distinction in Algernon's mind between Charles and the usurper Cromwell, who owed his authority to force, which gave no more legitimacy than birth. From this view he never varied in substance, though Charles's later breaches of the terms on which he had been restored (and they came very soon) caused Algernon also to hold that Parliament could depose him as legitimately as it had installed him; but until Parliament should do so Charles was indeed lawful. These views are so close to Vane's that one must seriously consider whether the two corresponded during the months leading up to the Restoration, and it was in reliance on them that Vane continued to live quietly in Hampstead until, a month after the entry of Charles, he was arrested. But of this arrest Algernon did not yet know.

He did not even know Charles had arrived in London until nearly a month after it happened. Immediately after signing the Treaty he decided he could no longer act as an ambassador and left for Sweden, where he spent more than a month on a round of formal visits and farewells, still comforting himself with the thought that his achievements might allow him to return home with honour, and even to a new post under the new regime. He did not arrive again at Copenhagen till the end of the first week in July, to find a letter from his father proposing he should come back to England. He even seems to have made arrangements to travel at least as far as Holland on the homeward journey. But towards the end of July he changed his mind, and decided for the time being at any rate to remain abroad. 'The letters of the two last posts', he wrote to his father, 'have put me out of that uncertainty and show me plainly what to expect.' Though he would have been willing to live quietly under Charles II he was now convinced that he would always be suspected 'and often affronted'. He had chosen 'voluntary exile, as the least evill condition that is within my reach.'[18] Some decisive news had reached him, and it was probably the arrest of Vane.

It was a sad end to his hopes of a conventional career, but before following him into his strange life of isolation and wandering as a political exile one should not forget his achievement as an ambassador, or its historical importance. Almost single-handed, and surrounded by difficulties and treacheries, he had fought through a lasting settlement between the jealous Scandinavian kingdoms, and ensured international access to the Baltic. From Sweden he had secured 'most favoured nation' treatment for England, and above all he had frustrated the Dutch hopes of controlling the Baltic trade through a satellite Denmark. The consequences were enduring: the maritime prosperity and expansion of England over the next two centuries was to depend on access to naval supplies from the North. It was the greatest diplomatic success of the English republic.

The Welcoming South

AT THE beginning of his exile he had the consolation that it might not last for long. Experience of the last twenty years did not suggest that the restored monarchy would prove more enduring than its many predecessors in power. He was at a distance from events, unable to judge the atmosphere in London, and probably ignorant of many of the important steps being taken to shore up the new regime: the decision not to unravel changes in the ownership of land and the elimination of the Army as a political force by paying it off on reasonably generous terms. When he planned his future during his last weeks in Denmark it was not as an active conspirator but as a dignified enemy of the regime that had now established itself in London.

He had had enough of northern Europe and 'all the drunken countries of Germany'. He had some knowledge of German but he recoiled from the hearty vulgarity of German society. After a year spent frustrating Dutch policy, he could hardly expect much of a welcome in the Netherlands, and he was 'not much inclined to France' – perhaps because of the possibility of extradition. The obvious haven would have been Switzerland, where several English republicans were now heading, but they were known regicides marked for death in the Act of Indemnity, and they would be dangerous associates. He decided on Italy, which he had visited as a boy, and whose language he knew. The great Sir Philip, too, had spent some time there.

His exact destination was decided on his first stop on his journey southwards, which was Hamburg. By sheer chance, he encountered a fellow-exile, Queen Christina of Sweden, who happened to be travelling homewards from Rome to make sure that her substantial pension continued under the new regime in Sweden. He seems to have got on well with that extraordinary woman, and had several conversations with her which much impressed him with her intelligence and knowledge of public affairs: in some ways she exemplified the qualities of womanhood he had once praised in the *Essay on Love*. Her visit to Sweden, she assured him, was purely private and she would soon return to Italy – 'There was but one place for me in Sweden,' she declared, 'and having resigned that I could not pretend again to it, nor content myself with any other.' He believed her, but, as he sadly adds, not just because she said so. 'I am,' he noted, 'in this year's employment grown much less credulous than I was.'*

She remained in Sweden for nearly two years and so far as we know they never met again, though Algernon may well have expected and even hoped they would. At any rate their meeting persuaded him that his destination in Italy should be Rome, about which the ex-Queen was able to give him much information and some introductions, including one to her mentor and lover, the curial Cardinal Decio Azzolino.

On parting from Christina (and his former colleague du Terlon who had taken on the responsibility of escorting her) he travelled southwards across the plains through Kassel and Freiburg to Frankfurt where he arrived early in September. Ravages left by the Thirty Years War were still visible, though it had been over for more than a decade. The people were poor, their dwellings wretched, and he particularly noticed the women, who 'have generally tanned, smoky faces, motions and actions more suitable to our sex than theirs, which may be caused by their ugly dwellings, poverty, and perpetual labour. All things belonging to husbandry are performed by them.' Anything that recalled England was eagerly recorded – the plains

---

* Nevertheless he should not have believed her. When she arrived in Sweden she suggested that if the child-king Charles XI died without issue she should be restored – after all she was not yet forty. But the idea was rejected.

round Brunswick struck him as being rather like Huntingdonshire, and the castle at Kassel 'doth overlook a river not unlike the Trent at Nottingham and a plain towards the south is like unto that which lieth between Nottingham and Leicester.' It was a comfort, too, to see the works of Baxter and other English puritan divines on the shelves of the local clergy on whom he sometimes called, and to be told by his hosts how useful they found them for their sermons.

He paused for a few days at Frankfurt, where he found the local wine excellent. Before pushing on to Augsburg, where letters were waiting for him, he wrote an oddly brief and generous little letter to his father directing that a legacy of £500 his mother had left him should be paid to his sister Dorothy, giving a full discharge for it. Possibly he still thought of it as a nest-egg safer in her hands than his father's, but there is no evidence that he ever saw any of it again, or even asked for it. It was still September, but he had been more than a month on the road, wholly without news, when at Augsburg he was faced with very unpleasant tidings indeed. In a long and grumpy letter from his father, filled with complaints about being left 'sick, solitary and sad' and reproaches about being omitted from the presents of wine and fish, he found a long account of dangerous rumours being spread about him in England. Their source was a diplomat whose name the Earl had caught as 'Peddicombe' but was probably in fact Pettekum, and they concerned Algernon's rash republican outbursts in Scandinavia, particularly the matter of the Album. The likeliest explanation for this apparently gratuitous malice is that 'Peddicombe' had been briefed by the Dutch as a revenge on the man who had so conspicuously got the better of them.

The Earl took it all very seriously. Until 'Peddicombe' set to work, he told Algernon, he still had hopes of arranging a reconciliation. Monk, now raised to a dukedom for his services, had offered to help, and the Earl himself had been planning to speak to the King – 'but since that I have heard such things of you that in doubtfulness of their being true, no man will open his mouth for you.' He was regarded as no better than the regicides themselves: 'There is as ill an opinion of you as of any, even of those that condemned the late King.'* The unspoken fear was that Algernon's

* Matters were made to look even blacker by the fact that the attendance book for the trial of the King was now in the hands of the Government and showed Algernon's presence at two early private meetings. It did not record his protest and withdrawal,

name might yet be added to the Act of Indemnity as 'excepted'. It was certainly not safe for him to return, and his family could not help him if he did.[1]

Algernon wrote to his father in passionate repudiation of his intentions, but could not (and would not) deny that the reports were literally true. Along with his pleas of justification he had to admit that his position was irreparable, and a return to the England of Charles II was out of the question. Then he wrote the letter to an unknown correspondent which has already been quoted, committing himself to opposition. We do not know whom he was writing to, but it was to someone on the other side of his life, and in it he speaks as a very different man – a passionate puritan, a committed republican, almost a member of a lifelong brotherhood. It was written before news of the final approval of the Act of Indemnity (and its exceptions) reached him, but after the arrest of Vane which almost certainly precipitated the outburst. Friends, he said, had advised him to return to England, since he was not 'excepted' and exile would permanently ruin him –

> but when that country of mine, which used to be esteemed a paradise, is now likely to be made a stage of injury; the liberty which we hoped to establish oppressed; luxury and lewdness set up in its height instead of the piety, virtue, sobriety, and modesty, which we hoped god by our hands would have introduced; the best of our nation made a prey for the worst; the Parliament, Court, and Army corrupted, the people enslaved; all things vendible, no man safe but by such evil and infamous means as flattery and bribery; what joy can I have? . . . Is it a pleasure to see all that I love in the world is sold and destroyed? Shall I renounce all my old principles, learn the vile court arts, and make my peace by bribing some of them?†

The independence of exile is far preferable to truckling and uncertainty:

> I hope I shall die in the same principles as I have lived, and will live no longer than they can preserve me. I have in my life been guilty of many follies, but as I think, of no meanness; I will not blot or defile that which is past, by endeavouring to provide for the future. I have never had it in my mind that when god should cast me into such condition, as that I could

---

and it would be easy to suggest that even a single attendance showed a common purpose with the other regicides, since the purpose was clear from the start.

† This letter, often reprinted almost as Algernon's declaration of faith, first appeared in a collection *The Familiar Letters of John Earl of Rochester and other Persons of Quality* (1694). It is undated, but was almost certainly written from Augsburg in September 1660. The addressee may have been Ludlow.

not save my life, but by doing an indecent thing, he shews me that the time is come, wherein I should resign it.

The greatest tragedy of all was not the return of the Stuarts but the treachery of Parliament in allowing it:

In all preceding ages, Parliament has been the palace of our liberty and the sure defender of the oppressed; they who formerly could bridle kings, and keep the balance equal between them and the people, are now become the instruments of all our oppressions, and a sword in the hand to destroy us ... I mean to owe neither life nor liberty to such means. When the innocence of my actions will not protect me, I will stay away until the storm be overpast. In short, where Vane, Lambert, Heselrigge, cannot live in safety, I cannot live at all. If I had been in England I should have expected a lodging with them, for though they may be first, I must expect to follow their example in suffering, as I have been their companion in acting.*

He was still, in his oddly chivalrous mind, willing to give King Charles himself, as an open opponent, the benefit of the doubt. In denouncing the toadies and self-seekers who had brought about the Restoration and now controlled events, the King must be regarded as still untested, and 'no man shall be a more faithful servant to him than I, if he make the good and prosperitie of the people his glory – none more his enemy if he doth the contrary.' It was still possible that Charles II of England would turn out like Charles X of Sweden: Algernon was never less than fair.

The commitment to opposition was to be kept for the whole of his remaining twenty-three years. No doubt he wished to escape the horrors that now threatened his old colleagues, but it is the letter of a potential martyr for all that. The Restoration's offer of reconciliation and indemnity, toleration and peace, had been fraudulent – and a decisive proof that similar offers which true republicans had always rejected had been fraudulent too. In the

---

* Vane, Lambert and Heselrige were all at that time imprisoned, and were to remain so for the rest of their lives. The allusion to them (and no other republican leaders, nor to any regicides) is significant for several reasons. It enables the letter to be dated between mid-July (the earliest that news of Vane's arrest could have reached northern Europe) and Algernon's awareness that the Act of Indemnity had been approved (not later than mid-September). It is also strong evidence of the letter's genuineness against any suggestion that it was fabricated after Algernon's own execution as part of his martyr cult. A fabricator would have been very sophisticated indeed to pick these particular three names; yet they were the three to whose situation Algernon would most closely have compared his own: clear of the direct taint of regicide and, though prominent republicans, entitled to benefit under any principle of general reconciliation.

great vote of December 1648 he had been on the right side.

In October he crossed the Alps, and after short stops at Venice and Bologna arrived at Rome.

There were good practical reasons for the choice, quite apart from the useful introductions he had obtained from Queen Christina. Rome was secure from the dangers of extradition and from the gunmen and kidnappers the English government was now sending abroad to hunt down its enemies, for the Papal government strongly resented interference from foreign powers on its sacred territory. It was also an admirable listening post for the international news and gossip which Algernon loved, and with which he filled his letters home, knowing his father's passion for it exceeded even his own. Moreover it was cheap, and although he notes that prices were a bit higher than they had been on his last visit fifteen years earlier, one could still keep two servants and live on five shillings a day.

Even so there is something bizarre in a stiff-necked puritan republican of strictly protestant stock not only settling at the head-quarters of Anti-Christ but seeming positively to enjoy it. Melancholy never left Algernon for long, but the two years he spent in Rome seem to have been very happy. And he spread himself: 'He has put himself here into a very great equipage, his coach and three lackeys: he is very gracious with some of the cardinals, which some attribute to his own parts and wit, others to some recommendation of the Queen of Sweade ...'[2] But this apparent inconsistency is superficial. Algernon's life-long attachment to the Cause was essentially an aristocratic choice, and although it was scrupulous to a point of extremity it contained nothing of the fanatical. Nowhere in his life is there evidence that he shared the crude anti-catholicism of so many of his English contemporaries, not even in the passages where one might expect to find it – his service in the Irish rebellion and, later, during the period of the Popish Plot. To him the Papal court was not the centre of an international conspiracy but an acceptable, even a necessary feature of the European scene.*

The reigning Pope was the mild, moderate and elderly Alex-

* It is of interest that one of the Sidneys' Montagu cousins, with whom Algernon's father kept up a regular confidential correspondence, was a Roman Catholic priest of some importance. Algernon would have known the Abbé Montagu, who before entering the priesthood as a result of visiting the convent of Loudun and experiencing its strange spiritual atmosphere, had served as an attaché in the Earl's embassy in Paris. Montagu went on to become a confidant of Charles I's Queen, Henrietta Maria, and after several secret visits to England on her behalf during the Civil War was made, by

ander VII, who had occupied the throne for five years at the time of Algernon's arrival and was to reign another seven, though he was already quite old enough to evoke discussion about his probable successor, which Algernon himself began by sharing. But he quickly noticed that the Pope's 'pale, sallow, and shrivelled face' gave a misleading impression of senility. His eye was bright and his movements brisk, and he was able to endure long taxing ceremonies without apparent fatigue. Indeed, both at home and abroad Alexander's was an active papacy, much concerned with the problems of Jansenism, the growing threat of French political power in Europe, and the adornment of Rome itself. One of the greatest architectural achievements of the Baroque Papacy, Bernini's colonnade in St Peter's Square, was commissioned by him and completed in the year of his death.

Algernon's letters home still recite his troubles, but his enjoyment of Roman society cannot be prevented from shining through. He was impressed by the punctilious and elaborate grandeur of the Papal court, and the cultured charm of its denizens. 'The company of persons excellent in all the sciences', he writes soon after arriving, 'is the best thing strangers can seek, and is never wanting ... I sought nothing here but rest and good company. I find reason to hope I may enjoy the one without molestation, and I do not know whether any place in the world doth afford the other in greater perfection.'[3]

He quickly began to make the acquaintance of the resident cardinals, and on the whole found much in them to admire. Cardinal Pallavicini's austerity was impressive – 'sixpence a day serves him for meat ... women never trouble his thoughts.' As for Christina's lover Azzolino, he took to him at once. They were almost the same age, for Azzolino, though a cardinal of six years' standing had been raised to the purple when only thirty – a remarkable tribute to his merits, for his family was not influential. He was a passable poet, a skilful administrator, and a close friend of the reigning Pope, whose election he had done a great deal to promote. 'His conversation is sweet and affable', wrote Algernon enthusiastically, 'wit sharp, subtile and dexterous.'[4]

Soon he had met so many cardinals that he decided to satisfy his father's appetite for information by providing twelve character

___

her influence, Abbot of Pontoise. Algernon, however, rather proudly denied owing any of his introductions in Rome to the Abbot.

sketches of members of the Sacred College with assessments of their chances at the next papal election. Along with Azzolino and Pallavicini, he considers Albizzi's 'free open nature', the 'gentle and affable' Sachetti, Barberini's 'sharpness of wit and invention'. Spada 'is subtle and likes to be thought so' but the weakness is compensated by his stock of knowledge and intense application to business. Perhaps Pio and Imperiali might suit other careers more than the Church, but the first would have made a very agreeable upper-class landowner and the other an excellent professional soldier. The only two receiving faint praise are Pallotta, who is dismissed as a muddler and fusspot, and the papal nephew Chigi, who on further acquaintance he finds a bit of a simpleton – 'rather innocent than good, or good than wise'.

None of these, however, for various reasons, could be regarded as strong candidates in a papal election. Cardinal Borromeo was his favourite, which is understandable since he had the qualities Algernon most admired. He was 'learned and upright, a principal ornament of the Sacred College.' His second choice proved to be the right one, and illustrates Algernon's compromise with the realities of politics. Cardinal Rospigliosi was the papal Secretary of State and 'a good man, rather regular and methodical . . . than of extraordinary acuteness . . . abilities rather acquired by practice, than the gifts of nature.' Nobody disliked him, 'and being known not to have an active dangerous head, he may perhaps be advanced before those that are more eminent.' Seven years later Rospigliosi duly showed the value of these qualities by succeeding as Clement IX.[5]

Algernon's admiration for the cardinals was a response to their kindness, for which he was always willing to make generous allowances. He had been told that Cardinal Barberini was not always sincere and sympathetic, but he had been so helpful that Algernon hoped the criticism was not true. What is more difficult to understand is why the Curia should have extended such a welcome to a penniless exile, in bad standing with his government, an extreme Protestant, without prospects, who had fought not only against his King but against the Catholic Irish. Indeed a young Irish priest, Father Plunkett, who was then in Rome and later became Archbishop of Armagh and a victim of Titus Oates, raised an agitation against him, but it had no effect. The possibility of a spectacular conversion may have crossed their minds, but although Algernon attended at least one of the great papal ceremonies and described it in detail to his father, he was careful to place himself as inconspicuously as possible and his account is entirely that of an objective spectator.

Naturally the Curia made its enquiries about him and the result was favourable. He had not, during his time in Ireland, gone beyond his duty in opposing the rebellion and his name was unstained by anti-Catholic atrocities. He was of high birth, and perhaps another turn of political fortune would restore him to influence. But there must have been more than this. Despite Algernon's solemnity and prickliness, he interested them. Perhaps they saw in him something of the stuff out of which martyrs are made.

He grew steadily happier and more tranquil. When company was lacking there were libraries and bookshops where he looked for the obscure desiderata his father now notified, such as the Life of Cardinal Vincentius Laureus by the Abbot of Pinarol, of which he found a copy at last in Cardinal Barberini's library. Though he thought it 'a slight thing' he provided his father with a lengthy summary and even offered to get the whole book copied. It had only taken him two hours to read, walking in the gardens of the Palazzo Barberini. The love of study was growing on him.

That letter to his father was written in April 1661, six months after coming to Rome, and as summer arrived to drive the upper classes to the hills he was offered the choice of two villas near Frascati. He selected the Villa Belvedere, owned by Prince Pamfili, and there spent a contented summer:

> Whilst everybody in Rome is panting and gasping for life in the heat ... I enjoy so fresh an air, as to have no reason at all to complain of the sun. Here are walks and fountains in the greatest perfection, and though my natural delight in solitude is very much increased since this last year, I cannot desire to be more alone than I am, and hope to continue. My conversation is with birds, trees and books ... I live now as a hermit in a palace. Nature, art and treasure can hardly make a place more pleasant than this. The description of it would look more like poetry than truth.[6]

He spent the heat of the day in study and writing, and put off exercise till the evening. In fact he was becoming quite captivated by study, and 'though one who begins at my age cannot hope to make any considerable progress that way, I find so much satisfaction in it, that for the future (though I had the opportunity) I shall very unwillingly put myself in any way of living that shall deprive me of that entertainment.' Indeed he was in some ways better equipped as a student than he admitted, for as entries in his 'Common-Place

Book' show, he could read with understanding not only Latin and French but Spanish, Italian and even German.

The so-called 'Common-Place Book' is almost certainly the product of Algernon's Roman years,* and provides the first solid evidence of his intention to write a work on political theory. It is a huge folio of nearly a thousand pages bound in vellum, and is clearly not just a common-place book in the usual sense of a depository for copying out favourite passages from miscellaneous reading. An ambitious plan underlies it. What its creator did was first to list some two hundred topics: 'Extraordinary examples of virtue and of fortune, and how these actions have had ill success' is an instance. With the topics as headings he assigned three or four pages of the volume to each, and copied into them passages he could find to illuminate the topic in question, thus creating a massive repertoire for the study of politics through history, which would be the ultimate work.

The plan was never completed. Many of the pages remain blank, and others have no more than the heading which still awaits a supporting text; but some thirty sections contain careful summaries of relevant historical reading in a surprising range of sources: medieval Spanish and Italian history; Roman and Greek history; the history of the Holy Roman Empire; and here and there some English history. Nowhere does he draw on contemporary events except (and this is rarely) to report general remarks people have made to him in conversation.

The historical summaries show the range of his sources and knowledge of languages, but it is the topics under which they are grouped that give the real clues to his thought. He was contemplating a study of the whole institution of monarchy, and nearly all his headings set kings in almost every possible situation, consider

---

* DL MSS U 1475 Z 1/10. The handwriting is certainly Sidney's. The vellum binding, strengthened with parchment strips cut from what seems to be a sixteenth-century manuscript, and the thick, handsome watermarked paper, suggest Italian manufacture. The extensive drawings on Spanish and Italian sources and references to what seem to be shelf marks make it clear that he was working in a library where these were readily available. All this, taken together with Algernon's statement that he first took seriously to study while in Rome, points to the book being the product of those years. Its massive weight would in any case have made it a most inconvenient piece of luggage, and the fact that it is now among the De L'Isle Papers suggests that on leaving Rome and its libraries he sent it home with other books we know he sent his father. Of course it may have been begun much earlier, and never left Penshurst; but the evidence points against this.

---

kinds of kings, and ways of filling thrones. He has headings for kings made prisoner, kings in exile, kings in relationship with each other and with representative assemblies; elective and hereditary kings; queens – a great deal about queens; the succession of infants and imbeciles; and such questions as whether there are any circumstances in which a king may break his pledged word.

Algernon was not good at formulating a single central theme in words, but the thought which supported the Common-Place Book is the same as that which is expressed in *Discourses Concerning Government*. Kings were human beings who also personified, as individuals, the states over which they ruled, and therefore were placed by their apologists outside the moral, or even the social judgments, applicable to human beings in general. Without such exemption, these apologists argued, a king could not perform his supreme purpose of acting in the interests of his people. This was the position Algernon planned to attack. A king indubitably had the same limitations as other human beings. The state, on the other hand, was not a human being or subject to those limitations. Hence a representative assembly, however it came into existence, was a more appropriate embodiment of the impersonal state. True, it too had to consist of human beings, and they individually were subject to the limitations which applied to human beings in general; but as a collectivity the assembly could act for the state without regard to any such limitations, for it was not a person. Its collective will was an abstraction.

That he had political theory in mind during this period is shown by a volume he sent his father from Rome, entitled *Discorso Politico nella Lingua Toscana*. The Earl endorsed it 'incerto autore' and was almost certainly right despite the suggestion by a later hand on the cover that it is not only in Algernon's hand but that he is the author. For anyone to compose a full-length work on political theory in a foreign language and then copy it in mannered script is so improbable a thought that it must be at once dismissed.*

During the early months of his stay in Rome he had heard nothing from his father, and often complained he was writing into the void. He even, in December 1660, came near a solemn rebuke

---

* DL 1475 Z 22. It has 326 pages of text and 38 pages of brief political maxims in a late humanist hand, clearly a copyist's. It has no resemblance to Algernon's writing, and the monogram at the end, in which one can fancifully trace A S, is used nowhere else by Algernon. The ascription to him is, I think, the work of an enthusiast.

to the Earl for his neglect: 'I shall with silence suffer what fortune so ever doth remain unto me. I confess I thought another conclusion might reasonably have been made upon what I had said, but I leave that to your Lordship's judgement and conscience. If you are satisfied in yourself you shall not receive any trouble from Your Lordship's &c.'[7] But gradually, thanks perhaps to the presents of books and his obvious success in Rome, relations improved. Some remittances were coming through, and there even seemed some prospect of recovering something from the Strangford estates, though even now Algernon could not find it in him to forgive Isabella for the tears and unkept promises which had made him behave so foolishly. He so warmed to his father that he offered him a choice from the stable he still owned in England, and was delighted to hear the Earl was pleased with the black gelding he had chosen. Algernon hoped his father would take what was left of the 'good store of mares and colts ... I believe the best in England of that kind'. He had always been a fancier of horses, but, he adds disconsolately, 'they will be worth nothing to me'.[8]

Happy though he was at Frascati the solitude brought out some of his usual introspection. Perhaps, he reflected, his experiences might have made a cleverer man more unhappy.

> I find stupidity an advantage; nature hath given me a large proportion of it, and I did artificially increase it to that degree, that if I were not awakened with the bitter sense of some mischiefs that my lady Strangford hath brought upon me I should rest well enough at ease, in a dull indolence, and never trouble myself with the thought of where I should have bread. ... I cannot but rejoice a little to find that when I wander as a vagabond through the world, forsaken by my friends, poor, and known only to be the broken limb of a ship-wrecked faction; I yet find humanity and civility from those who are at the height of fortune and reputation ... and since I cannot forget what is passed, nor be absolutely insensible of what is present, I defend myself reasonably well from encreasing or anticipating evils by foresight. The power of foreseeing is a happy quality unto those that prosper, and can ever propose to themselves something of greater felicity than they enjoy; but a most desperate mischief unto them who, by forseeing can discover nothing that is not worse than the evils they do already feel.[9]

A shipwrecked sailor on a raft, he reflects, is happier at night. By day he can see how hopeless the idea of rescue is.

But whatever he might say in his more philosophical moods Algernon could never stifle the feeling that he was destined for a public career. His incessant collection of political information wherever he happened to be, with a zeal which would have done credit to a professional journalist, was designed to increase his qualifications, and for a man who had lived through so many changes of regime, it was not unreasonable to think that after two years things might again be changing.

So he began to make plans on the basis of a return home within a year or two, when a substantial period of strict abstention from politics might allow him a fresh start. It needed to be fairly soon, for he saw middle age approaching, and noticed grey hairs showing among the auburn. He would pass a bit longer exploring the Mediterranean countries, and spend that winter in Naples, perhaps venturing as far as Sicily and Malta before returning to Rome in the spring of 1662. England might them be ready for him, and in the meantime he signed documents authorising the Earl to redeem a mortgage on one of the Strangford properties, in the hope it would provide him with a home.*

His last letter from Italy is dated from Frascati on 14 July 1661, and a long silence then suggests that for some time he was not in Rome or its neighbourhood. Whether he made his southern tour it is impossible to say. But by the spring of 1662 news was beginning to reach him which not only caused him to abandon any hope of a return to England but dealt him a personal blow which permanently changed him. Vane had been executed. He had been arrested in June 1660 on being included in a list of persons who, though not actual regicides, were considered to have been guilty of so much 'mischievous activity' during the republic that they should be exposed to penalties 'not extending to life'.

But Vane and Lambert (who was also on the list) had been the subject of particular venom during the debates on the Indemnity Bill, especially in the House of Lords, which had insisted on exposing them to the capital penalty as well, and eventually a compromise had been reached between the Houses that this should be so; but that, if as a result they were brought to trial (which was a matter for the King), the Houses would jointly petition for a waiver of the death penalty, which the King publicly undertook to grant. Vane

---

* Swingfield, in Kent. Strangford had raised money on it by the tortuous procedure of making Algernon, as his trustee, the mortgagor, and then pocketing the proceeds. Algernon hoped that if his father paid off the mortgage the property would revert to himself, but whether it would have done, since it still technically belonged to Strangford, was a nice point of law, which in the event the Earl decided not to test.

was then removed to prison in the Scilly Islands; but in the spring of 1662 was brought back to London and put on trial for treason. It was not easy to frame an adequate charge against him, since for technical reasons it had to be based on the highly artificial idea that Charles II had been reigning ever since the death of Charles I so that it was treason to keep him out of his kingdom.

Vane defended himself with skill and determination, arguing that it could hardly be treason to resist an absent king one had never undertaken to obey; and that obedience to a government in actual power had never been considered treason. If it were otherwise, there were plenty of people who could be similarly charged – Monk, for instance, and Montagu. No doubt he knew that like all treason trials it could only end in one way, but he could still at least rely on the public promise of a reprieve.

His confidence, however, was misplaced. The day after the trial began Charles II wrote Clarendon a letter which, though never known to Algernon, must be quoted to explain the correctness of the revulsion he felt for Charles:

> The relation that has been made to me of Sir Henry Vane's carriage yesterday in the hall, is the occasion of this letter, which, if I am rightly informed, was so insolent as to justify all he had done, acknowledging no supreme power in England but a Parliament, and many other things to that purpose. You have a true account of all; and if he has given new occasion to be hanged, certainly he is too dangerous a man to let live, if we can honestly put him out of the way. Think of this, and give me some account of it tomorrow, till when I have no more to say to you. C.R.[10]

Clarendon is thought to have hesitated over this chilling message, but in the closing speech for the prosecution the Attorney-General declared that Vane 'must be made a public sacrifice', without explaining why, and held a whispered conversation with the foreman of the jury before it retired. Vane was condemned, and refused to ask for a reprieve. 'If the King,' he said 'does not consider himself more concerned for his honour and word than I do for my life, I am very willing they should take it. Nay, I declare that I value my life less in a good cause, than the King can do his promise.' One of his friends suggested a large sum of money might change the King's mind but Vane vetoed the idea, saying that it would spoil the market when the King was already publicly committed to a reprieve.

His execution in June 1662 was generally condemned. Pepys was there, and noted Vane's courage, the frequent interruptions of his final speech by drums and trumpets, and Vane's final witticism when asked if he would pray for the King; 'You shall see I can pray for the King. I pray, God bless him.' 'The courage', Pepys wrote a day or two later, 'of Sir H. Vane is talked on everywhere as a miracle.'

The ruthlessness and dishonour involved are not easily explicable when one considers that equally prominent survivors of the past regime such as Heselrige and Lambert were allowed to live out their days as prisoners. It is necessary to infer that Vane inspired in Charles (and in some others) a particular fear and hatred that may well have gone back to the part he had played at the very beginning of the great Rebellion in contributing to the destruction of Strafford. Significantly, the scaffold was erected on the very spot Strafford had suffered and there is an ironical contrast between 'put not your trust in Princes', and 'I say, God bless him'. But above all the choice of Vane was symbolic. More than any of the surviving Parliamentary leaders he was felt to represent what had happened and his death was needed to expiate it. As one member of the House of Commons said, it was necessary 'to have somebody to die for the Kingdom as well as for the King' and the blood of the regicides alone was not enough.

This news transformed Algernon as a politician and a man. Harry Vane had been not only his chief but his hero, and the choice of him as a symbolic victim made Algernon realise that he himself was likely to remain a marked man so long as Charles was King. It had not been fairly done. A promise had been given and broken. At the end of his own life he looked back on it:

> Though I had ever opposed the then triumphing party, noe man had ever showed himself to be a fairer enemy, and I had done many personall and most important services, as well to the royall family as to such as depended upon it, I hoped that noe man would search into my personal thoughts, nor soe far remember my former actions, as to disturb me during a most innocent exile ... but I soon found that noe inoffensiveness of behaviour could preserve me against the malice of thoes who sought to destroy me; and was deffended against thoes designed to assassinate me only by the charity of strangers.[11]

From the late summer of 1662 Algernon ceases to be an exiled opponent of the restored monarchy and becomes an active conspirator against it. His judgement on Charles II, which he had suspended for two years, was made: the King was a cruel and treacherous tyrant, whose handsome ways and engaging manners made him more, not less, dangerous and contemptible. The long series of letters to Penshurst mingling complaints and attempts to please his father with political news and bibliographical presents, comes to an end, and his next written work is the admiring obituary of his hero in 'A Character of Sir Henry Vane'. He re-entered communication with the little knot of irreconcilable republican survivors who had found refuge in Switzerland. Late in 1662 or early in 1663 he moved northwards and recrossed the Alps, pausing on his way at Brescia to visit the shop of one of the most celebrated gunsmiths in Italy, Lazzarino Cominazzo, and purchase an extremely expensive pair of pistols.

The Refugees

WITH Algernon's departure from Italy he enters the true world of exile. The nature of the evidence about him changes, and we can no longer look for letters. Though he must have written many, their recipients prudently did not keep them, and only five survive that can with certainty be assigned to the next fourteen years. News of him is traced in intelligence reports, official communications, diplomatic memoirs, by those concerned to watch him. It was a life not only of exile but of conspiracy and, with Vane in mind, of emulation and vengeance.

Fortunately one of these five letters, written three years or so after he left Italy, is both autobiographical and introspective, and shows how the revolutionary Seeker had gained the upper hand over the aristocratic republican. It was written about 1666, probably to his Quaker friend Benjamin Furly,* and reviews all the changes in his fortunes and feelings since 'the great comply with thoes in power'. He had soon found 'I could not doe it. This persuaded me to absent myself, hoping that my enemyes would neglect me.' So he had spent almost three years, 'seldom much disturbed, but in the end, I found that it was an ill-grounded peace that I enjoyed, and

* See below, p. 149.

could have no rest in my owne spirite, because I lived only to myself, and was in no wayes usefull unto god's people, my countrey, or the world.' He must, he concluded, devote himself to 'the great and good work', however unfit an instrument he might be:

> I doe not knowe what success god will give unto oure undertakings, but I am certaine I can have no peace in my owne spirite, if I doe not endeavour by all meanes possible to advance the interest of god's people. Others may judge from whence this temper doth proceed, better than I can: if it be from god, he will make it prosper, if from the heat and violence of my owne disposition, I and my designes shall perish.[1]

When he crossed the Alps into Switzerland and his new life in the summer of 1663, he descended into surroundings which could not have been more different from the ones he had left behind him. Instead of the heat and grandeur of Rome, the hospitality and charm of the cardinals, the comfort and repose of the Villa Pamfili, there were the cool bourgeois Calvinism of the Canton of Bern and the company of hunted English remnants of the once Sovereign Rump, surrounded by mistrust, conspiracy, and personal danger.

Bern, which was a good deal larger than the present canton of that name, since it included what is now the Canton Vaud, was a formidable little republic with its own foreign relations and its own army. It was in a position to welcome and protect refugees for whom it had sympathy, and quite a number of Commonwealthmen had made their way there in the two years following the Restoration. Most of them had settled on the shores of Lac Léman in the Vaudois towns of Lausanne and Vevey, with the informal approval of the local authorities, to make up a not insignificant colony.

The most notable of them was Algernon's old friend, Edmund Ludlow, still using his rank of Lieutenant-General and tirelessly (though erroneously) reported by Charles II's spies as a constant visitor to England with far-flown plans to lead the veterans of the old army back to power. Ludlow was far too cautious to make any such journeys. As a regicide his life was forfeit. But he kept up an active correspondence with English sympathizers, and had chosen Vevey, with its good communications, for that very reason.

There were at least nine other republicans in the colony, some of whom had played prominent parts in Commonwealth politics. John Lisle had sat on the President's right at the trial of the King as Chancellor of the Commonwealth to advise on points of law, and had now been joined by his wife Alice. There were two other members of the Rump who had signed the fatal warrant, William Say, a lawyer, and William Cawley, whom Algernon must have known well at Chichester as one of that town's wealthiest and most influential citizens. Three others, though not actual members of the regicide court, were looked on as sharing its guilt – Edward Dendy, its Sergeant-at-Arms, and its two Clerks, Andrew Broughton and John Phelps. There were three other former MPs who had not been members of the court – Nicholas Love, Cornelius Holland, and Slingsby Bethel – and a single representative of the old Army, Colonel John Biscoe. Altogether it was the largest group of the old rulers of England still to survive, though there were many others scattered abroad.

The London government did not neglect them. Many different motives were at work, sheer vengeance being one. Both cavaliers and presbyterians had suffered much personally from Ludlow and his like. Then there was the need for a bogy with which, in a fickle world, supporters of the new government could be frightened. Finally, and perhaps most important of all, there was genuine fear. The government of Charles II in its early years was not a confident one. Its popular welcome and clothing of hereditary legitimacy did not make its leaders easily forget that only a short time ago they had themselves been an exiled, proscribed group hardly more numerous than the exiles of Vevey and Lausanne, with few friends and no money. From that low base they had recaptured power, and it did not seem impossible that their enemies might do the same. Indeed Ludlow and his friends did not feel the Cause was hopelessly lost so long as they stood firmly by its principles. In the light of later events they may appear a pathetic remnant, but when Algernon joined them neither they nor their enemies in London thought so.

Charles II's government brought pressure on all the countries harbouring republican exiles, including Bern, and had some success, for three regicides who had taken refuge in Holland were tricked into surrender, handed over by the Dutch, brought home, and executed. Other methods were also employed. Just about the time Algernon arrived in Switzerland an Irish adventurer named Macartey, but using the alias 'Riardo', settled on the banks of Lac Léman with a gang to mount operations of kidnapping and, if necessary, murder. They began work in the winter of 1663, and in July 1664 one of 'Riardo's' gunmen shot down John Lisle on his way to church at Lausanne, leapt on a horse led by a confederate a few yards away, and disappeared. It was one of the least savoury episodes of the Restoration, and strangely matched twenty-two years later when Jeffreys sent Lisle's now elderly widow to the scaffold for sheltering fugitives from the rout of Sedgemoor. Memories were long.

Algernon descended into this dangerous world at the end of July, or at latest during August 1663* and was welcomed as a considerable acquisition by the exiles, with whom he spent about three weeks. Even among Commonwealthmen (most of whom were country gentlemen) high birth commanded deference, and his diplomatic experience was especially valuable. Ludlow records his stay in almost grovelling terms – 'he was pleased to honour us with a visit ... assuring us of his affection and friendship, and in no way declining to own us and the cause for which we suffered ... he favoured us with his company.'[2] Algernon undertook to visit Bern and make representations to the cantonal government that they should extend official protection to Ludlow and his friends.

Ludlow's record of this visit suggests that Algernon was by no means short of money, and its source is one of the mysteries of his exile. One can accept that he not unreasonably paid himself in full for his embassy before he left from whatever public money was under his control, and he had only himself to support; but he had spent some three years of gentlemanly existence in Europe and done a good deal of travelling, and he must have been receiving a regular income, which can only have come from England. There are some traces of this in his correspondence from Rome, and when he became a marked man the invaluable Mr Hoskins, who was the Earl of Leicester's man of business, would have made sure there were as few clues left as possible. But there is one. In 1664 Lord Strangford's creditors forced him to promote a private act of Parliament enabling him to sell land to meet his debts, and after what seems to have been a good deal of argument in both Houses a provision was included enabling Algernon to benefit from the act. Considering the political cloud that was hanging over him Parliament was generous.

---

* Ludlow himself (Memoirs ii 345) places the visit in the late summer, though for some reason C. H. Firth in his footnote to the passage prefers the autumn. But by mid-September Algernon had left Switzerland, having cleared the way for Ludlow and other exiles to visit Bern and formally receive official protection, the cantonal letter being dated 13 September. Firth suggests this is a mistake for October, but it is difficult to believe so important a government document would be misdated, and the surmise does not seem to be supported by the Lisle letters to which Firth refers.

Although he did not stay in Switzerland for long, his utter commitment to the Cause in Exile was now complete. He would have agreed wholeheartedly with Ludlow's reply to a questioner at Bern who asked how it could have been that the apparently strong British Commonwealth was swept away almost without a shot being fired. In a classic statement of the Commonwealthmen's view of events since 1642 he pictured it as a long series of betrayals: by the aristocratic commanders in 1644; by the 'Presbyterian' compromisers when victory had been won; by the usurpation of Cromwell; and finally by the infamous coalition of 'Presbyterians' and military commanders that restored Charles II. It is a gross, even paranoid version of history, which had now become set in the minds of those loyal to the Cause, but it had as its centre something novel in politics – an ideology that was not primarily religious, yet was thought of as independent of political events and enshrining the indestructible truth.

Algernon had preceded his friends to Bern and did not wait for them, let alone go back to the shores of Lac Léman. He probably decided it was too dangerous, for it was easy to cross from the French side, and that autumn suspicious strangers began to be seen lurking in Vevey and Lausanne, causing Ludlow and his companions to live in a state of semi-siege and appeal to the local authorities for even more personal protection. In December there was an attempt on Ludlow's life. That Algernon was soon added to the list of targets may be gathered from a report sent by 'Riardo' to London the following summer: 'Si Cydnei est icy il est deguisse plus qu'a l'ordinaire, et je ne puis scauor au vray s'il y' est.'[3] Before leaving he presented Ludlow with the pistols he had bought at Brescia.

He went first to Augsburg, where he was shadowed by another party of assassins in charge of a Scottish officer called Andrew White, but eluded them, and by November was in Brussels. Algernon said later in his *Apology* that he was travelling on private business, but there can be little doubt that Ludlow was nearer the truth when he says Algernon 'thought convenient to draw nearer home, that if an opportunity should offer he might not be wanting to his duty and the publick service.' Ludlow always referred to conspiratorial journeys as if they were the most harmless official travel with all expenses paid at approved rates.

One of the first things Algernon did on reaching Brussels is in a way surprising: he arranged for his portrait to be painted by one of the best-known artists then working there, Justus van Egmont, a pupil of Van Dyck. The result, which is now at Penshurst, is dated 1663 and inscribed as showing the sitter in his forty-first year. It may seem an odd step for a political exile recently hunted by assassins, especially one so short of money as Algernon always maintained he was, but with politicians portraits and publication often have a political purpose. The miniature he had had painted before going to Denmark is essentially civilian and diplomatic, but the portrait of 1663 shows him in the breastplate of a soldier and a leader, and it could be engraved and circulated for propaganda purposes: the picture of a leader in the cause for the restoration of the English republic, for which he may reasonably have judged Ludlow was too cautious – and possibly too modest in his background – to make an adequate figure. Now that Harry Vane was dead, no surviving politician of the Commonwealth still at liberty could claim the same unblemished record of loyalty to the Cause with the same rank in society. The next three years were to be devoted to this new ambition.

The current international situation was therefore even more important to him than usual. England was again moving under popular pressure towards war with the Netherlands – a continuation of the Commonwealth's foreign policy which Charles II disliked but dared not resist. The Netherlands had insured against the prospect by a secret agreement with France under which Louis XIV would enter the war on the Dutch side if the struggle was at all prolonged. In this Louis was adopting the policy he consistently pursued for most of his long reign, which was to weaken and destabilise England while at the same time offering friendship and subsidies to its politicians. His aim was to neutralise England while he pursued his great ambition, the elimination of Spain from the southern Netherlands and their annexation to France. In the end it was to lead him into a disastrous miscalculation.

Most of this Algernon would have known. He was also well-informed about the state of affairs in England itself, though here his sources – 'his friends' as he called them – probably exaggerated the weakness of the government and the strength of the surviving opposition. There were indeed grounds for hope in Charles's wholesale betrayal of the 'Presbyterians' now that they had served their purpose in the Restoration: the revival of episcopacy, the massive ejection of dissenting clergy in 1662, the additional measures against non-conformity in the following years, the revived cult of monarchy and the outrageous corruption that surrounded it. Surely all these might rally the veterans of the old Army? The truth was — and here Algernon's informants would have been more muffled — that the government of Charles had succeeded with the Army where Parliament in 1647 had failed. The godly Army's 'industrial' demands which had originally propelled it into political power had been satisfied. Its old soldiers had a general indemnity as well as a fair proportion of their arrears, and, as a bonus, the freedom to trade without local restrictions in any corporate town. As for the officers, the estates and property they had acquired from the confiscation of cavalier and church lands were left with those who had got them, the only exception being property originally belonging to the King himself. The more extreme and sectarian old soldiers were easily isolated and their turbulence ruthlessly suppressed where it broke out. Ludlow and Sidney could dream about 'our old army' but the spirit that had maintained it had been suffocated and terrorised out of existence.

In the Netherlands Algernon found English expatriates very different from those he had left behind in Switzerland. They were numerous, and some of them were as deeply committed to the Cause as any of Ludlow's group: Michael Livesey, for instance, who had been one of the fieriest of the Independent M.P.s and a zealous member of the High Court of Justice; Cornet, now Colonel, George Joyce, abductor of Charles I and confidant of Cromwell, who for that reason was regarded in Whitehall as the equivalent of a regicide; and Benjamin Furly, a Quaker businessman who, in his quiet earnest ways gave much help and support to friends of the Cause. But there were many less reliable persons such as Colonel Joseph Bampfield, who had been employed on intelligence operations by both Charles I and Cromwell, and now commanded an English mercenary regiment in the Dutch army. Then there was the utterly unreliable William Scot, the son of Thomas Scot the regicide and briefly head of the Commonwealth intelligence service. Out of such diverse elements Algernon hoped for great things.

In December 1663 Algernon wrote to his father from Brussels — or rather he wrote to the English government, because at the end of this strange communication he asks his father to show it to Lord Sunderland, 'Saccharissa's' son, who was then at the beginning of his long and complex political career. He begins by referring to a suggestion, made by the Sidney family solicitor Mr Hoskins, that he should command a regiment to be raised in England for service in the Habsburg army against the Turks. Algernon's first reaction had been to say he was in no position to refuse any reasonable employment so he would consider the matter favourably; but further reflection has made him suspect that Mr Hoskins was acting for some higher authority whose motive was to remove him as far as possible from western Europe. This, therefore, is his considered answer:

> They shall have their end; I will serve them if they please, and upon more easy terms than are expected by others. I will undertake to transport a good strong body of *the best officers and soldiers of our old army*, both horse and foot. Though the obtaining of this would be a very considerable advantage unto me, and *some of my friends*, I do not ask it as a favour; I know neither they nor I shall receive anything upon that account. The first that I ever did ask, and the least that I ever can ask, (I mean assurance of being permitted to live quietly for a few months at Penshurst) not having been granted, I am like to make few requests for the future. But as I think that the advantage which the king expects by ridding the land of those persons, is the motive upon which this offer is made, I believe it to be a very considerable one, for they who find themselves suspected may possibly grow unquiet; the destroying of them will be a work of time, and not without difficulty and danger, and it cannot be expected, that they will of their own accord leave their country, unless it be with some man, of whom they have a good opinion, and all those are as little favoured as I am.[4]

The tone is ironically defiant and the words themselves almost a declaration of war, with such phrases as 'our old army', 'some of my friends', and 'a man of whom they have a good opinion'. The implication is that if he was entrusted with a regiment it might not be against the Turks he would lead it. He goes on:

> I doubt your lordship will be unwilling to propose this, lest it should make the king or his ministers believe that I am on better terms with my old companions than you would have them think me. I desire your lordship to wave that scruple; I have credit enough with them for such a business as this is; and if I were not thought at court to have far more than I have, they would not trouble themselves with me so much as they do.

Though the enigmatic tirade ends by saying that if he is given a regiment he will 'make use of it to carry me and a good number of those in the same condition so far from England that those who hate us may give over suspecting us', there is an additional reason for regarding even this as irony. Among the reports on anti-government plots reaching Whitehall early in 1664 there is one which makes the specific allegation that joining regiments to be raised for service on the Danube was a mere cover for conspiracy.

Early in 1664 Algernon withdrew to Germany with his companions Say and Biscoe. They were seen at Spa by an English agent, who reported they were considering a rising in Ireland; but much of Algernon's time was spent in writing, for which he had not lost his taste on becoming a conspirator, and the work in hand was his first major venture into political theory.

'Court Maxims', as it is known, was prepared for publication but its appearance was to be frustrated by circumstances, and it remained unknown until the printer's copy came to light three centuries later. It is a lengthy attack on the Restoration Monarchy in the form of seventeen dialogues between a supporter of Charles II and a Commonwealthman he improbably meets on a country walk and engages in conversion about why the Restoration seems to have fallen so far short of the hopes that greeted it. The outcome is a detailed discussion of the harmful effects of monarchy, followed by a well-informed survey of foreign policy. It begins politely enough but gradually the Cavalier throws aside the mask to reveal himself as a callous self-seeker and is denounced with ever-increasing fury by his opponent, driving home his central argument: a king, even if well-disposed, scrupulous, and patriotic, as by a happy accident he may be, *must*, if he is to survive, breed round himself a class whose very existence depends on supporting him. The motives of such a class are inevitably selfish and parasitic, and its morality therefore corrupt and against the public interest. It follows that monarchy is itself against the public interest, no matter who is the monarch, since it inevitably requires a corrupt class to sustain it.

'Court Maxims' advocates not only republicanism but alliance with the Dutch as the right policy for England. France, it maintains, is the real threat to Britain and the whole of Europe, and its king is the more menacing because he is efficient, patriotic, and public spirited: 'I can praise', Algernon's spokesman says, 'the courage of a lion.' It is folly to think of France as a reliable friend, and rushing into a commercial war with Holland is sacrificing the one sure ally. If Algernon did not succeed in injecting republicanism into the Whig tradition he at least provided one of the planks in Whig foreign policy.

He was not writing merely to pass the time. 'Court Maxims'

was designed as propaganda for the attempt on England he was now involved in, which was to be launched, if possible, with Dutch help, in the context of the impending war. During the first months of 1664 the cautious de Witt had avoided co-operation with the exiles, but on 19 August an English agent reported to Whitehall that things had changed. He begins with an obvious reference to the recent murder of Lisle in Lausanne, and continues:

> Their [the exiles'] counsels are now totally changed, and the thought of any sudden attempt is laid aside on account of a message from Holland that the Dutch will contribute largely to the promoting of any troublesome design against government, provided all matters are carried on by the joint counsels of a select party in England and Scotland, who shall correspond with those in Holland. Sidney and Ludlow are to be the chief. This project is highly approved . . .[6]

For some years past the Dutch army had included English and Scottish mercenary regiments, and these were now reorganized by de Witt to eliminate officers who might not be reliable if called on to serve in an expeditionary force to their native country. It was a notable departure from the traditional Dutch strategy against England, which had always been strictly naval.

Algernon probably returned from Germany to the Low Countries with the manuscript of 'Court Maxims' in his luggage towards the end of 1664 or early in 1665, just before the Second Dutch War finally broke out. 'Some of our friends,' wrote Ludlow, 'conceiving great hopes of the restitution of the Commonwealth, entered into a treaty with divers principal ministers [of the Netherlands] for securing some forces to join with our oppressed party in England against the common enemy.'[7] But he was deaf to Algernon's appeals to join him in Holland, and was the recipient of very waspish letters as a result. Whitehall followed developments with interest.

War was officially declared in March, but despite the attractions of using the exiles de Witt hesitated. The Dutch dispute with England was a maritime one, and the Dutch land forces were designed solely for the defence of the home territory. Looked at politically there seemed little merit in substituting a republic for the monarchy in England – the last republic had first offered the Dutch a bear's embrace and then made war. It had passed the Navigation Act and had been closer to the business world of the City than King Charles was ever likely to be. The proposed leaders of the new revolution in England had been members of the Rump and enthusiastic supporters of the First Dutch War. And then there was the Plague. It would be foolhardy to land an expeditionary force in such circumstances. So for a whole year de Witt kept the exiles waiting, perhaps seeing them more as a useful threat than as a real weapon. It would be better to wait until the French guarantee to enter the war was honoured.

The English intelligence service in the Netherlands was being improved. In January 1666 one Nicholas Arthur was planted at Amsterdam with a specific indemnity for anything he might do consorting with the King's enemies. At much the same time the celebrated Aphra Behn was launched in Antwerp on her career as a spy under the code-name 'Astraea' and gained the confidence of one of the conspirators, William Scot. As she archly wrote later on:

> Once Thirsis, by th' Arcadian King's Commands
> I left these Shades, to visit foreign lands,
> Imploy'd in public toils of State Affairs,
> Unusual with my Sex, or to my Years.

How good their information was can be judged by the fact that Nicholas Arthur was reporting the conspirators' next important move almost as soon as it took place. What should he do, he asked the Secretary of State, now that he had discovered the conspirators were in touch with France?[8]

One cannot help suspecting that de Witt, having discarded the idea of a Dutch-backed republican expedition, was using the Commonwealthmen for his own more immediate purpose of bringing the French into the war on his side as soon as possible. Louis XIV's heart was not in his commitment to the Dutch, and he did his utmost, even sending a special mission to London, to avoid the engagement which would limit the freedom of action he so much valued. He was extremely indignant therefore when he was informed in March that his ambassador at the Hague had been persuaded by de Witt to issue special passports to Algernon and Ludlow enabling them to come to Paris and discuss their plans with the French government. The unfortunate ambassador was sent a sharp rebuke for his premature action, and told that other arrangements would be made for Sidney and his friends to visit France if the King decided he wanted to talk to them.

Algernon had now gone far enough along the road of conspiracy to be firmly registered in Whitehall's demonology. That

Algernon Sidney, on the right, and his two brothers, Philip in the centre and Robert on the left. Painted by an unknown artist in about 1630.

Sir Philip Sidney, Algernon's great-uncle and the family hero.

Miniature of Algernon Sidney by John Hoskins, 1659. He too had a cleft chin.

Sir Henry Vane, the younger, by Lely. A fellow republican, executed by Charles II in 1662.

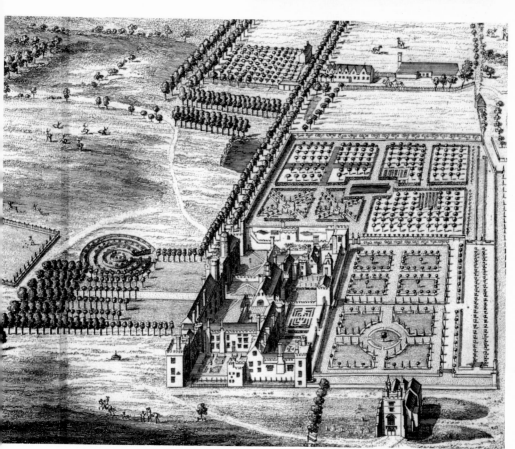

Penshurst Place early in the eighteenth century, from the engraving by Knyff/Kip.

The Swedes attack Kronborg in September 1658. Engraving by J. le Paultre after E. Dahlberg. This great Danish fortress dominated the Sound. Its capture changed the balance of power in the Baltic, leading to the three-power intervention and Sidney's mission nine months later.

Algernon Sidney in 1663, by Justus van Egmont.

Edmund Ludlow, Lieutenant-General, regicide and republican.

William Penn, the founder of Pennsylvania, by Francis Place

A joint meeting of English and Dutch Quakers, probably at Rotterdam, in 1677. Top left, hat in hand, is the brooding figure of Benjamin Furly, flanked on his right by the Dutch Quaker leader Jan Claus, and standing on his left, George Fox. William Penn is third from the right with George Barclay extreme right.

THE
Arraignment, Tryal & Condemnation

OF

𝕬lgernon Sidney, Efq;

FOR

High-Treafon.

For Confpiring the Death of the

KING,

AND

Intending to raife a Rebellion in this

KINGDOM.

Before the Right Honourable

Sir GEORGE JEFFREYS, Knight and Baronet, Lord Chief Juftice of *England*, at His Majefties Court of *Kings-Bench* at *Weftminfter*, on the 7*th*. 21*th*. and 27*th*. of *November*, 1683.

LONDON,

Printed for *Benj. Tooke* at the *Ship* in St. *Paul's* Church-Yard, 1684.

The Trial of Algernon Sidney, an early nineteenth-century painting recreating the scene, by S. Williams.

A medal struck after the Rye House Plot, showing the plotters as a seven-headed hydra, with the motto: 'They shall perish by the thunderbolt'.

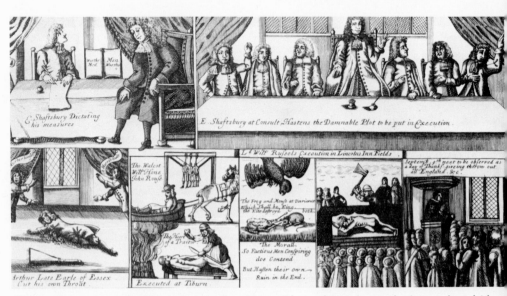

Government propaganda illustrating the Rye House Plot and its aftermath, from a broadside of 1683 entitled 'A History of The New Plot'.

same March it was decided in London to draw up a list of the less blameworthy exiles, offering them amnesty if they returned to England within a certain time limit. Algernon's name is on the first draft of this list, but was later erased and is not in the final published version. There can be only one explanation: he must not be given the opportunity of returning and pleading immunity. He was too serious an enemy.

De Witt, having as he thought palmed off Sidney and Ludlow on France, wrote to his ambassador in Paris on 4 March, and again on 11 March, to say that 'The Lord Sidney, accompanied by other disgraced Lords, set out in your direction in order there at the Court to propose a number of important matters.' He then asks van Beuningen to give them all the help he can, but is careful to dissociate the Dutch government from anything they may say: 'Of what representations they may put forward for themselves your Excellency will be the best judge'; and 'I do not know what representations he will himself make, but I am sure he will tell you.'[9]

Ludlow, earnestly pressed by Sidney and Say to join in the expedition to Paris, set out for a conference with them, but eventually decided to stay in his sanctuary at Vevey. Algernon wrote him a furious letter and then journeyed on with his companions. The others had to go to Mainz for fresh passports, which were not issued until France had actually entered the war at the end of April. They did not get to Paris until 6 May when they made contact with the Dutch ambassador, who arranged an interview for them with the French foreign minister, Lionne. 'Whatever emerges from it', van Beuningen wrote to de Witt, 'I will communicate to Your Excellency.'[10]

King Louis XIV was then only twenty-eight and at the height of his honeymoon with power. His head was full of plans, especially in the amoral world of international diplomacy which particularly charmed him. If Algernon had known their full extent he might well have hesitated, for they included a Catholic rising in Ireland and subsidies to the King of Denmark to impede the English trade in the Baltic which only a few years earlier he had worked so hard to guarantee. Nor, it seems from Louis' *Mémoires*, was Sidney the only English exile with whom the French were dealing.

Nevertheless Louis regarded Algernon as the most promising of what he describes as 'les restes de la faction de Cromwell', perhaps because he was 'un gentillhomme anglais', and he seems to have accorded him at least one interview, at which the proposals for a rising in England were discussed. They seem to have been ambitious, for 'grandes soulèvements' were promised, and a French subsidy of 100,000 écus was suggested. Louis thought it over, decided so large a speculation was not worthwhile, and offered 20,000 down with the rest payable on results. It was the way he would always deal with subsidies to the English opposition.

Algernon, as so often, had overplayed his hand, and found himself discarded by one potential ally, and shuffled off by another. The other exiles, as Ludlow makes clear, could not be brought into line. But it was just as well he did not accept Louis' offer. From the King of France's point of view the rising would be no more than a side-show whether it succeeded or failed: indeed failure might well be preferable to a substitution of Charles II by 'les restes de la faction de Cromwell'.

The overthrow of the restored Stuarts was in fact accomplished twenty-two years later by just such a Dutch-based invasion of England as Algernon had envisaged. But the episode is bound to raise the question whether, though vaunting himself so much as a patriot, he should be regarded as a traitor. In a legal sense he certainly was – he was discussing an invasion of his own country with foreign powers against whom England was actually at war. That he held political opinions with which the existing government disagreed can hardly be held as an excuse. His own ambition, not yet worn out by his many failures, urged him on. Yet when one has counted all this it would still be a misinterpretation of both the times and the man to see his dealings with de Witt and Louis XIV as in any sense disgraceful, whether in his own eyes or those of his contemporaries. England, his country, for which he had declared he stood during his last months in Denmark, and whose landscapes he had recalled in his travels across Germany, was one thing: Charles II was another. He had given no allegiance to him. He had offered it and been rejected, so he owed none. And in the seventeenth century, and especially for an aristocrat such as Sidney, allegiance was still deeply personal. It was his nature, and in a way his limitation, that he had as a young man given his allegiance to a Cause, and what was more an English Cause, which he could never abandon.

Gascony

AFTER his failure with Louis, Algernon was daily expected in the Netherlands by his friends and Whitehall's spy, Aphra Behn. Instead, armed with a special French passport,* he paid a visit to Montpellier, then still a strongly Huguenot town and the home of an English colony containing several sympathizers with the fallen republic. From there he sent an extraordinary message – it can hardly be described as a letter – but before considering its contents it is necessary to say more about its recipient.

Benjamin Furly is the one steady friend apart from Harry Vane that we know of in Algernon's morose and solitary life, and the two could not have been more different. Harry Vane had been a member of Algernon's own class and a few years older – just the model for an aspiring young soldier-politician: Benjamin Furly, on the other hand, was some thirteen years younger and the second son of a draper. His portrait shows a plumpish, rather clumsy-looking man with a round, ugly, but highly intelligent face under a thatch of dark hair which oddly enough is fully visible because, contrary to his

---

* The passport was issued at Vincennes on 2 August for a visit to Montpellier and subsequent return to Flanders. Meadley (p. 157) gives the date as 1663, but this is an error, for in August of 1663 Algernon had only just arrived in Switzerland, and there is no evidence of his being in contact with the French government till 1666.

Quaker principles, he holds his hat dangling before him in both hands.

His father had been one of the leading citizens of Colchester, and its mayor from 1650 to 1652, but his municipal career came to an end abruptly in 1655 when he was converted by the preaching of George Fox and, taking his whole family with him, became a Quaker. For a time he was imprisoned and barred from public office for refusing to take the necessary oaths. But the business prospered, and in 1658 his younger son Benjamin was sent to manage its affairs in the Netherlands, with the additional task of spreading the Quaker message there. He succeeded so well in both that before he was thirty he was one of the most prosperous foreign business men in Rotterdam and a leading figure in the Quaker congregation there. In 1665 his leadership at the Rotterdam Meeting became undisputed, and lasted for the next forty years.

Furly was a genuinely likeable and warm-hearted man, with a talent for making friends, and elicited lasting attachment not only from the sullen and headstrong Algernon but from the suspicious and timorous John Locke. Later in his life his Quaker extremism began to mellow, and although it was held with passion in his youth, as he showed in his violently worded pamphlet called *The Principle of the Hat,* he had none of the temperament of a fanatic.* Learning rather than controversy occupied his spare time, and he was a collaborator in a remarkable venture in comparative philology designed to justify Quaker linguistic usage. For this *Battledoor for Teachers and Professors to learn Singular and Plural* Furly collected no fewer than 249 grammars and dictionaries in various languages, which formed the core of a large library of more than 4,000 volumes sold on his death for over £8,000.

Furly was deeply concerned in the politics of opposition to the Restoration government, and appears frequently in Aphra Behn's

---

* It was a contribution to the current controversy among the Friends about whether the general rule that men should remain covered should be suspended during prayer. Furly argued strongly against those who favoured the exception, maintaining that uncovering, in whatever circumstances, was ordained by men, so uncovering in prayer was merely repeating a human custom. Anyway, what about women, what about Jews? The Quaker protest about hats was not so absurd as it may seem today. It was an attack on the elaborate code of manners by which deference and subordination were enforced. But it also reflects the sharp distinction Algernon made in his later writings between the Law of God (revealed and innate) and the Law of Man (conventional and procedural).

reports, where her source, William Scot, identifies him succinctly as 'The Quaker who the Fanatiques do so confide in'. He was more than their friend and confidant. For many years he lent them money, gave them house-room, handled their business affairs, and with his international contacts acted as their banker. He was the repository of their secrets, their trusted adviser, a solid resource in their shifting and uncertain world. 'Collonell Sidney,' Aphra reported on 22 September 1666, 'is in great esteem with de Witt and often in conversation with Benjamin Turly [she was always complaining about troubles with her cipher] the Quaker; being resolved to shape some designe for Ingland.'

By that time Algernon had returned to the Netherlands from Montpellier, and it is necessary to return to the message he had sent Furly from there. It is entitled 'A Prophecy' and, apart from his dying declaration, was the first of his works ever to be published, though it had to wait twenty-two years till Furly, on the morrow of the Glorious Revolution, arranged for its appearance simultaneously in London and Amsterdam.* Its single sheet is authenticated by Furly himself: 'This Prophecy I drew for myself out of the original hand of the Honourable A. Sidney Esq. which B. Furly found Yesterday among his letters which he had from him.' 'Yesterday', he noted, was February 18/28 1689.

The 'Prophecy' is couched in the language of the Apocalypse – appropriate enough for the year of the Great Fire and sporadic Dutch raids on England led by English officers. It talks of lions and eagles and lilies waging a world-consuming struggle, and the ultimate triumph of the Son of Man. Here is the less obvious side of Algernon the moody republican aristocrat: the 'Seeker' writing to the Quaker draper. Yet the expert on international affairs is not far away – so near in fact that Furly himself tells us Algernon's marginal notes for the interpretation of the vision. France (the Lily) will invade the Netherlands (the Lion), to whose aid will come the Eagle (the Habsburg Emperor). The Lily will triumph over the Lion but in the ensuing European War the Lily in turn will be defeated. The Son of Man (a new regime in England) will cross the

---

* *Copy of a Prophecy sent by the late Honourable Algernon Sidney Esq. in the Year 1666 from Montpellier to B. Furley of Rotterdam, and by him accidentally found among old Papers Feb 18/28 1689.* London, March 1689. There have been doubts about its authenticity, but I do not see why.

sea and crown victory with universal peace. Here, as so often, fanatical language is a political code.

Furly, on coming across this analysis of European politics twenty-two years later certainly felt it had come true. France did invade first the Spanish, then the Dutch Netherlands. The regime of the de Witts was destroyed. The Habsburg Emperor joined in the war. The Restoration monarchy was overthrown and England joined in the struggle which was to end the forward march of Louis XIV's France.

'Sidney', Aphra reported in August, 'is at present writing a Treatise in defence of a Republique and agst Monarchie, and designes soone or late for the Presse.'[1] Since Algernon was then in Montpellier, and before that had been some months in Paris, he could not actually have been writing it himself in Rotterdam. Nor is the manuscript of *Court Maxims* which we possess written in Algernon's handwriting. The first nine dialogues are in a hand which is so like known specimens of Furly's as to be indistinguishable. What had happened was that Algernon had left the manuscript with his friend to be prepared for the press. Nothing could show the closeness of the association between them more strongly. The pamphlet was intended for clandestine distribution in support of the movement Algernon was planning against Charles II. It was a close secret, which would have been entrusted only to a trusted sympathizer. It is even likely that in copying Furly also corrected and improved Algernon's original, for Algernon was a careless hasty writer, Furly an exact one.

This friendship, which began in 1665 at the latest, and probably much sooner, sheds light on several hitherto puzzling aspects of Algernon's later career. For instance it helps to explain how he kept going for so long financially without any apparent support from his family. It is not necessary to suppose that Furly actually gave him an income – a man like Algernon would not have accepted such an arrangement – but even in his impecunious exile he still had expectations on his father's death, and the Earl was now over seventy. Such security would not be unacceptable even to a less sympathetic banker than Benjamin Furly. But above all Algernon found in Benjamin a lasting friend, and this fills the darkest of the gaps in the story. That they corresponded we know from surviving letters in which, most unusually for Algernon, he addresses Benjamin as 'Dear Friend' and signs himself 'your affectionate friend';

and when Furly's library was sold copies of the report of Algernon's trial and of *Discourses Concerning Government* were found in it.

Although Algernon returned to the Hague in September 1666 the candle of his conspiracy was flickering out. The Swiss exiles were too cautious to move, the Dutch ones too unscrupulous and divided among themselves. Prominent among them was the dubious figure of Colonel Bampfield, whom Algernon rightly did not trust. In October he left for Germany: 'The phanatiques', Aphra reported, 'doe conclude [because the post did not come for weeks] that there are some troubles in England; they are not come to any resolution to doe anythinge nor can not, before Coll. Sidney's returne, who is expected some ten dayes hence, of what they doe you shall have advice.'² But he did not return. The conspiracy had lasted three years – ever since he had had his portrait painted wearing armour – and though he had written a book, negotiated with two foreign powers for an invasion force, and done his bad-tempered best to bring the disparate emigrés into some kind of combination, he had failed. He can be blamed for even trying, and should have known better, says History austerely, that he had not the qualities required to restore the Commonwealth. But looking round him he felt there was no one else. Ludlow was too cautious and undistinguished, Harry Vane had been slaughtered, Marten, Lambert, and Heselrige were finished. It had been as much a sense of obligation as personal ambition that had made him pick up the banner of the Cause when it was at its most hopeless.

The events he had foreseen in The 'Prophecy' were already in train, for that winter Louis was planning the invasion of the Spanish Netherlands which duly occurred in the summer of 1667 and inaugurated the series of wars which led to the destruction of the de Witts and the renaissance of the House of Orange. Shortly before Algernon left the Netherlands his boyhood acquaintance, Sir William Temple, arrived in Brussels as the British envoy and at once began to construct the tripartite alliance of Protestant powers (England, the United Provinces and Sweden) to resist the expected French onslaught. Temple must have known a good deal about Algernon's activities in the Netherlands, so would have treated him with caution if they met, as it is probable they did. The reserve would have been the greater because Temple was now on extremely friendly terms with Algernon's elder brother Philip, to whom he had rented his house at Sheen, and to whom he sent jaunty letters from Brussels, offering to send him a Spanish mistress who would enliven the quiet society of Surrey.*

So when Algernon wrote to Temple from an address which he hoped (wrongly) was unknown to the English intelligence service asking the courtesy of the diplomatic bag for a package he wished to send to Penshurst, Temple granted the favour but his reply was not encouraging:

> I am sorry your disposition of your fortunes have drawn you so far out of the reach of your friends' services, and almost correspondence; in which I doubt the difficulties may shortly increase, at least this way; for we are here at present in little hopes to see next month end without an advance of a French army into these provinces.[3]

By the next post he wrote to London reporting his contact with Algernon and seeking instructions.

If, at this point, Algernon had any idea of patching up peace with his family and the English government (which he quite possibly had), this was a complete rebuff, and he disappeared for more than a year, when he turns up in Montpellier again. How long he stayed there we do not know, but on 6 October 1668 he signed a certificate confirming that a local Scottish Protestant pastor, a 'M. David Abrenathée' was of ancient Scottish family. Such little services were expected of him as the son of an earl and a former ambassador, and the name was undoubtedly Abernethy.

He is next sighted in Paris in the spring of 1670 talking to the Huguenot Marshal Turenne, France's greatest soldier, about foreign policy on lines Turenne thought so interesting that he reported them to Louis, who in turn passed them on to London. One must always remember that in doing so Louis was serving his own purposes during the delicate negotiations leading to the secret Treaty of Dover and what Algernon is reported as saying may well have been improved from that point of view by the various hands through which it travelled. Nevertheless Algernon's opinions as recorded in the French foreign office are in shocking contrast to the pro-Dutch sentiments of 'Court Maxims', and his alleged willingness to collaborate with Charles II in a pro-French, religiously tolerant policy is an even greater breach in his reputation for personal consistency. Indeed so close are his opinions, as reported to Turenne, to the

---

* Philip had been quick to make his peace with the restored monarchy, and retired into private life, with his Cromwellian past forgiven. It was yet another source of ill-will between the two brothers.

policy actually agreed between the two kings in the secret Treaty of Dover that one suspects they were elicited by some partial (and no doubt allegedly hypothetical) disclosure of its main features, and so produced one of those policy analyses in which he was so facile, to suit his audience and the current state of play, but which did not deflect him in the least from his main objectives. If he had been given hints of the terms of the secret treaty he would at once have seen in them the possibility of using it as the basis of fresh subversion against Charles.*

Charles was not impressed, and told Arlington that he did not care in the least where Algernon lived so long as it was not England, where 'his pernicious opinions, backed by the courage and intelligence he has, could do much harm'. Arlington relayed this unconscious compliment to Paris on 4 August with the economical suggestion that Louis might be willing to provide Algernon with a small pension. Three weeks later Charles, no doubt feeling he had not been quite definite enough, ordered Arlington to tell the French that he did not wish Algernon to live in Paris, and the further away he was the better. If he had to be in France at all it should be in some remote province, such as Languedoc.

In the course of these exchanges Charles also said something odd, in referring to Algernon as his 'preserver'. It seems to have arisen from something said to him by either Arlington or the French ambassador suggesting some valuable personal service Algernon had once done the King. And in the last years of his life Algernon himself more than once referred to such a favour, though without ever saying what it was.

It is difficult to guess what it could have been, for their lives were spent not only in different political camps but, for the most part, in different countries, and there is no record of any meeting between them until the late 1670s. Yet one can hardly dismiss the evidence altogether, and there is one possibility to be considered. When Algernon was Governor of Dover during the 'Second Civil War' Cavalier raids from the Low Countries were planned, and one of these was to be led by Charles himself. The landing was to be in Kent; it was betrayed, and a trap was set, which in turn was betrayed, so that the operation never took place. If Algernon had revealed the trap set for Charles it would have indeed been a valuable service,

* See p. 181 post.

and would correspond to his quixotic character. Probably he would not even have regarded it as a breach of his duty, though Captain Cannon, if he ever discovered it, would have taken a very different view.

The fact that it is so difficult to trace Algernon after the collapse of his schemes to revive the Cause in 1666 does not mean that he was necessarily living in isolation and poverty. Limited his means certainly were, but he was a gentleman, and remained so; and he was now beginning in his grumpy way to enjoy cloaking his movements and intentions in mystery. In Paris he moved in the highest society, a friend of the Duc de Bouillon and other, Huguenot, noblemen, and may even have been received at court. He also had visits from his brothers. Robert Sidney came to France in 1668, and Henry, his youngest and most successful brother, in 1670.*[4]

Algernon and Robert, who had probably shared Lucy Walters with Charles II, met for the last time, for Robert was already a sick man and died later in the year, when his regiment, by a curious irony, was assigned to Harry Vane's younger brother Walter, who had made his peace with the government. Henry Sidney's visit, besides his interview with Algernon, marked his appointment as a junior official at the Paris embassy, the first step in a career which led to an embassy, a major role in the Revolution of 1688, an earldom on his own account, and the viceroyalty of Ireland under William III, making him the fourth member of his family to fill it in successive generations. It is very likely that as a young diplomat in Paris he played a part in the correspondence between the two kings about his elder brother, and in adjusting that awkward man's future.

The problem of finding a suitable place in France for Algernon to live seems to have been solved by the Duc de Bouillon, and religion and family connection explain why. Though he had himself conformed to Catholicism the Duke came of a notable Huguenot line which had been very much part of the international Protestant world. One of his great-grandfathers had been William the Silent, champion of Dutch liberation. His uncle was Marshal Turenne and he owned extensive properties in Gascony, including the pleasant but now sleepy town of Nérac, some seventy miles south-east of Bordeaux.

* Henry's discussion with Algernon was concerned with family matters and the possibility of Algernon's return to England with safe conduct. The Earl was engaged in one of his periodic reconstructions of his affairs, which provided yet another layer of disputes in the the family.

Nérac had not always been sleepy. Once it had been the second capital of the d'Albret kingdom of Navarre, and Queen Marguérite d'Angoulême, sister of King Francis I of France, had held her court in its little castle. There she had entertained the poet Clément Marot, sheltered the young Calvin, and written her collection of short stories, *The Heptameron*. Her grandson Henry, later Henry IV, spent much of his boyhood there and a sad little monument in the royal hunting-park still records the suicide of a gardener's daughter, the first of his many loves, when he failed to keep an assignation. When Henry became the leader of the Protestant cause during the Wars of Religion, Nérac was his headquarters, and in 1579 was the site of an important peace conference between the warring factions.

Under Henry's successors Huguenot Nérac had suffered. Its claim as a second capital had vanished when Navarre was united with France. Louis XIII demolished its walls, and Richelieu wanted to demolish its castle. During the Fronde it was sacked. Its municipal privileges were trimmed by Cardinal Mazarin, and its Protestant worship hedged about with oppressive restrictions. Catholic clergy were systematically imported, pressure was exerted to abandon the old faith. When Louis XIV visited it in 1659 the castle was so ruinous that the King had to put up in the mansion of the President of the Financial Court.

Nérac had passed to the House of Bouillon, but Algernon's friend the Duke never visited it, and left the management of his affairs there to an agent, Monsieur de Mazelières. The only member of the Bouillon family actually in residence was the Duchess, Marie-Anne Mancini, a niece of Cardinal Mazarin, whose infidelities had so embarrassed her husband that he consigned her to semi-captivity there.

The Duke thus had additional reasons for agreeing that Algernon should live at Nérac – probably in a house the Duke was in a position to provide. Besides obliging his exiled friend, and meeting the wishes of his monarch, he would have a reliable, independent observer in his remote possession to provide him with regular information about its affairs. That this was the arrangement is proved by the survival of one of the long news-letters about Nérac which Algernon wrote to the Duke's steward in Paris, Monsieur Bafoul.[5]

Nérac was Algernon's home for the next six or seven years. Quiet it no doubt was, as it is today, a charming town of old stone houses which crowd down to one bank of the Baïse, across which still lies the vast hunting-park of the d'Albrets known as the Garenne. In Algernon's time the Garenne still provided sport, and he spent several winters of solitary shooting in its woods. As a place of exile for a moody protestant aristocrat this decayed fragment of the world of the Reformation to which his own family, and above all the great Sir Philip, had always belonged, could not have been more appropriate.

The sparse hints we have do not allow a precise date for Algernon's settlement in Nérac. He tells M. Bafoul that he spent at least four shooting seasons in the Garenne, that he was there in 1674, and in January 1677, when he had just returned from a journey, presumably to Paris. Later, in his 'Apology', he said he had been eleven years an exile in a remote part of France, but this must start with his visit to Paris in 1666: late 1670 is the likely date for his settlement, or perhaps a little later. But it was nevertheless a long time, for it carried him to the age of fifty-four, old by the standards of the period. Yet his health remained good. Spare, greying now, he is as active as ever, shooting, writing, riding. In the voluminous correspondence of his lifetime, with its litany of complaints about circumstances and other people, there is hardly a syllable about not feeling well: and he is at his least self-conscious when he speaks of horses. He not only loved riding, but truly understood both horsemanship and horses.*

In addition to his roving commission for the Duc de Bouillon and his shooting he continued to be treated, as at Montpellier, as a person of status to whom English residents could turn for authenticating acts, as they would today to an honorary consul. On 13 May 1674 the Nérac records show an English couple being married in his house. Oliver Cheyney, son of Francis Cheyney Esq. of Eye in the County of Suffolk married Susan Grundy of Devonshire, both described as residents of Nérac, though what could have brought them there to have their wedding presided over by such an odd,

---

* The evidence for his stay in Nérac is his own report of four shooting seasons – the winters of either 1673–76 or 1674–77 – and two letters about a passport to England which are printed in his correspondence with Henry Savile (though they may not in fact be to Savile). There is a general agreement that these two letters as printed are misdated. The first, from Paris, has the date 14/24 November, and the second, from Nérac, 18/28 December, 1682, by which year Algernon had long been back in England. It is tempting to think the mistake is of one figure only, and to assign the letters to 1672, on the assumption that they are connected with the negotiations for the passport granted (and refused) in 1673.

sombre figure as Algernon is difficult to imagine. The *Essay on Love* had been a long time ago.

Nérac was not only a place of exile: in his opinion it was very badly run. The Garenne was infested with poachers, and correspondingly thin in game. The Duke's agent, de Mazelières, was a scoundrel and generally disliked (a view confirmed when he was assassinated in 1680 by some townsmen) and showed his religious impartiality, in Algernon's sarcastic words, by being willing to employ a Huguenot, as readily as he would a Catholic, if he was a forger, thief, murderer or poisoner. The Sous-Lieutenant Assesseur was an idiot, the principal advocate a man one would not entrust with a case worth sixpence, the brothers Casmont were of ill repute – one of them was suspected of murdering an officer in his bed – and the apothecary was 'turbulent'. Altogether, he advises M. Bafoul, Monseigneur le Duc ought to carry out a complete review of the arrangements for running his property in Gascony. As for his own hunting on the Garenne, he goes on, he is sure the Duke will not expect an exact account of the bag, but 'for my own satisfaction, I have enquired of my servants who inform me that over the past four years it has not exceeded sixty pairs of partridges.'

There were consolations, and one was the acquisition of a loyal secretary, who stood by him for the rest of his life. Joseph Ducasse was a Néraçais Huguenot of respectable family, and was taken on by Algernon as a personal servant very early in his stay, but gradually developed into a secretary and confidant. Somewhat younger than his master, he accompanied him to execution, and became the custodian of his memory, as well as the guardian of his papers. His knowledge of Algernon's political dealings during the last ten years of his life must have been very close.

In a much higher station of life there was the company of the Duc de la Rochefoucauld, author of the *Maxims*, whose family chateau was not far away, at Verteuil. Algernon was on visiting terms with de la Rochefoucauld, and found much there to admire. The Duke was now old, and was tortured by gout, but he still hunted, and he still wrote – in his visitor's opinion the ideal combination for an aristocrat. What was more his estates were well managed, his game well preserved – points which Algernon with characteristic lack of tact held up as models for the Duc de Bouillon. Here again we find the exile in the company of an aristocrat with Huguenot ancestry, for the Rochefoucauld family, like the de

Bouillons had been of the Protestant party in the previous century, and, the Duke himself had been a Frondeur.

Altogether the picture of Algernon's long exile in France is not quite that of the lonely, studious idealist which he often draws, and his legend has maintained. He was involved, though in a vexed way, with local life, and mixed in the very best society. His stay in Paris, and his visits there even after he had settled in Nérac, brought him a wide acqaintance.

But when all these allowances are made he must have had much time for thought and for writing, and to his life in Nérac must belong parts of what became his great work, *Discourses Concerning Government*. He claimed himself, when the manuscript was produced in court, that whatever he had written had been composed many years ago for his own satisfaction and drew attention to the yellowing pages and faded ink of the exhibit. Much of the material he had entered in his Common-Place Book during his stay in Rome, as well as echoes from 'Court Maxims' reappear in the *Discourses*, which suggests he had these manuscripts with him. The lack of a library would not have bothered him much. There were several great houses, such as the Château de Verteuil, where he could find books, and there is much in the *Discourses* by way of quotation that would be found on the shelves of any nobleman who had pretensions to education: Cicero, Livy, Tacitus, Aristotle, Plato, and above all the Bible. Indeed all these were available in excellent cheap pocket editions, mostly Dutch, which he could have carried with him. Often he quoted from memory, as any check of a sample of his quotations will show. Very few of them are accurate.

He wrote rapidly and in a passion of self-expression, hardly pausing, one feels, to check or improve. For much he needed nothing but his own experience and feelings. His view of Nérac is generalised into a view of France:

> We have already said enough to obviate the objections that may be drawn from the prosperity of the French monarchy. The beauty of it is false and painted. There is a rich and haughty king, who is blessed with such neigh-bours as are not likely to disturb him, and has nothing to fear from his miserable subjects. But the whole body of that state is full of boils, wounds, and putrid sores ...*.

* DCG ii 21. Later in this passage he gives reason to think it was composed in 1677 by quoting the alleged number of military executions during 'the space of fifteen years' which it would be natural to measure from Louis' assumption of full power in 1662.

The *Discourses* will call for consideration later, but in writing about their author's life while he was shaping them, passages such as this show how exile and disappointment, while embittering him, broadened him as well. Here he states the classic theory which, with all its defects, is still recognizable:

> Man is naturally free; cannot justly be deprived of his liberty without a cause; and does not resign it, or any part of it, unless it be in consideration of some greater good. This liberty, however, is not a licentiousness of conduct, but an exemption from all human laws, to which he has not given his assent. Nations have consequently a right to make their own laws, and to appoint their own magistrates, who owe them in return, an account of their actions. Magistrates are distinguished from other men by the power with which the law invests them for the public good; – and the people may proportion, regulate, and terminate that power as seems most convenient for themselves.[6]

The huntsman is back after a hard day's shooting in the snow, the neat sloping hand hurries over the paper oblivious of possible objections of 'just how?' and 'assertions need evidence', to produce something that not only rings, but resounded.

The letter of January 1677 to M. Bafoul ends on a triumphant note. After six pages of local news Algernon haughtily declares he is no longer interested: 'Quant au reste ie ne puis pas prendre interest a rien ici ou si l'en eusse iamais pris, les lettrs que ie recois d'Angleterre la sepmaine passsee m'en detacheroient.'* Seventeen years abroad were at an end: his passport to England was to be granted. After Elsinore and Copenhagen, Frankfurt and Rome, Brussels, the Hague, Montpellier, Lausanne, Paris and Gascony, it was to be Penshurst again. And Tower Hill.

---

* 'As for the rest I can't take interest in anything here I ever have done. Letters I received last week from England cut me off from the whole thing.'

The Exile Returns

ALGERNON always said afterwards, and may have come to believe, that the sole purpose of his return to England was to see his old father before he died and that the visit would be a short one. But one must always remember that while family matters often affected Algernon's political conduct, political and financial motives governed his relations with his family. He was no compromiser with his main principles and he had by now become a seasoned politician embittered by years of exclusion from the part in public affairs which he thought he deserved. The intention of a brief family visit must be treated with reserve.

The Earl was over eighty when Algernon learned the visit was to be allowed, and had long been almost a recluse at Penshurst. Visitors had not thought he looked well for some time. But he was not dying, and lived for nearly a year after Algernon's passport was granted. Nor did Algernon seem in any particular hurry to see the old man, for between his rather summary farewell to Monsieur Bafoul and his arrival in England, there are nine months largely unaccounted for.

The passport had been negotiated through Henry Savile, who was then deputising for Ralph Montagu as English ambassador in Paris. Both men were connections of Algernon's – one as a Montagu cousin, and the other as the brother of George, Lord Halifax, who was married to Algernon's niece. They formed two of a trio of ambitious young politicians who were in the early stages of a plan to ruin Charles II's current political manager, the Earl of Danby.

Whether or not Algernon had an inkling of these plans at this stage, he would have noted – and noted with alarm – a major international event which Danby had engineered in the summer of 1677 and which was to have a lasting, decisive effect in history – the engagement of King Charles's niece Mary to his nephew William Prince of Orange. No doubt many observers saw this as a realignment of English diplomacy towards friendship with the Netherlands, but that was not Algernon's view. To him it was a reunification of two branches of the same baleful family, both equally enemies of republicanism. Charles had betrayed his Restoration and murdered Vane. William's father had sought effective monarchy in the Netherlands, and William himself had risen to power on the horrific murder of the de Witts. Now there was a prospect of a Stuart monarchy straddling the North Sea. This view may be difficult to disentangle from the whig tradition we have inherited, but Algernon was not the only man in his time to hold it, and there was a good deal in it.

The engagement of William and Mary deeply alarmed King Louis for the same reasons. His unvarying policy was to induce as much instability and division as he could into the politics of neighbouring states. With the new situation in mind he decided to change his representatives in both London and the Hague, and to give them new instructions. The new ambassador to the Hague, the Comte d'Avaux, was to cultivate the republican opposition to William of Orange, and his colleague in London, the Sieur de Barillon Damoncourt, was to switch the French support hitherto given to Charles in the direction of his parliamentary opponents. Large funds were placed at the disposal of both envoys who, for more than a decade, almost became politicians in the countries to which they were accredited. It is not an accident that in Otway's *Venice Preserved*, staged in London in 1681, the leader of the conspirators is a foreign ambassador.

The return of Algernon to England could not have occurred without the knowledge, and probably the approval, of the King of France. Louis had arranged Algernon's residence at Nérac, and had seen the 'restes de la faction de Cromwell' as having some potential value in his own schemes. The new turn of events did not produce any diminution in his disapproval of Algernon's political credo but, as often happens in politics, their interests for the time being coincided. The nine months between Algernon's departure from Nérac and his arrival in England early in September gave time for many political consultations. These certainly included a prolonged stay in Paris, where he had conversations with the learned Jean-Baptiste Lantin, and very probably with Savile also.*

Now the Earl was indeed dying, and Algernon went straight to Penshurst where the family was beginning to gather. They included only five of the original eleven children: Philip, Algernon and Henry; Dorothy and Lucy. All the others except Ann were dead, including Isabella. One wonders if her husband Strangford, who had remarried, had the resolution to appear. Algernon saw his father the day before he died, 'thinking of nothing lesse than to trouble him with any concernments', and the dying man said, 'I cannot, indeed I cannot, I would if I could, I would if I could.' Yet another change in his Will was beyond him. On 2 November, just a fortnight after the wedding bells had rung out for William and Mary, Robert Sidney, second Earl of Leicester, died.

It must have taken Mr Hoskins some time to read the Will, for it runs to some eight thousand words and five codicils added since he had made this, the last of his many testaments,[1] in 1672. One thing it made absolutely clear: he had not forgiven his eldest son, and whatever he could leave away from him he did. With the title, Philip would have Penshurst and the other entailed properties, but nothing else. Dorothy and Lucy, having been provided for already, only got modest tokens of affection, and Ann a legacy of half what she would have had if she had married suitably.

All the rest – almost everything the Earl had power to leave – was divided between Algernon and Henry. Originally it had been divided equally, even down to the furniture, the library, and the papers, but in 1675, perhaps realising how contentious this might be, the Earl had made a codicil by which Henry was to have all his movable goods, Algernon a cash legacy of £5000, and the two were to share equally 'what I have charged upon my capital messuage of Leicester House and any other lands.' †

* The conversations with Lantin contain many reminisences and political remarks by Sidney, very fully described by Dr Scott in his work already cited.

† The distribution of the personal estate between the two younger brothers was far from equal, though Algernon (who had been told earlier about it by Henry) had

With these mysterious words the Earl launched his sons on several years of bitter litigation fought mainly between Philip and his two younger brothers, but also between Algernon and Henry over the personal estate. When Leicester Fields had been acquired nearly half a century earlier it had been open country, but now it was an urban site of enormous value, some of which was already developed with houses on short leases. Most of it, including Leicester House itself, was mortgaged, but the huge value of the ultimate development rights remained, especially as the original design of the house had never been completed. Philip's argument was that since Leicester House itself, being entailed, came to him, all rights over the rest of the estate came to him also, so the codicil was meaningless. Algernon and Henry maintained it gave them the development rights of the whole estate except the House itself, and so, in the end, Lord Chief Justice Scroggs and a jury were to decide. In the longer term that decision removed the Sidneys from the company of artistocratic families with major London estates and led to their decay in the next century. In the shorter term it made Algernon potentially – though never actually – a very rich man, and therefore increased greatly his political consequence. It was to be the fatal bait that tied him to England, whatever resolution he may have made for a quiet and studious retirement abroad.

Algernon was in an unusually buoyant mood on 20 November, writing to his old friend Benjamin Furly. He had already given his formal discharge for the £5000 legacy, and his letter is addressed from Leicester House itself, which he hopes his friend will notice as a pleasant surprise. The £5000 will be enough to buy himself a respectable place in a quiet part of Gascony and enjoy a comfortable retirement. True, there are some 'small contests between one of my brothers and me', but they will soon be settled, 'and then I shall have nothing relating to this world soe much at heart, as the desire of returning from hence.'[2]

Just as Algernon always explained his return to England by his father's approaching end, he blamed his decision to stay there on the litigation started by his brother, and his letter to Furly would certainly suggest to any ordinary reader (such as someone who intercepted it) that a strictly temporary visit followed by an innocent

assumed £5000 (in ready money) would be about half, and only asked for a little extra furniture and plate to furnish his house in France. He was furious on finding Henry's share was worth £25,000.

retirement was all the writer intended. But Furly was not an ordinary reader, and the letter contains one phrase which hints at a different intention, perhaps not yet fully formed: 'I can give you *noe other account* of my returne than ... my desire of being and rendering some service unto my old father'. There could in fact be another reason which he was not then in a position to mention.

The litigation with Philip and the lesser disputes with Henry were not the only family troubles in which Algernon was involved. Lord Strangford too arrived on the scene with a rehash of the twenty-year old quarrel over Algernon's trusteeship. Now an impecunious middle-aged roué, Strangford was the most indefatigable of litigants – as the records of the Court of Chancery testify.[3]

With the new year Algernon's jaunty mood began to change, all thoughts of permanent retirement abroad seem to have vanished, and he was beginning to see that it was not going to be easy to make ends meet. The £5000 no longer seemed so much as at first, and 'if I live upon the maine stock', he writes sadly to Furly, 'it will soon have come to nothing'. He was engaging in small business ventures, speculating a little bit on the foreign exchanges, importing brandy for possible sale, buying horses in Flanders for the Earl of Essex. But none of this made up the underlying reason for the prolongation of his stay in England.[4]

In a letter of January 29 he refers to the factors which had 'principally perswaded me to take the course I do intend', and (in a short note three weeks earlier) 'to think of passing my life in the place mentioned to you' – phrases characteristically veiled into harmlessness. His real plans had in fact been described to Furly more explicitly in an earlier letter, probably sent in December, which significantly has not survived.

He was being drawn further and further into the scheme for subverting Danby. If it succeeded it could result in a revolutionary convulsion similar to those the country had experienced in 1642, 1648–49, and 1659–60. Amid the various competing radiations of patronage and power thereby liberated, the Cause to which he had always been pledged would once more be present. 'Mr Sidney', Barillon was to write two years later to King Louis, enclosing an account of political disbursements,

> is a man who was in the first wars, and who is naturally an enemy of the Court. He has for some time been suspected of being gained by Lord

Sunderland; but he always appeared to me to have the same sentiments, and not to have changed maxims. He has a great deal of credit amongst the Independents and is also intimate with those who are most opposite to the Court in Parliament ... I gave him only what your Majesty permitted me. He would willingly have had more. ....[5]

Though this was probably the first payment Algernon had received from Barillon it was clearly in respect of earlier services, and his original involvement with French diplomacy can be traced back at least to the time he was writing to Furly at the beginning of 1678. This is made clear not by Barillon but by his opposite number in the Netherlands, the Comte d'Avaux.

From the moment of his arrival d'Avaux had set to work cultivating the Dutch republicans, and found a ready response. William of Orange's crusade against France was deeply distasteful to them, especially as the war it provoked came ever nearer their own frontiers, and they were alarmed by the additional strength William had gained by his marriage.* They were anxious to breathe life into languishing negotiations for peace which had already been opened.

Algernon had contacts with several of these Dutch republican leaders, as d'Avaux soon discovered, and sought to apply them to the advantage of France:

I spoke to − , one of the most considerable republicans in Holland: This man had an intimate correspondence with the leading men in the English Parliament; and by this means I signified to Colonel Sidney, a famous republican ... that as long as the Prince of Orange remained so powerful in the States General, nothing could be more prejudicial to the Parliament of England, or the republic of Holland, than to allow the King of England to make an alliance with the Prince of Orange, for it was certainly intended to hurt the common liberty; that the grandeur and power of the French monarch, the pretext of this union, could not possibly be more prejudicial to either state, than such an alliance, which they ought to prevent, with all their strength and vigour. Colonel Sidney wrote to his friend, that he was strongly convinced by the reasons advanced, and that he had likewise communicated them with success to the majority of the Parliament. Nevertheless he informed him at the same time, that the French King began to give powerful succour to the King of England; that he had sent

---

* Their alarm was justified. In the treaty following the marriage the heads of the two branches of the Stuarts had included a secret article agreeing to give mutual support to each other against any insurrection in either of their respective countries.

him lately a considerable sum of money; and that if the King of England, by the assistance of his most Christian Majesty, should be able to do without his parliament, in that case he would become absolute sovereign; and this would oblige them to make an alliance with the States General.[6]

One cannot fail to be impressed by the range and coordination of French diplomacy; and d'Avaux was so pleased with his efforts that in his memoirs he claimed they were the chief influence leading to the defeat by the English Parliament of Charles's plans (if he ever really had them) to come into the current war on William's side, and therefore to the peace treaty that summer which virtually made Louis master of Western Europe for the next ten years.

Even allowing for the natural exaggerations of retired diplomats, what d'Avaux says throws a flood of light on Algernon's real reasons for staying in London, the extent of his political contacts, the importance which at any rate the French attached to him, and his own aims. It also shows that he knew or strongly suspected the secret which Ralph Montagu was to spring on Parliament in December 1678, and thereby ruin Charles's parliamentary manager Danby: that the apparently pro-Orange policy of Charles and his minister had been accompanied in parallel by the negotiation of a secret subsidy treaty with France and was, in short, a sham designed to deceive Parliament into granting money for an army with which to support the Dutch.

How far back this knowledge on Algernon's part went and what plans he built on it, cannot be established with certainty: very possibly back to the time when he was still in France during the summer of 1677 and actually met Montagu; but his letter to Furly of 29 January 1678 contains a specific claim to inside knowledge. 'I heare as well as other men', he then wrote, 'that which is sayd concerning the warre, and think it noe hard matter to learn as much as most other, or perhaps I may saye as any knowe, and yet I am in noe ways able to give a judgement whether we shall have a warre or not.'[7]

By the Spring he was speaking even more clearly, for on 3 April he assured Furly that if the peace party in the Netherlands persisted in spite of 'the secret negotiations with the French, ancient and new jealousies of the tow houses of Stewart and Nassau, or other reasons ... you may look upon peace as a thing certaine, and order your affairs accordingly.'[8]

Should we therefore describe Algernon, during these years, as in effect a French agent? Despite the contacts with French diplomacy and the subsidies which later generations of historians were so shocked to discover, that would not only be an over-simplification but contrary to his character and conduct both earlier and later. He was playing his own game, which was, if possible, to subvert Charles and his system of broken promises, and to do that he would accept help from any ally whose aims for the time being coincided with his.

In principle he detested and opposed all that Louis XIV stood for, and had lived long enough in France to know all about the persecution of the Huguenots and the sufferings of the general population in Louis' pursuit of glory and conquest. But along with this went a kind of grudging respect for a king who devoted his life to making his country great. The overthrow of Louis was in his eyes impossible, even if it had been his duty to attempt it; but it was not his duty.

So he remained in contact with Barillon, though the man filled him with almost physical revulsion. In a letter to Savile he gives a vivid portrait of the ambassador –

> You know M. de Barillon governs us (if he be not mistaken) but he seems to be not so much pleased with that, as to find his embonpoint encreased by the moistness of our air, by frequently clapping his hands upon his thighs, shewing the delight he hath in the sharpness of the sound that testifies the plumpness and hardness of his flesh: and certainly, if this climate did not nourish him better than any other, the hairs of his nose, and nails of his fingers, could not grow so fast as to furnish enough of the one to pull out, and the other to cut off, in all good companies, which, being done, he picks his ears with as good a grace as my Lord Lauderdale.[9]

The interpolation 'if he be not mistaken' says a great deal. Algernon's fastidiousness and reserve make one think of him as a lonely figure and, in the sense that he had few intimate friends, this is true; but his range of acquaintance and contact was very great, and was one of the reasons Barillon valued him. His family connections admitted him to most of the great houses. His elder sister Dorothy watched over him with an almost motherly care. With two opposition noblemen, the Earl of Essex and Lord William Russell, he was on friendly terms. He also renewed, probably through the venerable Dr Owen who had once helped to reconvene the Rump, his acquaintance with many of the veteran sectaries of the old days, such as Colonel Michael Danvers, once an officer in the New Model, and now leader of an Anabaptist congregation in Whitechapel; Major Wildman, the plotter whose commission also dated from Parliamentary times; Robert Ferguson, the most tireless of conspirators; and Lord Howard of Escrick, who had once belonged to Cromwell's life-guard and more recently, owing to the premature death of his brother, had succeeded to a peerage.

But at this time two particular names stand out, one by its presence, and the other by its absence in this range of acquaintance: those of William Penn and Anthony Ashley Cooper, Earl of Shaftesbury.

Algernon was almost certainly introduced to Penn by Furly, probably before coming to England, for Penn and Furly were great friends, and Penn had visited Holland to see Furly in the summer of 1677 when Algernon was on his unrecorded travels. Very soon afterwards Furly became principal agent on the Continent for organizing the settlement of Penn's favourite project of a new, free, Quaker colony in North America, so that Pennsylvania owes to Furly its strong tradition of Dutch and German nonconformity. During several critical years Penn was to be one of Algernon's closest friends and collaborators, though in some respects they differed greatly and in the end they quarrelled. To some extent they coincided in their religious views and even shared acquaintanceships, for Penn had known Algernon's nephew Sunderland long ago, and had been sent down from Oxford for corresponding with the dissenting pundit Dr Owen. Penn was well off, a shrewd business man, and as such helped Algernon, but although he was punctiliously defiant in matters of religion, in matters of politics his eyes were on one objective alone: toleration. For its sake he was willing to collaborate with those whom Algernon regarded as his deadly enemies, and as a young man he had sat at the feet of the Huguenot professor Moyse Amyraut who taught passive obedience to princes. Nevertheless, in the storm that was brewing the friendship of Penn was to be an important influence.

So was the deep hostility and distrust which existed between Algernon and Shaftesbury, now the most prominent leader of the opposition. That story went back to the days of the Civil War and the Commonwealth, when Algernon first knew him and first began to distrust him. Shaftesbury had served Cromwell and held high office under Charles, and now, in 1678, approaching the end of his career, with his life sustained by a silver tube inserted by his medical adviser and secretary John Locke to drain the poison from his bile duct, he was preparing a new bid for power. Under him Algernon never had been enlisted and never would be. The contrast with Algernon's attitude to Louis XIV is interesting, even paradoxical, for both Shaftesbury and Louis could have been regarded as allies against the hated regime, and the conclusion must be not only that Algernon's hatred and distrust were profound, but that they were reciprocated.

On this scene, in the early summer of 1678, burst the allegations of Titus Oates and his imitators that there was an insidious and ubiquitous Catholic Plot to destroy the regime and indeed subvert society. Such hold did this gain over the public mind that the Plot assumed a life of its own, ever developing new instalments until it became a kind of horrendous 'soap opera'. Even the most sceptical ignored it at their peril, and from whatever seedy source it was originally promoted, its strength was such that political leaders of all shades quickly realized it could neither be contained nor denounced and the only course was to try to steer it in the direction which suited their particular interests. Shaftesbury was the first to perceive this truth, and though the origins of the scare cannot be traced to him, he quickly put his sails into its wind. The Government, seeing the danger in which it stood if it showed the slightest weakness towards an alleged Catholic conspiracy, vied with the opposition in hounding those whom Oates and his imitators denounced.

Algernon never said or did anything to suggest he doubted the genuineness of the Plot. On the contrary he expressed absolute assurance as to the guilt of Oates's victims, and in a long discussion with a sceptical van Beuningen, the Dutch ambassador in London, he maintained complete confidence in it. Yet although it was clearly a threat to the government against which he was working, and (as we shall see) he was well acquainted with Titus Oates's mysterious legal adviser Aaron Smith, he took no active part that can be traced in the anti-Catholic rabble-rousing of the next two years.*

It seems improbable that a man so well-informed as Algernon could have believed the increasingly crude and lurid stories of the

---

*In this he differed very much from his friend Lord Howard of Escrick, who made his political name as a zealous member of the House of Lords Committee investigating the plot.

informers. After all he had spent two happy years in Rome and had personal affection and esteem for many of its cardinals, especially Cardinal Barberini, who as Cardinal Protector of England might be supposed to stand at the very centre of a conspiracy to reconvert the nation by force. Algernon's attitude to the Catholics in Ireland had been rational, and he shared his friend Penn's views of religious toleration. But every one of these reasons was also one for fearing that a single false step would attract a denunciation for being involved in the Plot himself – and all the more so since the confusion of the public mind was lumping Quakers with Jesuits in its panic against any deviation from orthodoxy.

Barillon describes in loving detail the negotiations leading up to the exposure of Danby for secret dealings with France. In England one can never be sure of anything, he wrote to Louis, and Montagu was asking a great deal for the risks he was taking, 'but this accusation cannot be entirely fruitless, because it is not destitute of foundation'.[10] The implied reference to Oates and his stories is obvious. The beauty of the thing, as Barillon pointed out, was that in the present situation any attempt on Charles's part to rescue Danby would bring him into conflict with an infuriated Parliament, from which his only escape would be total dependence on France.*

Montagu sprang his mine in December 1678, and very soon, as Barillon had foreseen, Danby had to go and the Government to compromise, with even Shaftesbury being briefly admitted to office. But the most important consequence was to give the thundercloud of public emotion generated by Oates two foci instead of one. Oates had concentrated on the menace of the Pope and his agents: now the much more real power of the King of France was added to the brew. Hence emerged the slogan against 'Popery and Arbitrary Power' for those who were just beginning to be called Whigs; and domestically the fire of the opposition was concentrated on two targets: the Duke of York, the flagrantly Catholic heir to the throne; and the fallen Danby, who should now be impeached, on the ugly precedent of Strafford nearly forty years earlier. Let the King, it was

---

* Montagu asked for £3000 a year for life secured on the French Exchequer and vested in trustees, or the lump sum equivalent, if his revelations produced the resignation of Danby within six months. If they did not, he was to have French protection for life, and a more modest pension. His political career was in the end crowned with a dukedom from Queen Anne.

said, try to save either of them at his peril. No doubt this would drive Charles further into dependence on France, but such dependence had already been exposed with damaging effect, and it could be exposed again.

Alarming symptoms of the old days began to appear. The House of Commons, once so loyal, but much changed in its membership since it had been elected in 1661, reverted to the habits of the forties and fifties by appointing days of fasting and humiliation. The chained barricades symbolizing the independence of the City of London, which had not been seen since the days of General Monk, began to reappear. Early in 1679 King Charles brought an end to the proceedings against Danby (it was too late to save him as a minister) by dissolving Parliament and set a new election for March that year.

At this point Algernon began a series of news-letters addressed to Henry Savile, now again in charge of the Paris embassy and at a distance from the battle. They maintained the pose of modesty and isolation which was now second nature with Algernon – 'we simple people', he says, 'we of the vulgar'. 'Many things may pass in the town that you may be willing to hear but come not to the cell of your humble servant.' But the self-depreciation is hardly genuine, for the letters are packed with political information set out in his best mordant manner, and he must have been at full stretch. At one point he confesses to being almost asleep as he writes, and we can picture him crouching by candle-light with the faithful Ducasse in attendance, and wrapped against the cold in 'the best and warmest Indian gowne' which he had asked Furly to get for him in Amsterdam.

The news he sent Savile is abundant, and must have required many contacts to collect, but nowhere does he mention that he was himself planning to re-emerge into open politics as a candidate at the election which had now been called. A seat in the Commons and its privileges would undoubtedly help him in his financial difficulties and the troublesome litigation that beset him, but there is no evidence that this was his main motive. A return to the House of Commons would be absolutely consistent with the principles and the pattern of his unhappy life, and at last a state of affairs again existed which might bring triumph to the Cause for which he had suffered so much.

He was to fight in all the three remaining elections of Charles

II's reign, and in his own eyes to win every time, and every time the prize was to be snatched away by petitions from his opponents and sudden dissolutions before those petitions could be decided. It is a great pity that Fate seemed to fight against him, for once in Parliament he would have made his position clear. He might even have thrown light on one of the main mysteries of his career – his own solution to the problem of Charles I in 1648. When Henry Savile heard from his brother Lord Halifax, of what seemed to be one of Algernon's electoral successes, he commented that the best reason he could think of for wanting to be in the House himself was curiosity to know what Algernon would do there.

He chose Guildford for his first attempt, with his friend William Penn as backer. The electorate was quite a large one, though as in many other constituencies nobody was quite sure how large, since there had not been an election for seventeen years. Nevertheless he had collected promises of 140 votes, which would give him a substantial majority over his opponent Mr Dalmahoy, and applied well in advance for the freemanship of the borough, which the returning officer (who was in the Dalmahoy interest) insisted was necessary for all candidates. But when he appeared with Penn on polling day, the returning officer told him the magistrates had not yet reached a decision on his application. On his demand to be admitted a freeman then and there the returning officer flatly refused, and added insult to injury by denouncing Penn as a suspected Jesuit and proffering him the oath against transubstantiation to be instantly sworn. Penn, as a Quaker, would swear nothing whatever and left the scene, so the rest of Algernon's supporters decided to abstain under protest. Dalmahoy was then declared elected on votes which (so Algernon said afterwards) included those of the inmates of the local almshouse and the keeper of the Crown Inn, who had been told his bill for electoral refreshments would not be paid otherwise.[11]

There was a consoling letter from Penn, hoping 'a disappointment so strange doth not move thee . . . Thou, as thy friends, had a conscientious regard for England; and being put aside by such base ways is really a suffering from righteousness.' There should be a petition, with leading counsel – perhaps the great Sir William Jones – employed. He could personally lobby the opposition leaders – Buckingham, Essex, Halifax, Holles, Shaftesbury . . . 'for to me it looks not a fair and clear election'.[12] A petition was duly on the table when Parliament met towards the end of March, along with some fifty others about disputed elections.

But it was never reached. Only two months later, having made history by passing the Habeas Corpus Act and defying any compromise with the King over the Shaftesburyite demand that the Catholic James should be excluded from the succession, Parliament was dissolved without being able to attend to the afffairs of Guild-ford. Another election was set for July.

For his second attempt Algernon considered various seats, among them being Bramber, a nice little town in the territory of his brother-in-law Sir John Pelham, and conveniently near Penn's house at Warminghurst. He decided, however, not to stand there himself, probably because he knew his brother Henry was also interested in it; but he succeeded in offending Henry just the same by making a speech there on behalf of Sir Charles Woosley, another veteran of the Commonwealth, who was also a candidate, and distributing some money to the rural electors. Henry, though absent throughout the campaign attending his duties as ambassador in the Netherlands, was elected, but family relationships were not improved.[13]

Instead Algernon decided to present himself to the electors of Amersham, who even two generations later were regarded by the local incumbent as 'exceedingly zealous and very fanatical'. There was a strong local community of Quakers, and one of the county seats was held by the opposition champion Tom Wharton. Altogether Algernon's chances against the Tory Lord of the Manor, Sir William Drake, seemed promising, even though Sir William lived at neighbouring Shardeloes and had sat for the place since the Restoration.

Algernon appeared at Amersham with a large number of local votes already promised and two campaign managers – a City business man named Harford and the veteran Anabaptist, Colonel Michael Danvers. Sir William later complained that some of Algernon's supporters shouted he was a papist and a pensioner, which Algernon primly passed off by saying that while 'he in no way approved of the licence usually taken in such cases of using ill language', there was nothing he could have done about it, and 'Sir William must suffer as well as others'. He would pass over what Sir William's supporters had said about him.

Polling presented particular difficulty because there were two lists of electors, the 'short poll', which included only householders paying local taxation, and the 'long poll', which included a good many other inhabitants. Sir William favoured the 'long poll' because it gave votes to many of his non-ratepaying tenants and dependents, so it was taken first, but Algernon won by 79 to 64. The 'short poll' was then appealed to, and Algernon won again, by 39 to 28. Each individual vote in each poll was hotly disputed by the losers, and at last the returning officers (there were two, one Whig, one Tory) reached different conclusions and returned both candidates, leaving the House of Commons to decide between them. But it was generally considered that Algernon had won, and he left Amersham in triumph, donating ten pounds for immediate distribution to the local poor. The gesture did not escape Sir William's agents, as material for the inevitable petition.[14] 'The most remarkable thing about the election', wrote one political observer, 'is the success of Colonel Sidney at Amersham, where he was brought in by the activity of two or three persons, though he was wholly unknown there.'[15]

But Parliament did not meet. For more than a year, from the autumn of 1679 to the autumn of 1680, the King deferred it while the Shaftesburyite agitation rampaged in the streets and the victims of the 'Plot' were hurried through the courts to the gallows. Charles also had a serious illness, which left him a changed man and added to the excitement over the succession. The question whether Algernon should take his seat for Amersham was one of the many matters still to be decided.

Until the very end of this turbulent interval Algernon took no conspicuous part in politics, and no part at all in the agitation organised by Shaftesbury. He was probably opposed to the simple cry to exclude the Catholic Duke because he foresaw that if it succeeded it could only lead either to the puppet monarchy of Monmouth manipulated by Shaftesbury or the still worse succession of Mary dominated by her husband William of Orange. Paradoxically, therefore, he favoured the solution (also proposed by Halifax) that would subject James on his succession to restrictions imposed by Parliament, for these would survive to give a continuing purchase over the monarchy and perhaps, if James sought to defy them, open the road to the republic which was Algernon's objective.

This is the most likely explanation for an interview he had with Charles II which he describes, but does not date precisely, in his *Apology*, as occurring between the summer of 1678 and the autumn of 1679. It is the only occasion, so far as we know, on which they ever met, and although Algernon's account of it makes it out as very much a man-to-man affair, he was probably under some form of temporary arrest, for the King accused him of being party to a protestant plot. This, Algernon says, he strongly denied, pointing out that for a dissenter such as himself to be involved in a plot would only drive the King into the arms of the Catholics – a practical argument the King seems to have conceded; but the interview left Algernon with a suspicion that the government was contemplating ways of using the current atmosphere of conspiracy to destroy him.

The possibility of 'turning the plot' against its own champions was indeed one of the defensive measures being considered by the hard-pressed government. But if such a counter-attack was to succeed it needed authoritative justification of the ground on which the regime now stood politically. Nearly twenty years had passed since the Restoration, and since that time the basis on which Charles ruled had insensibly changed from kingship by invitation to kingship by hereditary right. It was to this alteration in the character of the regime that the 'Exclusion' agitation was a challenge, for though it was aimed ostensibly against the succession of James and was envenomed with anti-Catholic prejudice, it subverted also Charles's claim to sit at the political table in his own right as his father's son, and not as the (possibly revocable) nominee of 1660. This is the political context which explains the appearance, in the winter of 1679–80, of that celebrated work *Patriarcha: a Defence of the Natural Power of Kings against the Unnatural Power of the People*, by Sir Robert Filmer Bt. Nothing else can explain the abrupt disinterment of a work which had lain unpublished for more than forty years, and drew on a political tradition current nearly a century earlier.*

Faded, pedantic, extreme, even absurd as it was, *Patriarcha*'s publication at this time was an act of calculated defiance, and a far from unsuccessful one. Three editions were called for in the year of its appearance. Filmer's appeal to the family as the natural unit of society, his commonsensical argument that man far from being born free, comes into the world a helpless being utterly dependent on his

---

*It seems likely that *Patriarcha* had been available to the Government from the Restoration onwards, and that its publication had been considered as early as 1662. A preface by Peter Heylin commending the work is annexed to the edition of 1679. Heylin, who died in 1662, was an extreme Laudian clergyman and a close friend of Filmer, as whose literary executor he seems to have appointed himself.

parents, struck a deep response in a society where relationships and inheritance were supremely important to all but the poorest. He also managed to insinuate that doctrines of contract between King and people and presumed states of nature not only lacked any historical foundation, but were products of Roman Catholic casuistry designed to justify the Pope's claim to supersede Kings. The theory of absolutism which Filmer constructed out of these materials was certainly flimsy, reaching a grotesque pinnacle, ridiculed by his opponents, in the assertion that hereditary royal power was conferred by descent from Noah. Just the same the best minds in the opposition at once acquired copies and set about answering the book.

Locke, then Shaftesbury's secretary and medical adviser bought a copy of *Patriarcha* in January 1680 and began writing the reply to it which was later published as the *First Treatise on Government*. His friend Tyrrell worked even faster and issued *Patriarcha non Monarchia* in 1681. Algernon too bought a copy of the earliest edition.* [16]

There is no direct evidence for thinking Sidney had seen the work in manuscript, but there is no question that, for Algernon, Filmer was not merely an ideological opponent but a hated enemy he had known and could almost see before him as he wrote the reply to which he now devoted himself. For years he had been accumulating material in defence of his own assault on monarchy as a system of government. Now he began assembling and adapting it for a gigantic work which would devastate for ever the apologists for Divine Right and place republican institutions on a firm foundation. It is the most telling proof of *Patriarcha's* political significance that the enterprise of answering it cost Algernon his life and earned him fame – not indeed as an author, but as a hero.

Discourses Concerning Government (the title given to Sidney's massive work when it was published fifteen years after his death) stated the theme he always returned to during the remaining years of his life, but it was also the work of a life-time, and the opportunities for writing had to be fitted into many other kinds of intense political activity. In 1680, though Parliament had not yet met, he considered himself to be the member for Amersham, and became more and more conspicuous in the ranks of the opposition.

He was better able to sustain this by a victory in the courts over his elder brother. On 7 January 1680, almost the very day John

---

* His quotations from *Patriarcha* in DCG (though frequently inaccurate) are clearly based on the 1680 text, and not on the later, and improved, edition.

Locke acquired his copy of *Patriarcha*, Lord Chief Justice Scroggs and a jury decided that the Earl of Leicester had indeed left the Leicester House rights to his two younger sons, so they were both £2000 a year richer. Algernon had refused to be present in court when the decision was given, but could not restrain an uncharacteristic hoot of laugher at Philip's expense when he was told the news. From now on he was comfortably independent, relieved of humiliating attendance on the nose-picking French ambassador. Quite soon he had houses both in London and the country, a stock of plate, and a decent stable.[17]

Algernon's energy (for all this time he must also have been labouring on his great treatise) is the more extraordinary because that spring he had for the first time been far from well. His kindly, gossipy sister Dorothy discovered 'he was living on nothing but gruel' and persuaded him to come down to the country to recover. When he came he talked waspishly about politics and politicians in a way that rather shocked her, but she was careful not to contradict him, having long known that contradicting any of her difficult brothers did no good.[18]

Two political dramas were played out on the streets of London that summer and autumn: one, the more spectacular, was the demonstrations raised by Shaftesbury and his followers round the demand for Exclusion and the continuing cry for Catholic blood: the other was the opposition campaign to capture the powers of the City of London Corporation so as to make the capital a bastion. This was a far more serious threat to the Government than the processions of Shaftesbury's 'Green Ribbon' men in which Algernon took no part; but he had a major part in the victorious elections of the City Sheriffs that summer. It was a great step forward for the opposition cause, and for the plans which its republican wing were now harbouring.

The importance of the Sheriffs lay in their being the principal executive officers of the capital, including Westminster and all the adjoining county of Middlesex. Without their participation no sentence of a court of law could be carried out, no jury assembled, no elections held for the eight parliamentary seats representing the metropolis north of the Thames. In effect the King's writ could not run in London without their consent. The rising had started in London in 1642, and the hope of Algernon and his friends was that it would start there again.

The opposition candidates that summer were substantial business figures. One was Henry Cornish, a chief financial backer of the Whig cause and one of the richest men in the City.* The other was Algernon's old friend from the days of the Commonwealth and exile in Lausanne, Slingsby Bethel, who was an austere and unswerving republican. Since the Lausanne days he had written *The World's Mistake in Oliver Cromwell* and a pioneering work in economics, *The Interest of States and Nations* in which he argued that autocracy was harmful to national prosperity. He had long abstained from active politics, and it seems likely that Algernon had a hand in the candidature of a man so much after his own heart. He turned out in support of Bethel and incurred accusations of leading a riot at the height of the turbulent election, though he maintained 'he was only looking out of a window'. He did not add that he was also making a speech.

It was the most rowdy election there had been in London for many years, but also the most democratic. After much excitement over procedure, and two successive polls, Cornish and Bethel were elected, and London became a place of safety for opposition politicians, a hive for anti-government propaganda, and a stage on which to mount publicity-seeking court cases such as the presentation of the Duke of York as a Popish recusant and the Duchess of Portsmouth as a common nuisance.

As the time for Parliament to meet approached it was becoming clear that the opposition was not firmly united under the banner of Exclusion so enthusiastically waved by Shaftesbury, and towards the end of September Algernon had a private interview with Barillon in which he urged a very different policy. He did not mention the idea which Charles II himself was soon to put forward, of restricting the powers of a Catholic successor by Act of Parliament instead of excluding him altogether, but what Barillon reported to Louis on the interview shows that anxieties about Catholicism were the last thing Algernon had in mind. No record, perhaps, demonstrates more clearly his absence of fanaticism and anti-Popish prejudice. It was very like what he had said to Turenne in Paris nine years earlier.†

---

* In the day of its triumph the Government did not forget Cornish. He was hanged outside his own house in 1685, after the defeat of Monmouth's rebellion.

† See pp. 154–55.

The best possible outcome of the crisis for France, he told the ambassador, would be a republican England, and the worst, 'a reunion of Britain under a Protestant king authorised as the Prince of Orange would be' by the Exclusion of James.* That would not only destroy the liberties of Britain and the Netherlands but unite their resources against France, whereas an English republic would be in constant rivalry with its Dutch counterpart. This glimpse into the future is not only a tribute to Algernon's insight into international affairs, but to his percipience about the domestic situation. English Catholics, he told the ambassador, would never get relief from an English King, whether openly a Catholic or not, because public opinion would never accept it from a King who was or was suspected of being a Catholic. Such relief might indeed come from a Republic, and as proof Algernon pointed to the tolerance of the republican Netherlands, where no one could doubt the protestant convictions of the government. Barillon thought there was some force in the arguments, though he concludes deferentially that 'Your Majesty knows better than anybody what solidity there is in these reflections.' Louis might have been wise to take more notice of them.[19]

Such a conversation would not have taken place if Barillon had not seen Algernon as representative of a significant body of political opinion. 'Obscure and concealed persons' Barillon calls them, but as an example he includes Dr John Owen, the 'Patriarch of the Sectaries', who had as much religious and political influence in London as its bishop. He could have added the veteran Agitator, John Wildman, now again an M.P.; William Penn, who was currently consulting Algernon about the constitution of Pennsylvania; and perhaps even Aaron Smith, the son of a 'Model Army' chaplain and recently legal adviser to Titus Oates. These republicans were meditating a revolutionary tactic if, as was rumoured, the King dared not hold the Parliament in the Whig-dominated capital, but convened it in Oxford, his father's old stronghold. That could be made the spark of conflict in which the Commons could set themselves up once more in sovereign isolation in London, there to hold

---

* The inevitable consequence of the Exclusion Bill as it stood, though little mentioned. The candidature of Monmouth was espoused by Shaftesbury, but could only have been achieved by more parliamentary action.

an inquest on the whole course of politics since the Restoration, from which Shaftesbury would not escape unscathed.*

The King, however, did not yet feel strong enough to call a Parliament anywhere but in London, where it at last assembled in October 1680, with the petition about the representation of Amersham to be settled along with some fifty others. It became the subject of a bitterly fought partisan struggle, not between Whig and Tory but between the two wings of the Whigs.

The Committee on Elections reached the Amersham petition on 10 November and went into it at unusual length, hearing witnesses on both sides and even allowing its report to be printed – a sure sign that it was of wider public interest than most petitions. In the end the Committee came down in favour of Algernon, but left the final decision to the House, so that until the House chose to discuss it he could not take his seat. By now, of course, the renewed debate on the Exclusion Bill dominated the programme, but even allowing for this there is clear evidence of systematic obstruction to the seating of a man who was, with some reason, suspected of not being sound on that great measure. When the Committee's report came up it was to be considered 'tomorrow', 'Monday next', 'tomorrow first business', and after four deferments was not reached until 11 December in a House crowded with nearly three hundred members – far more than would have attended for a merely local dispute. They must have been overwhelmingly Whigs, for they decided without a dissentient voice that Sir William Drake had not been duly elected and that the franchise in Amersham lay with the 'short poll'. But when it came to what might be thought the merely formal resolution that as a result 'Algernon Sidney Esq. hath been duly elected a member of this House for the Borough of Agmondesham' a vote was called, and the resolution was defeated by 191 to 83. So there was an order for a new election at Amersham.

That the majority in this division consisted mainly, if not entirely, of Shaftesburyite Whigs is proved not only by the fact that they were the most numerous body in the House, but by the presence of William Harbord, one of the most prominent Whigs in the House, as one of the majority tellers. The 83 votes cast in the minority

---

* See the opening passages of Robert Ferguson's MS printed as Appendix I to *Robert Fergusson the Plotter* by James Ferguson (Edinburgh 1887). Anything Ferguson says must be read with caution but his analysis of the situation in 1680 is extremely convincing.

measure the true support for the Old Cause and perhaps the high-water mark of republicanism in an English parliament. It can easily be believed that, from distrust of Shaftesbury, Algernon now moved to profound hostility for the man who had once more frustrated his hopes. Yet he did not give up. When, almost immediately afterwards, the King dissolved Parliament and called another General Election, Algernon was once more a candidate for Amersham.

And all this time page after page in Algernon's sloping hand was being added to the mountainous manuscript of his great historico-theoretical work on government. Very few such books can have been written so close to the active politics to which they relate by an author so deeply concerned in them.

Discourses Concerning Government

*D*ISCOURSES *Concerning Government* cannot be treated like other
books, for one principal reason. It was unfinished, and un-
revised. Sidney was working on it when he was arrested, with some
of the manuscript on the desk before him and some of it in an open
trunk at his side. He had not made up his mind whether to try to
publish it at all, and when it was published certain passages we
know he wrote were missing. What liberties his editor took with
the manuscript are unascertainable, for no original manuscript survives.* History put Sidney himself on a pedestal, but made a sad
mess of his book, if indeed book it can be called.

As we have it *Discourses Concerning Government* consists of three
huge parts described as 'chapters', though each is divided into
numerous sections long enough to be chapters in their own right,
and looked at as a whole it is very difficult to trace any unfolding
of arguments towards a conclusion, any structure such as one would
expect from a trained mind. It is certainly evidence of wide reading,
but closer examination removes any claim to scholarship. The

---

* For a more detailed account of these problems see Notes on Sources. No two
editions of DCG are quite the same in text and pagination and all are now antiquarian
items, the last having appeared in 1772. My references are therefore limited to Chapter
and Section.

numerous inaccuracies which so worried Sidney's most careful editor, the reverend J. Robertson, can be excused on the ground that Algernon never had a chance to remedy them.* But the piling up of authority and quotation suffers from another and graver defect. Algernon uses it not so much to explore or develop ideas and arguments, as to reinforce and buttress those he had already asserted. In this he was working very much in the methods of the contemporary preachers whose two-or-three-hour sermons delivered some simple religious or moral lesson surrounded by a galaxy of learned illustration.

If *Discourses Concerning Government* is not to be read for the logicality of its arguments or the exactness of its scholarship, it cannot claim either to be a great work of controversy, for it is much too long. It certainly delivers an eloquent barrage of argument and ridicule at Filmer, which by the time it is over leaves very little of *Patriarcha*'s structure standing. But Locke did the same job with a great deal more skill and economy, and both men use similar arguments – sometimes even their words come so close that one feels they might have seen each other's work. Sidney felt passionately about the long-dead Filmer – far more passionately than did Locke – and though the spleen had a contemporary political purpose its source lies deeper. He saw Filmer as embodying the negation of the Cause to which he had sacrificed his life and his prospects, and in which he had come devotedly to believe.

But the compensating strengths of Sidney's book are its style and its purpose. Take this characteristic passage as an example of his purely literary gift:

> Besides, good and wise men know the weight of Sovereign Power, and misdoubt their own strength. Sacred and human historys furnish us with many examples of those who have fear'd the Lustre of a Crown. Men that find in themselves no delight in doing mischief, know not what thoughts may insinuate themselves into their minds when rais'd too much above their Sphere. They who were able to bear adversity, have bin precipitated into ruin by prosperity. When the Prophet told Hazael the Villanys he would

---

* 'Balthei and Amalthei', Robertson moans in his preface, 'for Balthi and Amali, Almoranides for Almoravides, Chilperic the Third for Childeric the Third ...' Sidney was hopelessly confused about the details of the Anglo-Saxon kings, and even misquotes his opponent Filmer. Perhaps his worst error is pouncing on Filmer for a misreference to Aristotle when the reference is in fact correct. But Robertson was a true scholar, who had written a dissertation on the supersession of 'th' by 's' in English orthography.

commit, he answer'd 'Is thy Servant a dog, that I should do these things?' but yet he did them. (iii. 41)

Or this as an illustration of his invective power:

> I should have thought that Princes, tho Tyrants, being God's Vicegerents, and fathers of their People, would have sought their good, tho no advantage had thereby redounded to themselves, but it seems no such thing is to be expected from them. They consider Nations, as Grasiers do their Herds and Flocks, according to the profit that can be made of them: and if this be so, a People has no more security under a Prince, than a Herd or Flock under their Master. Tho he desire to be a good Husband, yet they must be deliver'd up to the slaughter when he finds a good Market, or a better way of improving his Land; but they are often foolish, riotous, prodigal, and wantonly destroy their Stock, tho to their own prejudice. We thought that all Princes and Magistrates had bin set up, that under them we might live quietly and peaceably, in all godliness and honesty; but our author [Filmer] teaches us, that they only seek what they can make of our Bodys and Goods, and that they do not live and reign for us, but for themselves. If this be true, they look upon us not as Children, but as Beasts. (i. 27)

This powerful style, and his whole obsession with writing, was, one feels, put at the service of a personal rather than a political need: the need to explain to himself, if not to others, what the Cause was, and why he had devoted his life to it; and so perhaps, on a deeper level, to solve the personal problem with which Filmer faced him, and which must have tortured a man of his upbringing and principles. He could not deny the natural authority of his father as not only binding but lifelong. It made him what he was. How was it to be distinguished from the authority of government? This is what gives his book its historical, and to some extent its biographical, importance. With all its faults it is the best account we have of what the Cause was, written by its life-long champion. In this task Sidney produced many passages of almost Miltonic nobility, and a view of social institutions which may not have been unique, even in his own time, but which unlike most contributions to political theory in the seventeenth century was drawn not from speculation, but from history, direct observation and personal experience.

Religion plays very little part in Sidney's picture of the Cause. True, he quotes more often from the Bible than from any other authority, but it is predominantly from historical books of the Old Testament, for Jewish history would have carried greater authority with him and his audience than any but Roman. Prophecy, preaching, poetry and revelation find no place in his exposition, save in one important respect.

In questions of moral conduct there was 'a perpetual and universal Law given by God to mankind, and of no value against it, since man cannot abrogate what God has instituted, nor one nation free itself from a Law which is given to all.' (iii. 9) That Divine Law was to be found in the Bible and in our consciences, and it was the responsibility of human institutions to observe and enforce it. Thus murder, theft, adultery could never be lawful. But there was also Law that was entirely human, 'the constraining power' exercised by the institutions men themselves created. The same institutions that had created human laws, or their successors, could change them, for they could never (unlike Divine Law) be perfect, and at different times, in different communities, they would vary. Human Law was in the sphere of human reason, and laws were 'written reason'.

Here he followed Vane, who had written, in *The People's Case Stated*, that

> the power which is directive and ascertains the rule for morality and obedience is in the Law of God; but the original source whence all just power arises, which is magistratical and coercive, is from the will or free gift of the people, who may either keep the power in themselves, or give up their subjection and will into the hands of another.

Human law was not given by divine authority or imposed by kings, priests, or philosophers, but emanated from the society to which it applied and by which it could be altered. It could not change human nature, but it must regulate society to produce the state of affairs in which civilised relationships were possible and could develop:

> Whilst every man fears his neighbour, and has no other defence than his own strength, he must live in that perpetual anxiety, which is equally contrary to that happiness, and that sedate temper of mind which is required for the search of it. The first step towards the control of this pestilent evil is for many to join in one body, so that every one may be protected by the united force of all, and the various talents that men possess may by good discipline be render'd useful to the whole; as the meanest piece of wood or stone being placed by a wise Architect conduces to the beauty of the most glorious building ... Magistrates are political architects; and they only can perform the work incumbent on them, who excel in political virtues. (i. 1)

This passage at one point comes so close, even in its words, to the language of the American Constitution that it can hardly have been without its influence on those who framed it. It also implies an aristocratic view of those qualified for government which is thoroughly Platonist.

The idea of human law as a rational system of procedures designed to protect civilised life is conventional enough. It is Sidney's view on the nature of the institutions men create to make, change, and enforce human law (and particularly that part of it which regulates the government itself) that is far more original and interesting, because he supports it entirely from history and observation. Man, he maintains, is naturally free, with a freedom of which he cannot justly be deprived 'unless it be in consideration of a greater good, which he proposes to himself.' Such a concession of liberty need not be conscious or deliberate, and the new-born child, on whose total absence of freedom Filmer had built so much, would, if rejected by its natural parents, yield a ready obedience to anyone else who would give it food or shelter, without any question of a 'contract'. Thus, though naturally free, men had a propensity to form societies for their own protection and comfort, and from these societies arose human law and civilised government. These societies were of infinite variety within time and space, and were subject to constant change by those who belonged to them, even though as law developed, such change was regulated by legal procedures.

Each such society collectively developed an upper tier which constituted government, which might indeed be monarchical, as with the ancient Jewish or Roman kings: but such societies did not on that account yield up the freedom which had originally been pooled by their individual members. Just as laws could be changed (if proper procedures were followed), so the people could change the government they had created. Thus the important contract was between the individual members of the society, and if there could be said to be a contract between the people and their government it was unilateral in the sense that it could be enforced by one side only – the people's. As he was to summarise his thesis in his dying speech: 'Magistrates were set up for the good of nations, not nations for the honour or glory of magistrates.'

There was thus, in any nation, an immanent constitution which continued to exist whatever regime was in power, and by it the regime could be changed and called to account. It was the true source of legitimacy and of the obligation owed by the people to the laws and to the magistrate, and could be discovered by a study of the blend of custom, consultation and procedure which had established itself historically in each community from the smallest up to the nation as a whole. Thus Sidney, though he often refers to 'the people' as the ultimate arbiters of governments, was far from being a democrat, or in social terms a revolutionary. He did not believe (like Harrington) that there was a mysterious truth in popular opinion. When giving evidence to the Committee investigating the Amersham election he maintained there was no general rule about who had the right to vote in an election: each community, each constituency, had its own method of electing a representative, and all of them were valid until they were lawfully changed.*

For Sidney this immanent constitution was the republic, and in that sense only is he to be called a republican. He did not see 'the republic' as an alternative form of government to monarchy, though he would indeed have maintained that a form of government without a monarch was preferable, and closer to the reality of political society, than a monarchical one. The immanent constitution could create a monarchy, but it did not thereby cease to exist or lose its power to call the monarch to account or substitute something else in his place. A breach of this principle was usurpation and tyranny, such as that inflicted by Cromwell, but even in the teeth of usurpation the immanent constitution, 'the republic', would not perish because it was grounded in the way people actually behaved.

This provided Sidney with one of his most effective weapons against Filmer. English history, Sidney pointed out, had produced many kings such as William I, Henry IV and his line, Henry VII and his – whose hereditary claims could not stand scrutiny, yet they had been accepted as lawful, and Filmer could only defend them by an appeal to their success in arms. If so, should not Filmer have accepted the authority of Cromwell, and the whole doctrine that might was right? He, Sidney, had never done so, but he had accepted Charles II, and the ruin of his own prospects, because the installation of Charles had the authority of a lawful Parliament.

In this republican doctrine Sidney designated Parliament as the supreme manifestation of the immanent constitution so far as England was concerned. It was not an advisory body, to be sum-

---

* The same view is to be found in DCG iii 38.

moned and dispensed with, but a continuing expression of legitimacy, founded in the communities which, to Sidney, were the
people. 'The Parliament and the people have the power of making
Kings.' (iii. 30) In his eyes, as inheritor of a Tudor tradition, the
utterance is less strange than it seems at first sight – and indeed a
mere statement of fact – for Henry VII had insisted that his dubious
hereditary title should be endorsed by Parliament, and his successors
had always employed it to reinforce their decisions. If, like Frank-
enstein, they thereby created a monster which devoured their Stuart
successors, Sidney can scarcely be blamed.

To him Parliament existed in complete independence from the
monarch, from whom it needed no summons and need accept no
dissolution. Even an enforced dissolution did not end its authority.
It was not an assembly of delegates, though certainly the fact that
its members were chosen by an electorate meant that those who
failed to satisfy the voters should be replaced by other, better men.
But once elected Sidney, like Burke a hundred years later, saw
members of Parliament as owing their primary loyalty to the nation,
not to their respective constituencies:

> 'Tis not for Kent or Sussex, Lewis or Maidstone, but for the whole Nation,
> that the members chosen in those places are sent to serve in Parliament: and
> tho it be fit for them as friends and neighbors (so far as may be) to hearken
> to the opinions of the electors for the information of their judgments, and
> to the end that what they may say shall be of more weight, when everyone
> is known to speak not his own thoughts only, but those of a great number
> of men; yet they are not strictly and properly oblig'd to give an account of
> their actions to any, unless the whole body of the Nation for which they
> serve, and who are equally concern'd in their resolutions, could be
> assembled. This being impracticable, the only punishment to which they
> can be subjected if they betray their trust, is scorn, infamy, hatred, and an
> assurance of being rejected, when they shall again seek the same honor. And
> tho this may seem a small matter to those who fear to do ill only from a
> sense of the pains inflicted: yet it is very terrible to men of ingenious spirits,
> as they are suppos'd to be who are accounted fit to be entrusted with so
> great powers. (iii 44)

Here one can see the practical politician rather than the theorist,
in awareness that members of Parliament did not speak their own
thoughts only and that defeat at the polls was a very serious penalty
for anyone temperamentally drawn to political life. It applied, in
Sidney's opinion, as much to kings as to parliamentarians, and he
records with approval a remark made by Charles X of Sweden

(which he had perhaps elicited himself) that having been raised to the throne as a poor man 'he had but one work to do, which was so to reign that the Swedes might never repent of the good opinion they had of him.' (iii 31)

During the long interval between July 1679 and October 1680, when Algernon regarded himself as the Member for Amersham in a House that did not meet, the King began his counter-offensive. He recruited several of the politicians who had conspired for the downfall of Danby, including Algernon's nephew Sunderland and his kinsman Halifax. He shifted his inconvenient brother James off the scene to Scotland and entered into secret negotiations with Louis for a further subsidy while at the same time (through Algernon's brother Henry at the Hague) trailing the idea of cooperation with William of Orange to contain Louis' ever-growing power. Plans were begun to recapture London by obtaining a friendly Lord Mayor at the next election, and it is noticeable that in the continuing propaganda war, of which Dryden's *Absalom and Achitophel* (published in 1680) is the most brilliant product, Slingsby Bethel the Whig Sheriff receives prominence as 'Shimei'.*

Progress was also made with the idea of 'turning the plot' against the opposition. That the mood was right for such a re-direction of public emotion against the unconforming can be judged from the entry Evelyn made in his diary on the day the aged and totally innocent Catholic Lord Stafford went to the block. Charles had declined to save him, and the execution was supervised by the whig Sheriffs Bethel and Cornish. Evelyn had once been a firm believer in Oates's revelations, but now he commented that 'such a man's testimony should not be taken against the life of a dog.'

---

* It is significant that apart from City figures the cast of *Absalom and Achitophel* is taken almost entirely from the Shaftesburyite agitation. No figures from the 'Commonwealth' opposition are included unless one counts Howard of Escrick. It points to an appreciation by the government that its opponents were divided.

The Rye House Business

WHEN Parliament met again on 22 March 1681 it was found that the 'short poll' at Amersham had once more done its duty by producing claims by both 'Algernon Sidney Esq, and Sir William Drake kt' to have been duly elected, but the only importance of the dispute – which there was to be no time to decide – was that it produced a lasting and justifiable belief in Algernon's mind that he was, and remained, a member of Parliament.

It is difficult to regard this, the last of Charles's Parliaments, as anything other than a defiant demonstration on the King's part which he felt strong enough to plan in advance. He convened it at Oxford – causing many members to have doubts whether they could constitutionally attend or not; it was surrounded by carefully disposed troops; the government's attitude was from the first uncompromising; and a sudden, dramatic dissolution after one week's sitting was rapidly followed by a long and carefully drafted manifesto justifying the King's decision. Within a fortnight of the dissolution the manifesto was on its way to all the parishes of England to be read from the pulpit on the next available Sunday.

In the week they were allowed to sit, the parliamentarians showed that this session would mark the beginning of a new stage of defiance on their part also. There were proposals for 'An Association for the Defence of the Protestant Religion' – menacing words which had been used in 1588 and were to be used again in 1688 to mean a general mobilization – and after being formally dissolved some members of the House of Lords lingered in their chamber in the hope of provoking some demonstration of autonomy. When, in the end, the parliamentarians and their retinues streamed back to the comparative safety of their London stronghold, they had not accepted defeat.

This was to be the background for the final act of Algernon's tragedy, a drama of undeclared war, fought indeed without armies, but a struggle none the less in which the purpose of each side was to destroy the other. In this struggle the prime objective of the government was to recapture the capital, and the main (though far from the only) weapon employed was 'turning the plot' against its opponents by substituting them as the targets for the popular forces originally stirred up by Oates. If this accounts for much of the murkiness of the political drama that followed, it also throws light on a real drama mounted that autumn by Aphra Behn who had now turned to literature and the stage for her living. In her protégé Otway's melodramatic tragedy *Venice Preserved* the action is impelled by a conspiracy of malcontents under the guidance not of a religious figure but of a foreign ambassador whose address to his colleagues shows the sort of plot the government now wished to implant in the public mind:

> The public stock's a beggar, one Venetian
> Trusts not another. Look into their stores
> Of general safety; empty magazines,
> A tattered fleet, a murmuring unpaid army,
> Bankrupt nobility, a harassed commonalty,
> A factious, giddy, and divided senate,
> Is all the strength of Venice. Let's destroy it . . .

The public mind had begun to be impressed by the protests of the later, and quite innocent, victims of Oates and his fellow-witnesses, but it still hungered for the excitement of court drama and mystery 'The Plot' had bred, and though the modern mind may think of left and right as opponents widely separated by a central ground, the average seventeenth-century Englishman made the much simpler distinction between conformity and deviancy; and deviancy for whatever reason was suspect. One only has to add the peculiar gratification taken by the public in seeing yesterday's hero turned into today's villain to understand the path on which the government now set out.

The counter-attack's first victim was a straightforward case enough. Stephen College, a demagogue known as 'the Protestant Joiner', had addressed the crowds outside the Parliament at Oxford, and was charged with treason. When it became clear that it would be impossible to get a conviction in London, he was promptly 'extradited' to Oxford, tried, and hanged. Aaron Smith was his legal adviser, and was pilloried for it.

The next victim, though uninteresting in himself, was far more important as a sign of the times and in Algernon's tragedy. Edward Fitzharris was an Irish Roman Catholic who had embarked on the career of an informer, and in 1680 he fell (or pushed himself) into the hands of the Whig authorities in London as a suspected Popish conspirator; but on finding he had connections with the Government, Sheriffs Cornish and Bethel began to suspect something else, namely that the 'plot' he had to reveal would, at the right moment, be announced as a Whig forgery designed to destroy innocent Catholics, and so 'turn the plot' against the Whigs themselves. There was probably something in these suspicions, for once the Fitzharris case became a cause célèbre, as it quickly did, the Government moved as quickly as it could to get him not only out of Whig hands but out of the world altogether.

The wretched man twisted in every direction, denouncing one side and the other in turn, until, under the management of the chaplain of the Tower of London, he made statements implicating various Whigs, including the two Sheriffs themselves. He was then quickly tried and executed before he could change his story again. The chaplain of the Tower was promised the next vacant deanery, and Mrs Fitzharris was given a pension in return for her late husband's papers.

Among those implicated by Fitzharris was the man who was to prove Algernon Sidney's Iago, William, Lord Howard of Escrick, and like Iago, Howard was an engaging, companionable fellow. 'A man of very pleasant conversation', wrote Burnet, 'he insinuated himself so into me that without being rude it was not possible to avoid him.' Burnet was shrewd enough to mistrust him, despite his charm, and Dryden put him into *Absalom and Achitophel* as 'canting Nadab'.

He had a curious background. His peerage had originated in

the reign of James I and the ascendancy of the Duke of Buckingham, whose follower the first Lord Howard had been. But the first Lord Howard had not been loyal to the Stuart line, and from the start embraced the Parliamentary Cause with an enthusiasm which he carried to the point of getting elected to the House of Commons when the House of Lords was abolished, only to earn the distinction of being expelled three months later for corruption. His second son William served for a time in Cromwell's life-guard, plotted against Cromwell, and after a brief membership of the Convention Parliament that recalled Charles II, plotted against him as well. On succeeding to the peerage, which descended on him unexpectedly, he thrust himself forward in the witch-hunt against the Catholics, and became chairman of the House of Lords Committee investigating 'The Plot'. Now, thanks to the testimony of the unfortunate Fitzharris, Howard of Escrick was lodged in the Tower himself, and was no doubt subject to the ministrations of its chaplain. He did not emerge for some time.

Algernon had known Howard for many years, and was a victim of his undoubted charm. With all his sullenness and dignity one of Algernon's endearing characteristics was that he would exert himself – often to an unreasonable extent – on behalf of people he liked, however unworthy they proved to be. One remembers how he lobbied for the release of his devious aunt, Lady Carlisle, and how he involved himself in a financial mess helping his sister Isabella and her unscrupulous husband Strangford. It was the same with Howard. He lent him money (something Howard was always short of) and he did his best to get him out of prison by pestering influential relations such as Sunderland and Halifax, even though they were working for a government he bitterly opposed. Nobody, wrote Burnet, 'but a monster of ingratitude could have made him the return that he did.'

Released Howard duly was, in September 1681, and Algernon congratulated himself. But whether this generous gesture by the Government can be attributed to sympathy for Algernon or conviction of Howard's innocence or to some other motive is quite a different question. During his stay in the Tower, Howard would have been subjected to considerable pressure as a very suitable instrument to 'turn the plot', and the probability that he accepted the commission is high.

In the first half of 1681 the government had been made to

realise that time and patience would be needed to re-establish its authority. They tried a direct blow at Shaftesbury by accusing him of treason, but after a spectacular enquiry a London Grand Jury threw it out. That summer two new Whig Sheriffs were elected to secure the machinery of justice in London to the opposition for one more year. Dissidents were still safe in the capital, schemes and pamphlets multiplied and, as Howard mildly remarked later on, there was 'a greater freedom and a liberty of speech with one another than perhaps hath been used formerly'.

This was the context of the systematic attack on municipal privilege – and above all on the privileges of London – that the government now began. The motive may have been reconquest rather than conquest, but the technique has a strong resemblance to the methods then being adopted in France for subjecting recent conquests to searching legal scrutiny in the hope of extending them by establishing possible dependencies and semi-dependencies. Just as Louis XIV's 'Chambres de Réunion' added to his territory by legal research, Charles's writs of 'Quo Warranto?' attacked municipal privilege. Indeed they penetrated further, for along with municipal privilege went the election of many members to Parliament. In this sense the move was a direct assault on Algernon's notion of an immanent republic. In several passages of the *Discourses* he alludes, though in general terms, to this struggle, maintaining that municipal privilege, far from being a gift of the King, was an element in the general pool of liberty.

But the basis of the attack on municipal charters was that what the King had given freely, he could freely, and without compensation, cancel, and many municipalities preferred surrender and petition for a new charter to the expense and obloquy of a contest. Gradually this campaign was pressed further and further, not only in England, but even across the Atlantic against the charters of the New England colonies. It was Filmerism in action.

Algernon had not been idle in opposition in the months following the retreat from Oxford. He had, among other things, helped to compose the reply to the King's manifesto which was later polished by the great Whig lawyer Sir William Jones and published as a *Just and Modest Vindication of the Proceedings of the Last Two Parliaments*.* It is a highly effective piece of political writing, and

* Burnet had no doubt that it was a collaboration between Algernon, Jones, and Jones's pupil Somers; and it bears distinct traces of Algernon's style. Barillon's despatch

even in the middle of the next century was considered to state the constitutional issues then at stake better than any other.

Shaftesbury still had many political assets – in Locke a genius for his secretary, in Ferguson an effective if devious chief of staff. He still had, or claimed to have, a citizen army of Londoners at his disposal. But despite his triumphant rescue from the charge of treason in the summer, the chill of it had shaken him and he had tried (and was known by some of his colleagues to have tried) to strike a bargain with the King. His scheme for using Monmouth, the illegitimate royal duke, as a figurehead did not convince other politicians. Algernon said he did not care who was King – whether it was James Duke of Monmouth or James Duke of York. As a political chief he much preferred a man of his own class, an opposition aristocrat so far untarnished, Arthur Capel, Earl of Essex.

Arthur Capel was ten years younger than Algernon and had the same studious, introspective temperament. There were many things to draw them together. Arthur's grandmother had been a Montagu, and his wife was one of Algernon's Percy cousins. He had followed in Algernon's footsteps as ambassador in Denmark, and his success there had gained him, though still a young man, the Lord-Lieutenancy of Ireland. His four years there gave Ireland its most conscientious and humane government since the rule of Strafford, and the best the Restoration government gave to any part of the British Isles. In 1681, though a zealous Protestant and no longer Lord Lieutenant, he tried to intervene with Charles to save the life of the totally innocent Oliver Plunkett, Archbishop of Armagh, only to be told that a reprieve would be seized on by opposition propagandists as proof of Catholic influence at court.†

However there was one reason why it is at first sight surprising to find Arthur Capel and Algernon Sidney as the political allies they became in 1681. Capel had not only served the Restoration loyally in high office: his father had been one of the most devoted supporters of Charles I and had gone to the block in 1649 as one of the leaders of the disastrous 'Second Civil War'. The sacrifice had earned the

of 5 Dec 1680 records Algernon's close political relations with Jones and we know that Jones advised Algernon on his family litigation. The suggestion, though often made, that the work is by Ferguson does not bear examination.

† This was the same Oliver Plunkett who twenty years earlier as a young priest in Rome had denounced Algernon in a sermon. He in his turn had been denounced, quite falsely, by two renegade Irish informers as being concerned in the Popish Plot. His sacrifice to prejudice is one of the most shocking episodes of the reign.

family an earldom at the Restoration. Nevertheless from the end of the Oxford Parliament onwards Arthur Capel became more and more closely identified with the opposition, especially that part of it in which Algernon was a leading figure. That in this partnership Algernon was dominant there is no doubt, and if one is looking for a Brutus in the story that followed he is Arthur Capel, not Algernon Sidney.

During 1681 the Whig garrison of London seemed to be holding their ground – with two new Whig Sheriffs elected the assault on Shaftesbury was beaten off. The Common Council refused to send a congratulatory message to the King on his firm action at Oxford, and voted a protest instead. But this defiance was carried by only a small majority – 91 to 77 – sure evidence that the political nerve of the councillors was weakening. In the autumn the Government managed to get a friendly Lord Mayor, and in the New Year it was emboldened to extend its enquiry into municipal privilege to the charter of London. The rewards of this strategy soon became apparent: in the summer of 1682 the judges declared that the King indeed had the power to withdraw London's municipal privileges, and soon afterwards, in an election which by any standards was a scandal, the Government regained control of the administration of justice with the appointment of two Tory Sheriffs. To achieve the desired result the Lord Mayor set aside the open poll and insisted that he had the right to nominate one Sheriff himself and preside over a private poll for the other.

By the autumn of 1682 the opposition leaders, with London no longer safe for them, began to realise that the retreat from Oxford had been a mistake. They now had to face the King with diminished and demoralized backers, for while the City magnates might put up money they would do so only for a competent upper-class leadership with backing in the provinces. Moreover no rising against the monarchy had ever succeeded without some backing from outside England, and no such help was to be hoped for (or desired) from William of Orange. There remained the Covenanters of Scotland, but they were themselves in retreat, they expected money, and Scottish intervention in English affairs was never popular.

Both factions of the opposition – that still dominated by Shaftesbury and that which had Algernon and Arthur Capel as its focus – began to consider where they should turn next. Hence arose the consultations which were readily penetrated by informers and collectively have come to be known as 'The Rye House Plot'. The Governmental strategy of 'turning' the original Popish Plot against the Whigs was put into operation against a real, not an imagined, enemy.

This strategy required that the events to be ultimately paraded before the public should appear as forming a closely integrated conspiracy with as many dramatic features as possible, and this image – particularly the image of an assassination plot – has succeeded in a measure in imposing itself on history. But even the tainted and fragmentary evidence that we have does not provide any picture of an integrated episode under central direction, and in this broad sense one can say there was no such thing as 'The Rye House Plot' at all: not even a plot with various sub-plots, for the different anti-governmental activities described by the witnesses turn out, on examination, to have no connection with one another. What we have, rather, is a picture of a desperate and disorganised opposition threshing about in various directions to escape the net its members began to see closing in on them.

'The Rye House Plot' in its narrow sense was a plan to assassinate the King and his brother using a Rye House owned by a Commonwealth veteran near Hoddesden in Herts on a route from Newmarket to London. Plenty of exciting corroborative detail about such a plan was later produced by witnesses who said they had heard it from other people – the exact arrangement of the line of men with blunderbusses, the farm cart to be used to block the narrow road, the arguments about just whose hand should deal the fatal blows. But if such a plan was even talked about no steps were ever taken to carry it out, and no hint of it seems to have reached the ears of any of the opposition politicians.* The Rye House itself must therefore be dismissed from Algernon's biography as quickly as it has entered it. What is left is the activity of the opposition politicians themselves during the autumn of 1682 and the first six months of 1683.

Shaftesbury retired to a secret address in Wapping as soon as

---

* Algernon would certainly have rejected the idea, and so would Monmouth. The first was far too pernickety to countenance a murderous ambush, and for Monmouth it would have been parricide, and what was more, parricide of the man to whom alone he owed his political importance. In pure political terms it is difficult to see that any insurrection claiming popular support could hope for success starting from such an episode.

he heard that Tory sheriffs had been elected, and transmitted his views to his colleagues through his henchman Ferguson. With his health forsaking him and his nerve gone, he still talked about a rising, and it seems to have been discussed under cover of a wine-tasting at which his main political allies Monmouth, William, Lord Russell, and Lord Grey of Wark were present. The meeting had elements of a trap, for the wine-merchant Sheppard afterwards turned out to be one of the Government's most useful informers. But neither Algernon, who continued to live quietly in Monmouth Street, nor Arthur Capel attended, and there is no evidence that they were even approached.

Whatever was said at the wine-tasting (and some parts of it doomed Russell) nothing came of this last effort by the Shaftes-buryites. Shaftesbury himself fled to Holland not long afterwards where, in January 1683, he died, leaving a vacuum in the leadership of the opposition.

Into this vacuum Algernon was induced to step, perhaps by the ambition and sense of duty he had shown when he did the same thing in 1665, perhaps by a consciousness of his mission, and very probably under the influence of his Iago, William Howard. Howard at any rate, on his own evidence, built the bridge between Algernon and Monmouth, the significant survivor of the Shaftesburyite wine-tasters, by the simple expedient of telling each that the other was anxious to meet him, even though they scarcely knew each other. Thus the Shaftesburyite cabal of the autumn was revived into a winter union of constitutional monarchists and republicans.

Monmouth later summed up Howard by saying he was 'zealous for no government save that under which he could get most', and no doubt his calculations included the possibility that a combination of the two wings of the opposition gave it a better chance of winning; but if it did not, all the principal enemies of Charles would be involved in a common ruin from which he could gain. So Algernon and his republican allies were steered by Howard into alliance with a man whose only political significance was his illegit-imate royal blood; and Monmouth, along with his hapless friend Lord Russell, just when they were thinking of giving up the whole game, were lured into coalition with a man who despised royal pretensions.

The meetings of this group seem to have started in February 1683, and by the end of March, according to Lord Grey of Wark, who was then invited to join the group by Monmouth, they had assembled four or five times, and decided on much the same pattern of insurrection as the Shaftesbury group had contemplated before Christmas, but with one addition: they proposed to enlist the support of the Scottish Whigs, and in particular the Earl of Argyll.* An emissary to Scotland was therefore needed, and Algernon suggested Aaron Smith, whose expenses he volunteered to pay. Next day he went to his bank, accompanied by Howard, and withdrew the required sum of £40, mentioning Aaron Smith's mission to Howard as he did so. Howard later had the clearest recollection of the incident for it was an 'overt act' and he was familiar with the law of treason.

The conspirators might agree on the English centres of revolt (London, Cheshire and Devonshire) and the need to bring in the Scots, but divisions on policy had emerged almost immediately, and before any operations could begin there had to be a manifesto stating their objective. Russell, for one, saw great difficulties about this, and when Grey joined them, appealed to him to support him and Monmouth in insisting on the preservation of the monarchy and opposing the Commonwealth faction. If they could not agree to follow the programme agreed at Sheppard's wine-tasting, he would abandon the whole project.

The conflict came to a head early in April when the anti-republican faction met separately to discuss their plans for a meeting of the whole group later in the month. Ferguson and another veteran Shaftesburyite, Rumsey, now back from Holland, were also present and had news of the Scottish end of the plot, with which they were in touch. Indeed some Scots emissaries had now arrived in London, and according to Grey, who had seen them and had not been impressed, they also were against raising the old republican standard.

* Grey of Wark, *The Secret History of the Rye House Plot*. London 1754. Not published for seventy years, this consists of the statement made by Grey, as a prisoner after Monmouth's rebellion, to Sunderland, then Secretary of State. It was thus, like the evidence given at the trials of Russell and Sidney, given by a witness whose life depended on it. Burnet, who was not in this situation when he wrote some years later, knew several of the principal conspirators well – notably Russell, Essex, and Algernon himself; and provides a great deal of interesting detail, including Howard's contrivance of the meeting between Algernon and Monmouth. Ferguson's narrative, *Concerning the Rye House Business*, is also that of a prisoner, but relates only to the events before Shaftesbury's flight. It is printed by J. Ferguson as an appendix to his *Robert Ferguson* (Edinburgh 1887).

The consultations of the anti-republican faction ended with expressions of confidence that the republicans would certainly be outvoted at the full assembly of 'The Cabal', especially if Howard was not there – indeed Grey said he would not attend if Howard came, so little did he trust him.*

The meeting of the full Cabal took place at Russell's London home, Southampton House, later in April. There was a certain formality about the proceedings, and the language used about the Cabal's origins by those who took part provides significant echoes of the old Councils of State. 'It would be necessary', Howard said later in his evidence against Russell, 'that there should be some general council that should take upon them the care of the whole', and when a little later he referred to 'the party concerned with Lord Shaftesbury', the Lord Chief Justice interrupted. 'What party?' he demanded. Howard was quick to see the danger and replied 'We were not chosen by the community but did erect ourselves.' But Algernon and those who thought like him probably saw it in a different light. All who were there had sat (or in Algernon's case had been elected to sit) in one or other of the Houses of Parliament that had assembled at Oxford; and he, at any rate, well remembered how in 1659, from a beginning almost as small, the whole Rump had been re-embodied to return in brief triumph.

Only five persons were at the meeting of the full Cabal in April and Algernon found himself outnumbered. The only other republican was Hampden, the most junior member of the group, for Howard sent excuses, and Essex said he would be late: it is not clear if he ever came at all. Algernon's reaction was characteristic: disregarding the fact that Russell, not he, was the host, and that he was in a minority, he opened the proceedings with a long speech explaining why he considered the proposed rising lawful, and dwelt on Scottish support as the indispensible factor. Their highest priority should be raising money for it.

When Algernon stopped, Grey asked whether an agreed declaration of policy should not come first. 'Col. Sidney muttered to himself for some time, and truly what he said I know not; all I could distinctly heard was, that my Lord of Essex and my

---

* Here I have relied on Grey's narrative rather than Howard's evidence against Russell and Sidney where they differ, as they do in material respects. Howard was very much influenced by a desire to minimise his own part.

Lord Howard not being there, it was not a proper time to talk of a declaration.'

The King, Algernon went on, had broken the terms on which he had been brought to the throne, and the kingdom should be settled in a parliament which would decide the future constitution. When the others tried to insist that nevertheless their programme should include the preservation of the monarchy in some form, 'Col. Sidney said he had heard, when wise men drew their swords against their king, they laid aside the thoughts of treating with him,' and positively refused to talk about it. They turned to discussion of who should be the Commander-in-Chief, and what his powers should be, and again Algernon showed that his position was still what it had been during the great controversies of the late 1640s. Whoever was made Commander-in-Chief – and he personally favoured Monmouth – he must be subject to the Council (namely their group) until a properly constituted parliament had met.

Despite being in a minority Algernon seems to have won, for a fortnight later there was a further meeting at which two of his major points were carried: he and Essex were to draft a manifesto, and arrangements were put in hand to raise a large sum in the City as a subsidy for the Scots. So, at any rate, Grey (who was not at this meeting) says he was told by Russell. The rising was timed for June. Still later Grey says he was told by Monmouth that all was going smoothly, the 'Cabal' was in complete agreement, he expected the rising to be almost entirely bloodless, and it would be followed by an acceptable settlement between King and Parliament.

We have only Grey's word for it that these remarks were made – and at the time he recorded them he was trying to save his own life at Monmouth's expense – but even if he was speaking the truth, there is much better evidence for holding that insurrection was far from ready to explode that summer. No arms, apart from two unserviceable cannon dug up in Major Wildman's cellar, were ever found, no preparations at any of the proposed foci of rebellion in Cheshire and the West Country were ever noticed, no treasonable correspondence ever came to light, no money-raising operations in the City were ever detected, and when the arrests began in June the Scottish emissaries Cochran and Baillie of Jerviswood were still in London.

And something else had happened which would have made any plan for a Whig insurrection a certain failure. After a decision by the courts that the charter of the City of London was potentially forfeit the City Council had surrendered, and the King's terms were harsh; the Tory Lord Mayor and Sheriffs would remain in office until the King authorised fresh elections, and even then, if he disapproved their result, he would make his own appointments; even junior jobs in the City, such as under-sheriffs and Coroners, would be subject to Crown approval, and in due course the King would make further and more detailed regulations for the government of his capital.

This collapse of City resistance was what scared secondary figures from the Whig underground. Keeling, the bankrupt anabaptist oilman, turned informer on 12 June, the very day judgment was entered against the City's privileges. Two more such figures, Rumsey the former Cromwellian officer and West, the shady attorney, came in on 23 June, three days after the Common Council voted to seek terms. Most of their information concerned conversations they had heard about plans to assassinate the King and the Duke of York, and some of it related specifically to the autumn of 1682, thus implicating Monmouth, Russell, and Howard of Escrick. The two arms of the Government's strategy – attack on municipal privilege and 'turning the plot' – closed simultaneously.

XVI

Trial

A LGERNON was arrested having lunch at his house in Monmouth Street on 26 June 1683. He was attended by Ducasse,
and had been working on his book, for some of the manuscript was
on his desk and more was in an open trunk beside it. The Privy
Council Messenger carrying the warrant for arrest (it was signed by
four councillors, including Algernon's relations Sunderland and
Halifax) was quickly followed by the Clerk to the Privy Council
himself, Sir Philip Lloyd, armed with a search warrant. Sir Philip,
watched by Algernon, Ducasse, and the two maidservants Grace
Tracy and Elizabeth Penwick, went over the whole house, exam-
ining 'many secret places', but decided to limit his seizure to the
papers on the desk and in the trunk beside it, which he put into a
pillowslip, tied and then suggested Algernon should seal the knot.
Algernon, suspecting a trap, refused, so Lloyd sealed it himself and
escorted his prisoner to the Privy Council, where four councillors
asked him questions about Aaron Smith and visitors to Scotland
'unto which I returned answeares with all the respect I could, and
without prejudice to the truth.' He was then remanded to the
Tower.[1]

Algernon's calm indifference, which is vouched for by several
witnesses, was shared by only one other victim of the wave of

arrests[2] in late June and early July – Arthur Capel. Monmouth achieved a diplomatic disappearance, for his whereabouts remained known to the authorities; John Locke quickly packed his bags and took the next boat to Holland; Russell, when he was arrested, remarked to his wife that he was as good as a dead man. Howard of Escrick visited as many houses as possible 'raising his hands to heaven' (as Burnet reports) 'that there was no such thing as a plot' and then went into hiding, which proved to be a cupboard behind the chimney piece whence he was dragged whimpering. One is left with the strong impression that those who had been in any way involved with Shaftesbury were aware of the danger in which they stood; but those who had been clear of him felt they had not yet broken the law.

Howard's behaviour was peculiar. The day after Algernon's arrest he called at Monmouth Street professing complete astonishment and hoping his friend would soon be released, for there was certainly no plot and there was nothing more unpleasant than being in the Tower, as he knew very well. One would do anything to get out of it. Algernon had been most kind at that time and he would like to do anything he could to help – for instance if there were any papers not taken away by the authorities he would be glad to take them to a place of safety, along with any valuables in the house, such as Mr Sidney's silver, and would send his coach at once. Ducasse replied that he had no orders to allow anything to be removed, and advised Howard to make himself scarce, since the house was watched. Immediately after his arrest on 9 July he made statements to the investigators implicating Russell, Sidney, Essex, and Hampden (all by that time arrested) in the plans for insurrection.

It would be oversimplifying things to say that Howard was a government agent from the first, just as it is impossible to believe that the possibility of a betrayal did not govern his behaviour throughout the period following his release from the Tower in the autumn of 1682. He was playing a dangerous game, and knew well that his own life was forfeit unless he could bring down greater victims. But two facts tell strongly for holding that the destruction of Algernon Sidney – or at any rate the power to destroy him – guided him throughout. One is his gratuitous introduction of Algernon and Monmouth early in 1683 after the collapse of the Shaftesburyite consultations; and the other is the line of questioning about Aaron Smith and the Scottish connection with which Algernon was faced immediately after his arrest. At that time none of the ostensible informers had mentioned the Scottish connection and no other source but Howard himself can be identified as the reporter of the one act by Algernon which could be construed as treasonable: the payment of Smith's travel expenses to Scotland. One of the specific questions put to Algernon on his first apparance before the Privy Council concerned this point. And Howard alone, on his own admission, was responsible for reviving the conspiratorial meetings after Shaftesbury's flight.*

Trials for high treason in the seventeenth century had something in common with bull-fights. The rules were elaborate and well understood by the audience, and proper skill and finesse had to be shown by the prosecutors and the judges. The victim was allowed to earn applause for courage and even ferocity, but his end was inevitable, no matter how brave his fight.

Treason, unlike other crimes, was defined primarily by intention, so there had to be specific acts by the accused which could be described as showing a treasonable intent. In other crimes, such as murder, intention could be assumed from the act itself unless the prisoner could prove the opposite. But in treason intention had to be inferred from the context of acts which might in themselves seem harmless, and the question 'Did these acts show treason?' was all-important. The recital of facts and their implications in an indictment was therefore framed by the prosecution with particular care. The rules seemed to be designed to protect the prisoner, but in fact faced him with a cruel dilemma.

The indictment was kept from the prisoner until he arrived in court, and even then he was not allowed a copy, nor were his counsel, if he had any. But when he heard it read he was entitled to argue that the facts recited and their context did not amount to treason; and he could even have counsel to argue it. But it was a dangerous step, as the judges always pointed out, for the court would not listen to a prisoner saying 'I don't accept this, but even if I did ...' If you disputed the implications of the facts alleged in the indictment as a matter of law, you must accept the facts set out in it. The judge would then decide whether those facts showed

---

* That some contemporaries suspected Howard as an *agent provacateur* is mentioned by Burnet, who only dismisses the possibility on the ground that when all was over Charles II expressed nothing but contempt for Howard. Well he might. Howard was to spend the rest of his life shunned by society.

treason or not, but if it went against you that was the end of the matter. You had accepted the recited facts, they amounted to treason, you were guilty, and the court would go straight to sentence.

The alternative to 'demurring' as this was called, was to plead 'not guilty', and thereby accept that the allegations amounted to treason. That meant encountering the well-trained witnesses for the prosecution speaking to the carefully selected facts. For this counsel was not allowed. After that you could call your own witnesses if you had any, and make a speech. Verdict and judgement would then follow.

One other rule existed on the side of the victim. In cases of treason, as distinct from other crimes, one single witness to the facts was insufficent: there must be two. But over the years the safeguard had been much eroded, and two witnesses to the same act would do. So would two witnesses to connected facts, such as the purchase of a knife and a declared intention to use it. Some lawyers thought the two-witness rule was satisfied even if the jury disbelieved one of them. But two witnesses there had to be. The doctrine had scriptural authority in the case of Susannah and the Elders reported in the Book of Daniel, and had been embodied in the statute law of England in the reign of Edward III.

The prosecution of William, Lord Russell, presented no diffi- culties from this point of view, and his trial came on within a few weeks of his arrest. The case against him was based entirely on events of the previous autumn, before the flight of Shaftesbury, for which there were plenty of witnesses, including Sheppard, the wine merchant at whose now famous wine-tasting Russell had been present, another informer, Rumsey, and others. But the star witness was Howard of Escrick, now clearly under government control, who testified at length about how he had been present as an active conspirator at all the meetings, and had acted as an intermediary between Russell, Monmouth and Shaftesbury in trying to reconcile their differences.

He was giving evidence when the trial was suddenly inter- rupted. A courageous juryman complained that the witness's voice was trailing away, and could not be heard. 'Pray, my Lord', said Chief Justice Pemberton courteously, 'raise your voice, otherwise your evidence will pass for nothing.' Howard apologised for seeming shaken, but he had just been told that the Earl of Essex had been found dead in his cell at the Tower with his throat cut.

The sensational end of the man who had been destined as the next victim obscured the remaining stages of Russell's trial and even its inevitable conclusion. Naturally the Whigs at once claimed Essex had been murdered, and it is indeed true that his successful trial would have presented difficulties; but suicide is more probable. That studious, worthy, hardworking man, with his Cavalier background and tortured principles, was not built for the appalling prospect with which he was faced: not merely the prospect of execution, but execution as a collaborator with the forces which had executed his own father, a traitor to his family and his own traditions. Charles II said afterwards that Essex had been rash, and might have expected a pardon. 'I owed him a life', are the words he is said to have used – an interesting expression of the way he approached these matters.

No clemency, however, was intended for Algernon. Like Harry Vane he was regarded as too dangerous, too inveterate an enemy, to be allowed to escape, and now Russell had been struck down as the most prominent available symbol of the Shaftesburyite wing of the opposition, an equally prominent victim was needed from the republicans. Even so the Crown's lawyers, led by the Attorney-General, Sir Robert Sawyer, found serious difficulties in mounting a satisfactory case. The consultations in which Algernon had taken part all belonged to the early months of 1683, and for these none of the informers except Howard himself could give any direct evidence. Howard, it is true, had obligingly but irrelevantly dragged Algernon into his testimony against Russell, but the most that could be done with the other witnesses was to create a general atmosphere of conspiracy. Howard could prove only one 'overt act' – the despatch of Aaron Smith to Scotland at Algernon's expense. So where was the second witness to that, or to another, or to a connected act of treason?

The contents of Sir Philip Lloyd's sealed pillow-slip must at first have seemed to provide very little help with this problem. It contained no ciphers, no military plans, no conspiratorial letters, only what seemed to be part of a treatise, some of it yellowing and dog-eared with age, aimed against Filmer's *Patriarcha*, and a paper professing to be the constitution of a country called 'East Jersey'.

The hope of representing the paper about 'East Jersey' as a scheme for the revolutionary constitution the conspirators wanted to impose on England was put aside when it was found to be a contribution to Penn's colonial constitution-making. But much of the summer and early autumn was spent wading through Algernon's material about Pepin le Bref and Saul, Brutus and the Gracchi, the Saxon Witenagemote and the medieval monarchies of Spain, in the hope of identifying passages which could be convincingly described as treasonable, while Algernon remained in the Tower.

Although he knew well enough that a man once placed on trial for treason rarely escaped, he remained confident for a long time that a sufficient case to mount a trial at all would never be established, and a series of letters from him, written at this time, has survived which shows his changing moods and intense preoccupation with his defence.* That they survive at all is surprising, for they are all (except the very last) addressed to his colleague John Hampden, grandson of the Civil War hero, who was now also under arrest and a fellow-inmate of the Tower. He was in the end to escape trial for treason, for although Howard's evidence told as much against him as against Algernon, the indispensable 'second witness' could not be contrived.

In other passages of his life – confronting Lord Inchiquin, Cromwell, and Montagu, speechifying at Amersham, laying down the law to his fellow-conspirators in Southampton House – one can always suspect in Algernon an element of posturing and aggressiveness, or at any rate of over-conscious dignity. Looking back on his career he often criticised himself for impetuousness as his greatest failing. But in these letters, calmly discussing his defence and hoping to survive, he faces the possibility of conviction with a stoicism which justifies his subsequent reputation:

> I can resign myself into the hands of god [he writes in the first of the letters] to be disposed of as to life or death as he pleases and am very much comforted by that which you say of the prayers of good people. If I know myself at all, I love them and never embarke into any publick action upon any other motive than a desire of doing them good, and if they are on my side towards god I hope I shall not be much troubled whatever my lot may be among men.

In the same letter he gave Hampden a pledge that was rare for the slippery times they both lived in:

---

* Glynde MSS 794, East Sussex Record Office. The series, which belongs to the Hampden family archive, consists of ten letters and was not known to any of the earlier biographers of Sidney. The first can be dated as September 1683 and the last bears the date 22 November, the day after he had been sentenced to death.

I have sent word to such of my relations as seem desirous to be usefull unto me, that whatever they endeavour to do for me they should do the same for you, and that I would not give him the name of a friend whoe is not so to you. This course, by the help of God, I shall hold, and hope never to doe anything soe unworthy of a gentleman and Christian, as to divide your concernments from my owne, unlesse it doe appeare that the comradeship of them will be to your prejudice.

He had heard, of course, about Howard's betrayal, and was remarkably restrained on the subject:

My morals doe not incline me easily to pardon a man that hath behav'd himself as the gentleman I mention'd unto you . . . but for the same reason that one of the worthiest men that I was ever acquainted with in my life, having a great wit at law . . . refused an attorney recommended to him under the name of an easy honest man . . .

He remained optimistic that there would be no trial since Howard was the only witness the crown could muster.

Aaron Smith was the obvious second witness, for he was now in custody too, and attempts in this direction seem to have been made by an emissary of the Solicitor-General. 'You know this rogue Sidney is a traytor', the prisoner was told, 'and you may make yourself what you will, if you will discover what you know of his design against the Government.' Smith replied that 'he could not say a word that could touch a hair of Colonel Sidney's head.' As for his journey to Scotland, he did not deny it, but he had never heard it was a crime to travel there.[3]

The Attorney-General, Sawyer, was one of the ablest legal minds of his time, and had led the Government's case against the City of London to victory, as well as the successful prosecution of Russell.* But the Government was not, in Algernon's case, relying entirely on its Attorney-General. *R. v Sidney* was to be the first major case presided over by Sir George Jeffreys, and to it he owed his spectacular promotion in a single leap from the bar to be Lord Chief Justice of the King's Bench on 29 September 1683.

Jeffreys had planned a meteoric career when he was still at school, and was called to the bar when he was only twenty. The City of London made him their Common Serjeant at the age of twenty-three, six years later he became Attorney-General to the Duke of York, soon afterwards Recorder of London, and at thirty-

*He had a troublesome political past to live down, having been an advocate of Exclusion in its early days, and was reputedly the draftsman of the first Exclusion Bill.

two Chief Justice of Chester. Then, in 1680, had come a check when the second Exclusion Parliament, disapproving of his behaviour as Recorder of London, had deprived him of the post and administered a stinging rebuke which he had to receive on his knees. The wounds to his ambition and self-esteem were salved for the next two years as Sawyer's junior, supplying the venom in the trials of Stephen College, Fitzharris, Plunkett, and Russell.

The spectacular promotion of Jeffreys was due partly to governmental dissatisfaction with the judge at Russell's trial, and a sense that it would not be safe to entrust him with the more difficult trial of Sidney. Lord Chief Justice Pemberton had shown unusual consideration for Russell, and had ostentatiously left the jury to decide whether 'compassing the king's death' covered the consultations at which Russell's presence was proved. So at the end of September the Attorney-General's junior at the age of thirty-five became the youngest Chief Justice in modern English history. The King was at first hesitant, saying Jeffreys had 'no learning, no sense, no manners, and more impudence than ten carted whores', but agreed.

The news soon reached Algernon in the Tower, and he saw at once what it meant. 'I do already see enough,' he wrote to Hampden, 'to assure us of a good issue if we could have judges of understanding and honesty, but we must expect that all possible care will be taken to give us such as have neither. You know what advances have bin of late towards that good work.'

Even so, right down to the middle of October, Algernon was extraordinarily sanguine about the outcome. 'I growe to be very confident', he wrote, 'that such rules being observed against us as the law requires it is not possible to bring us into danger.' He had had a letter from a friend in Gascony offering a house 'I knowe very well, and it is a good one, about seven leagues above Bordeaux', where perhaps Hampden might join him, 'and we may probably expect as much peace, safety and convience ... as in any place I knowe.' He intended to apply for bail, and saw no reason why it should not be granted.

Jeffreys had been appointed to make sure of a conviction, and his own future would depend on the outcome of this, his first important case. He entered at once into consultation with the Attorney-General, and carefully read the papers that had been seized in the raid on Algernon's house. 'There is not a line in the book, scarce', he later told the jury, 'but what is treason.' Two passages he noted particularly:

> The power originally in the people of England is delegated unto the Parliament. [The King] is subject unto the law of God as he is a man; to the people that makes him a king as he is a king ... He must be content to submit his interest unto theirs, since he is no more than any one of them in any respect than that he is, by the consent of all, raised above any other ...

and

> We may therefore change or take away kings, without breaking any yoke; or that which is made a yoke, but ought not to be one: the injury is therefore in the making or imposing, and there can be none by breaking it.

Round the writing of these words Jeffreys span a new doctrine which solved the two-witness difficulty. If they had been uttered in a speech, published in a pamphlet, or even included in a private letter those would all be acts which could be proved by witnesses, and that the words themselves were treasonable he had no doubt. Merely to think them was treasonable, even though thinking could not be proved, and so could never be brought to court. But surely *writing them down*, even without any intention of communicating them to anyone, was also an act, and could be proved by the handwriting? If so, the documents themselves would constitute the necessary second witness, and Algernon was lost.

In the absence of any authority for such an extension of the law, Jeffreys invented a maxim which in Latin, 'scribere est agere', has a wonderfully authentic ring: 'to write is to act'. No law-book contains it, and the Attorney-General, though adopting the substance of Jeffreys' argument creating the second witness, almost ostentatiously avoided his former junior's new piece of legal coinage.

By the time the prosecution had settled on their strategy, Algernon had been some three months in the Tower in comparative isolation. Preparations for his defence must have been made already by his friends and the leaders of the bar, Serjeants Pollexfen and Rotherham; and the great Mr Williams had been retained, but he was not allowed to see them until 30 October.[4] It seems that by then he had heard about the Crown's line of attack and they tried their best to pacify his indignation at the thought of his own writings being used against him. It was, they assured him, no more than 'a dirty corrupt practice consisting only of a few new-found tricks to elude and overthrow the law.' He should on no account admit he had written the documents – such an admission would play straight into the enemy's hands. He must instead take every possible technical point: challenge the indictment, object to the proposed jurors, argue whether a book could be an 'overt act', and much else on which Mr Williams had prepared a full technical brief.*

Algernon's instinct was to reject this advice:

> I do not yet knowe how my Councell will suffer me to proceed in this businesse, but confesse ... I am much inclined to admit [the papers], and telling the utmost nature, meaning, and intention of them, to put it upon a special Plea, that if such papers, so written, are Treason, I am guilty, if not not.

He was far from sure, anyway, whether at the age of fifty-nine he would be nimble-minded enough – even with the whispered prompting which was all Williams would be allowed to provide – to handle the technical brief. It would make him seem evasive and even cowardly if he hid behind legal niceties. He would be denying authorship of his own book.

> I think I have god to be the defender of my innocence. If he will that I persist in it I hope he will give me grace to submit and strength to suffer, and having, though with such frailty, hitherto endeavour'd to uphold the rights of mankind, and particularly of my owne country, doe not find in my owne hart any great unwillingness to be made a sacrifice of our expiring liberty. Let my blood lye where god will lay it, and I think it will be heavy.

Yet in the end he was overborne and accepted the advice of his defenders. After all, Harry Vane had put up a brilliant legal defence and gained much respect for it. Such unrepentant regicides as Scot and Harrison, despite their courage, had somehow rather lowered themselves in public esteem by their embittered defiance.

He was not given long to reflect on all this: within a week of seeing his lawyers for the first time he was led to Westminster Hall for arraignment, the first stage of the proceedings.† The haste with which the Government was now moving is shown by the fact that

---

* It runs to many pages and is printed in full in Howell's *State Trials*.

† There were three separate stages in what we would today call a trial: the Arraignment, at which the charges were put to the prisoner and he was called upon to plead, at which stage he could dispute the indictment on legal grounds. If he then pleaded 'Not Guilty' the 'trial' in the strict sense followed, with the jury considering the evidence and returning a verdict. Lastly came the separate stage of 'Judgment' at which, if the verdict had been 'guilty', the prosecution demanded sentence. Here again further legal argument 'in arrest of judgment' was possible.

the Grand Jury was still hearing Howard of Escrick's evidence in support of the indictment on that very morning, and the indictment itself contained a serious slip which could have invalidated it if it had been noticed by the defence in time.

The arraignment began at ten in the morning of 7 November. On the bench with Jeffreys were three other judges: Wythins, Walcott and Holloway. The prosecution was led by Sawyer, and the Solicitor-General Finch. Formally speaking no one could appear for the defence, but Mr Williams was stationed conveniently near the dock. The long and involved indictment came down to two allegations – that the prisoner had personally arranged a treasonable journey by Aaron Smith to Scotland, and that 'on the thirtieth day of June [this was the error, for Algernon had been arrested on 23 June] in the five and thirtieth year of the said Lord the King that now is, did make, compose, and write ... a certain false, seditious, and traitorous libel in which ... is contained as followeth these English words' – namely the passages about the accountability of kings which have already been quoted.

Algernon then tried to attack the indictment without losing his right to plead. None of the people he was alleged to have conspired with was named in it, the allegations about the manuscript had nothing to do with the allegations about conspiracy. This was the one point he could not be allowed to win, and Jeffreys made this clear, no doubt cursing himself inwardly for the slip in the date which, trivial as it was, could not have been resisted if it had been raised, and would have destroyed the whole indictment. However, it was overlooked until it was too late:

L.C.J.: You must plead or demur.

Col. Sidney: My Lord, if I put in exceptions to the bill I do not plead till those exceptions are overruled. This was the case with Sir Henry Vane ...

It was certainly a mistake to mention Vane.

L.C.J.: Sir, I must tell you, you must either plead, or demur ... If you can assign any matter of law, do. But otherwise, what kind of a thing would it be? All criminals would say, in all cases, I doubt whether the Bill be good or bad, and after I have thus considered of it I will plead. You are misinformed, and thus the court tells you ...

Wythins J.: If you demur and show what your causes are, we will assign you counsel.

Col. Sidney: I desire you would not try me, and make me run on dark and slippery places. I do not see my way.

L.C.J.: Do not apprehend yourself to be so, as if the court would run you on any inconvenience. But they are bound to see the methods of justice preserved.

Algernon tried to persist, and produced a paper, no doubt prepared in advance by his lawyers, to dispute the indictment without prejudicing the right to plead, but Jeffreys refused to look at it except on the basis that if he ruled it was a refusal to plead he would proceed straight to sentence. This gave a cue to the Attorney-General to object to Williams coaching the prisoner, whereupon Jeffreys sternly told Williams not to interrupt the proceedings. Sidney characteristically had a fit of petulance. 'Why, then, if you drive me upon it, I must plead. Not guilty.' 'If you be not guilty', replied Jeffreys blandly, 'I pray God you may escape.'

The prosecution then asked for a week's adjournment, and Algernon for a fortnight, which was granted, but requests for a copy of the indictment and counsel to argue points of law were refused on the tortuous ground that Algernon himself must first satisfy the court that points of law existed to be argued. Then Jeffreys, having won the first and decisive round, allowed himself the luxury of apparent generosity by offering to have the indictment read again, this time in Latin. 'Those things that you may have by law', he remarked politely, 'God forbid that you should not have the benefit of them.' But as the clerk read, Algernon asked for a reference to a statute to be clarified, and the Lord Chief Justice's politeness vanished:

L.C.J.: When you come upon your trial, Mr Attorney will tell you what statute he goes upon. And he may give in evidence any act of parliament that comprehends treason ... He must take notice of his trial this day fortnight. Lieutenant of the Tower you may take the prisoner back again.

The trial proper began at 10 o'clock on 21 November with one more attempt to dispute the indictment, which Jeffreys waved aside as already settled, and began work on the difficult task of assembling a jury. The jury panel of more than a hundred still survives[4] but many of those listed were too prudent to appear, and it is noticeable that the more gentlemanly names are listed last. Algernon's lawyers had clearly managed to see it beforehand, and his subsequent complaint that it contained the names of many who were not freeholders and 'of the meanest callings, ruined fortunes, lost reputations and hardly endowed with such understanding as is required for a jury ... for a business of five pounds' had considerable justification.

Jeffreys refused to accept challenges based on absence of free-hold, on the ground that the necessary enquiries would be an intolerable waste of time. Nevertheless thirty-five jurors were successfully challenged before the jury was complete, and according to Luttrell, who was present, it was 'a very ordinary one too.' One was a cheese-monger, another a 'horse-rider', and the prisoner remarked he 'might as well be tried by his own groom'.

At last the prosecution brought on its evidence, beginning with its squad of informers, who did not do very well. 'Pray', the Solicitor-General asked the first of them, 'give an account to the court of what you know of a generall insurrection intended in England.' Sidney was quick to interrupt, and before the witness West could reply, put in 'What he knows concerning me'.

L.C.J.: We will take care of that, that no evidence is given but what ought to be.

When Sidney tried to press the argument of relevance, Jeffreys reminded him that his friend Sir William Jones had been allowed to ask just such general questions when prosecuting alleged conspirators during the Popish Plot; but West was eventually forced to admit that though he had heard from various people that Sidney was implicated in a plot he had never met him over the entire period. He was quickly dismissed and replaced by another informer, Rumsey, who said he had heard of Sidney's involvement from West:

Col. Sidney: My Lord, I must ever put you in mind whether it be ordinary to examine men upon indictments for treason concerning me that I never saw, nor heard of in my life.

For a moment Jeffreys faltered –

L.C.J.: I tell you, all this evidence does not affect you, and I tell the jury so.

Col. Sidney: But it prepossesses the jury.

At last the prosecution produced Howard of Escrick, their one relevant witness, who gave his well-rehearsed story of how, after the collapse of Shaftesbury, the conspiracy had been revived, omitting, of course, the fact that he was primarily responsible for the revival. He plodded on through the story of Aaron Smith and then Sidney was invited to cross-examine. His reply was –

I have no questions to ask him.

It is his strangest contribution to the trial. The Attorney-General grinned at the jury and remarked, 'Silence – you know the proverb'. But it was not surrender, for later in the trial Sidney mounted an effective attack on Howard, both with his own witnesses and in his final speech. Sir John Hawles, who was Solicitor-General to William III and wrote a long legal opinion on the case, thought Sidney's failure to cross-examine Howard was correct for, ''tis well known 'tis no prudence to ask a thorough-paced witness a question'.[5] It seems far more likely that the true explanation lies in the arrogant detachment in which Sidney always took refuge when he was frustrated in the certainty of rectitude. Arguing with Howard, after his unbearable betrayal, was something he could not bring himself to do.

Formal evidence then followed. Sir Philip Lloyd proved the seizure of the papers produced, a bank clerk was called to prove Algernon's handwriting. A juryman who was either totally unable to follow the case or had noticed the mistake in the indictment asked Sir Philip which June had been the date of the seizure. 'Last June', Sir Philip innocently replied, and the point dropped again.

In fading November light the clerk then read long extracts from *Discourses Concerning Government* on which the prosecution relied, and the Attorney-General asked the prisoner if there were any other passages he would like read. It was an obvious trap, for any display of familiarity with the manuscript on Sidney's part could have been twisted into an admission of authorship, so his answer was evasive: 'I do not know what to say to it, to read it in pieces thus.' Jeffreys became more daring. 'I perceive you have disposed of them under certain heads: to what head will you have read?' At this point Algernon must have been tempted to abandon his strategy and attempt a defiant defence of his own book, but again he tried ambiguity: 'My Lord, let him give an account of it that did it.' 'We will not delay Colonel Sidney from entering upon his defence', said the Attorney-General.

Algernon's long speech in his defence, which was punctuated by a great deal of sparring with Jeffreys, concentrated on two points – the unreliability of Howard's evidence and the fact that there was no other witness. Jeffreys insisted that the court would settle the issue of whether Howard was the only witness in due course, and that Sidney should speak to the evidence that had been given.

> Col. Sidney: You confound me. I cannot stir. You talk of a conspiracy. What is a conspiracy to kill the King? Is there any more witnesses than one for levying war?
>
> L.C.J.: Pray do not deceive yourself. You must not think the court and you intend to enter into a dialogue. Answer to the fact. If there be not sufficient fact the jury will acquit you. Make what answer you can to it.

No wonder Sir John Hawles, in his review of the case, considered that Sidney had been 'talked to death'.

Undeterred, Sidney delivered a sober attack on Howard as a self-confessed conspirator whose own life was at stake. Before his arrest Howard had solemnly denied there had been any such thing as a plot, and now, to save himself, he gave evidence against those he knew were critics of the government. He had admitted after the trial of Russell 'that he could not get his pardon till he had done some other jobs, till he was past the drudgery of swearing.' Could such a witness, uncorroborated, be believed in a capital case? As for the manuscript, while still keeping up the fiction that it was not his, he embarked on a defence of it.

The manuscript looked an old one 'writ perhaps these twenty yars' and seemed to be 'an answer to Filmer,* which is not calculated for any particular government in the world' but asserts legitimacy of all authority, however acquired, and could have been used to justify the regime of Cromwell 'though he was a tyrant and a violent one – you need not wonder I call him a tyrant, I did so every day in his life.' Was it a crime to argue against such a book? It must now have been getting dark outside, and Jeffreys grew impatient.

> I do not know what the book was an answer to. We are not to speak of any book that Sir Robert Filmer wrote . . . Spend not your time, and the court's time in that which serves no other purpose, than the gratification of a luxurious way of talking that you have. We have nothing to do with his book; you had as good tell me again, that there was a parcel of people rambling about, pretending to be my Lord Russell's ghost, and so we may answer all the comedies in England . . . Do you own the paper?

Again Sidney refused, and tried to argue against the whole

---

* This could have been attacked, for Filmer's book had been generally available for only three years.

219

confection as 'a whimsical imaginaton ... pieced and patched to make a contrivance to kill the king.' Was it not 'a right of mankind, exercised by all studious men, that they write in their own closets what they please for their own memory, and no man can be answerable for it unless they publish it'?

> Pray do not go away with that right of mankind [replied the Lord Chief Justice piously] that it is lawful for me to write what I will in my own closet unless I publish it. I have been told, Curse not the King in thy thoughts, not in thy bedchamber, the birds of the air will carry it ... we must not endure men to talk, that by the right of nature every one may contrive mischief in his own chamber, and he is not to be punished till he thinks fit to be called to it.

Algernon exclaimed that this was worse than the Inquisition, which led to one of the few inteventions by Mr Justice Wythins, begging him not to pollute an English court of law with such a precedent.

Witnesses for the defence were then produced, most of them to describe the conversations they had with Howard before his arrest, when he had energetically denied there was any plot at all. They included three members of the House of Lords (Anglesey, Paget, and Clare), two relations of Howard's (Philip and Edward), and three members of Algernon's own household – Ducasse and the two maidservants. Edward Howard courageously finished his evidence by saying that if he had the honour to be serving on the jury he would not believe a word Lord Howard had said – which caused Jeffreys to exclaim 'This must not be suffered', and the Attorney-General to suggest the witness should be bound over to be of good behaviour. But the most effective of these witnesses was a man named Blake who confirmed that Lord Howard had said he could not expect pardon 'till the drudgery of swearing be over'.

As the evening wore into darkness the jury was subjected to a short final speech from Sidney, and an immense review of the case from the Solicitor-General, which must have taken at least an hour to deliver and at last gave the tortured legal argument on which the Crown relied. If a conspiracy to rebel existed, whether it resulted in any rebellion or not, it amounted to a plot to compass and imagine the death of the king, for one must assume that those who planned intended the ultimate consequence of their plan. As for the attack on Howard's credibility, his earlier denials of any conspiracy were just what one would expect from a man so deeply implicated, and in no way undermined his evidence. Looked on as a whole the evidence about Aaron Smith and the evidence of the book could be seen as two aspects of the same treasonable plan – two acts, and two witnesses to them.

When the Solicitor-General had sat down Jeffreys delivered his summing up. It also was long, and meant to be so, for part of the technique was to exhaust both the prisoner and the jury. Bull-fights are never adjourned to give the bull a second wind, and Jeffreys intended to get his verdict that night. He began by saying he would rather many guilty men should escape than one innocent man suffer.

As a matter of law, he told the jury, merely planning to levy war was not treason if no war was levied. The prisoner was right about that, so Howard's evidence by itself was not conclusive; but in combination with what was said in the documents about the possibility of deposing kings it provided the necessary element of conspiracy to 'compass and imagine the king's death'. To argue that the documents were merely private memoranda on political theory was irrelevant, even if true. A treasonable letter was undoubted evidence, and one kind of writing could not be distinguished from another. *Scribere est agere.*

The witnesses apart from Howard, he conceded, had said nothing to implicate the prisoner directly, and the jury should pay no attention to hearsay, but what they had said about a general conspiracy was relevant if Howard's evidence that the prisoner had taken part in it was accepted. Howard's evidence might have been attacked on the ground that he was a conspirator himself, but it was every man's duty to discover treasons; 'and for a man to come and swear himself over and over guilty, in the face of a court of justice, may seem irksome ... it is therefore to his credit that he is an unwilling witness' who 'wished the drudgery of his swearing was over.'

Before the weary jury were sent out Mr Justice Wythins, on behalf of his brother judges, said they agreed with the Lord Chief Justice's view of the law and in a few pithy sentences told the jury how they should approach the case:

Says Colonel Sidney, here is a mighty conspiracy, but there is nothing come of it. Who must we thank for that? None but the almighty Providence. One of themselves was troubled with conscience and comes and discovers it. Had not Keeling [one of the informers] discovered, God knows whether we might be alive at this day.

It was nearly six o'clock, and quite dark outside when the jury retired, and they took only about quarter of an hour to reach a verdict of Guilty.* Algernon heard it with complete calm, requested that each juryman should be asked his opinion individually – a request that was naturally refused – and was led back to the Tower to await sentence. Luttrell, who sat through the whole eight hours of the trial, was struck by the prisoner's tranquillity and the fact that he 'smiled several times'.

* The official record says half an hour – Luttrell, an eye-witness, fifteen minutes.

XVII

Judgment

THE equanimity Luttrell had noticed in Sidney during the trial was not a pose, and not many men would have sat down the day after such a punishing experience to write the letter which is the last in the series he wrote from the Tower. In the same sloping, steady hand it gives a sober appreciation of his position and his feelings, yet with a warmth and intimacy we find nowhere else in his correspondence.

It is not addressed to Hampden, with whom he always starts 'Honoured Sir', but to 'My most deare friend and kinsman'. It ends with the hope that 'you will pardon and remember, that noe man had a more faithfull and affectionate friend', and in the course of it he writes that 'when I grew first acquainted with you, I discovered those qualities in you that I had most loved in men, and by experience finding that I had judged rightly, grew to have more kindnesse unto you than ever I had to any man, and I do not think that anything would break it but that which is now shortly to ensue.'

Algernon would never have used the word 'kinsman' in any but its literal sense, and there must have been very few among his many kin for whom at that moment he would have felt the warmth this letter shows. It speaks of long friendship, predating Algernon's exile, and for that reason alone cannot relate to his Savile nephewsin-law, even if they had not at the time been serving the detested government, or to his Montagu connection. But there is one candidate so convincing as to be irresistible: Algernon's cousin Henry Neville, whom he had helped into Parliament in the great days and who was still loyal to the Cause. They had always been close, and as recently as 1680 Neville had published a republican pamphlet, *Plato Redivivus*. It would be republished in 1698, the very year when Algernon's own *Discourses* at last were printed.

The letter shows that Algernon intended his kinsman to be his heir, and although a will he had made the previous March was now invalidated by his conviction, he was sending it to his brother Henry ('he having himself behaved well to me since I am in prison') hoping he would find a way of giving effect to it. All he could now do was to enclose three bills of exchange he happened to have by him. 'Pray doe not in this mistake me: I doe not think to endeare my memory unto you though I were to leave you forty times as much, but such things as are usuall men must be suffered to passe.'

At this point he was interrupted by visitors, and by the time they had gone the light was beginning to fail, and so were his eyes – after such a lifetime of writing one is hardly surprised. He resumed next morning, to go over once more the detailed injustices of his trial which now bulked larger in his mind than its outcome. Then came more visitors, and by the time they had gone it was 'too late to saye unto you a tenth part of what I would. Let this, then, suffice. Somme propositions have been made unto me for saving my life, but I do not think them reasonable or decent.' He had refused to agree to anything except a formal petition for a new trial.[1]

The second batch of visitors had been lawyers, and they had brought an astonishing piece of news: the Duke of Monmouth, denounced as the arch-conspirator Sidney was to die for supporting, had reappeared from hiding, presented himself to the King, grovelled, and been forgiven. He had even undertaken to satisfy the public that the plot he had himself taken part in had really existed. This discreditable episode had been arranged before Algernon's trial. Monmouth had already written two letters (drafted by Halifax) to the King promising eternal loyalty to both Charles and James, and begging for forgiveness, and in reply the King had demanded a complete public submission and full details of the conspiracy. This duly happened on 24 November, three days after Sidney's conviction, and was clearly timed to ensure that that case had been disposed of: for Monmouth had made one stipulation – he would not give public evidence against any one of his former colleagues.[2]

Algernon's philosophic calm on hearing the news was extraordinary. 'What effect this may have on others', he wrote, 'I cannot tell, but if this be his temper it can hardly be good', and adds 'Why he did not appear before my triall I cannot tell.'

Even now, no firm answer can be given to that question, and the only rational explanation is that though Charles II was determined to destroy Sidney, he was equally determined to save his favourite offspring. To reconcile these inconsistent needs the pardon of the leader of the conspiracy could not precede, for it would have made impossible, the trial of a subordinate. Algernon may well have reflected sourly that Monmouth was quite possibly his own nephew, and not the offspring of Charles II at all.

Two days after Monmouth's public surrender Algernon was led once more into court for his final confrontation with Jeffreys. This third stage – judgment – was no formality, but the nearest approach seventeenth-century justice made to an appeal, and Jeffreys was to need his utmost resources to deal with it. All the points already made against the indictment – and some new ones – were raised, and so was the composition of the jury, but those were all ruled out as having been already settled. Then the prisoner played his one new card –

> My Lord, there is one person I did not know where to find then, but everybody knows where to find now, that is the Duke of Monmouth; if there had been anything in consultation, by this means to bring anything about, he must have known of it, for he must be taken to be in prosecution of those designs of his; and if he will say there ever was any such thing, or knew anything of it, I will acknowledge whatever you please.

Jeffreys was clearly stumped, but knew what he had to do:

L.C.J.: That is over; you were tried for this fact: we must not send for the Duke of Monmouth.

Col. Sidney: I humbly think I ought, and desire to be heard upon it.

L.C.J.: Upon what?

Col. Sidney: If you will call it a trial –

L.C.J.: The law calls it so.

Mr Justice Wythins: We must not hear such discourses, after you have been tried here, and the jury have given their verdict; as if you had not justice done you.

Mr Justice Holloway then made another of his rare interventions:

I think it was a very fair trial.

When Sidney persisted in demanding a fresh trial Jeffreys delivered a lecture on the majesty of the law, the patience with which the case had been heard, the accountability of judges to the powers of heaven and earth, and the impropriety of arraigning the justice of the nation. Sidney asked one despairing question before being silenced – 'Is writing an act?' Jeffreys took refuge in mystification. 'Yes', he replied, 'it is agere': and when Sidney said 'I must appeal to God and the world, I am not heard', went on to pass sentence of death, accompanied by a long, and in the circumstances insulting, homily. 'Mr Sidney', he concluded, 'you are a gentleman of quality, and need no counsel from me: if I could give you any, my charity for your immortal soul should provoke me to it. I pray, God season this affliction to you!' The prisoner should be hanged, drawn and quartered.

Sidney had already nerved himself for the moment, and replied with a prayer:

Then, O God, O God, I beseech thee to sanctify these sufferings unto me, and impute not my blood to the country, nor the city through which I am to be drawn; let no inquisition be made for it, but if any, and the shedding of blood that is innocent must be revenged, let the weight of it fall upon those who persecute me for righteousness sake.

Jeffreys was nettled, especially perhaps by the reference to the City, and could not resist a final sneer. 'I pray God work in you a temper fit to go to the other world, for I see you are not fit for this.' But Algernon had the last word. He held out his hand towards the bench and said:

My Lord, feel my pulse and see if I am disordered. I bless God, I never was in a better temper, than I am now.

Then he was taken away.

Almost at the same time Monmouth was granted a pardon, and the Government arranged to insert a notice of his admissions in the *London Gazette* which would, they hoped, convince all who doubted the genuineness of the 'Protestant Plot'. Poor Hampden was deeply alarmed at the thought that he might now find himself facing a capital charge, and Monmouth's chief adviser, Sir James Forbes, told his principal he would never live down the discredit if he allowed the admissions to stand. Within a week of his surrender, but sure that his pardon could not be revoked, Monmouth withdrew all the admissions he was alleged to have made, quarrelled with his father, and left the country.

In these extraordinary circumstances Algernon's advisers thought a petition for mercy would stand some chance of success. The King was said to be nervous about the way the conviction had been obtained, and to have remarked that Howard was 'so ill a man that he would not hang his worst dog on his evidence.' There was a widespread feeling that if Monmouth, guilty on his own admission, was pardoned, the sentence on Sidney could hardly be carried out with justice. It is possible that if the petition had been in sufficiently grovelling terms and contained enough admissions to make a suitable publication, it would have succeeded, but here Sidney's advisers came up against his obstinate sense of honour, which would allow no admissions, no apologies. A petition was put in (only the signature is in Algernon's hand) but the language is no more than respectful, and the main argument is the pointlessness of executing a man already elderly. Perpetual banishment, it suggests, would be the appropriate sentence.[3]

Charles was not, and did not think he could afford to be, a merciful man, and since his severe illness of 1680 Dr Welwood had noticed even a change in his outwardly easy-going temperament, 'for from an easiness and debonnaireness that was natural to him he came at last to ... express a severity in his disposition that he had been averse to before.' The petition showed no useful political advantage; and he was under pressure from Jeffreys, who was treating the execution as a matter of confidence in his appointment, and threatened to resign if it was not carried out.

The words 'carrying out the sentence' are ambiguous, for Jeffreys wanted Algernon not only to die, but to be hanged, drawn and quartered. He was therefore extremely annoyed to receive a letter from the Secretary of State, Sir Leoline Jenkins, dated 'This star'd night 1 Dec. Past Six', telling him that he expects the King will remit all the sentence, 'saving that of beheading him'. Jeffreys insisted that the full sentence should be handed to the Sheriffs in advance of the King's letter modifying it. Jenkins irritably agreed, adding 'but the sooner Mr Sidney hath notice of the time the greater is the charity, and it will prevent a clamour.'

Algernon was neither a popular man, nor in the mould of the

zealous religious orators the city crowds still loved. But the sense of injustice over his treatment was spreading. Evelyn, that sensitive barometer of respectable opinion, had been shocked when the plot had come to light, but was disgusted as a guest at a City wedding two days before the date set for the execution to see Jeffreys and Wythins in the highest of spirits, dancing with the bride and 'exceeding merrie'. They stayed till eleven at night 'drinking healths, taking tobacco, and talking much beneath the gravity of judges'.[4] Sidney, he reflected, might have been an inveterate enemy of the government, but he was a 'man of great courage, great sense, great parts' and had been condemned on the evidence 'of that monster of a man, Lord Howard of Escrick and some sheets of paper taken in his study'. Those words, or others like them, were to be repeated again and again, and were to harden as an instance of a dilemma in political thought which the English tradition has never been able to decide: the choice between conscience and allegiance.

Algernon himself was now obsessed with the sense of injustice. Almost to the end he was writing – perhaps dictating – to Ducasse. He felt that in rejecting his defiant instinct to plead guilty he had committed himself to a traditional battle of skill and nerve against Jeffreys and the prosecutors which, the more he thought about it, he felt he should have won, and deserved to win. He had been beaten by chicanery, bullying, sharp practice. He had kept his temper, played by the rules, behaved with dignity, and the other side had not. He would be a martyr, certainly, but an indignant and protesting one, not asking for mercy or admitting his faults – above all not forgiving those who had hounded him insultingly to his death – and he would be a witness for the cause to which he had always been loyal.

In this spirit he composed the long document called 'The Apologie of Algernon Sidney in the Day of His Death' which he entrusted to the faithful Ducasse, now his only outside visitor. It begins with a few, but valuable, pages of autobiography, but most of it is devoted to the iniquities (and the political importance) of his trial. Jeffreys, he had heard, had

> bragged to the king, that noe man in his place had ever rendered unto any king of England such services as he had done, in making it passe for lawe that any man might now be tryed by a jury not consisting of freeholders; and that one witness, with any concurrent circumstance (as that of buying a knife) was sufficient to convict him. In this he seems to have spoken very

modestly; for he might have said, that he had overruled eight or ten very important points of lawe, and decided them without a hearing; whereby the lawe itself was made a snare, which noe man could avoide, nor have any security for his life or fortune, if one vile wretch could be found to sweare against him such circumstances as he required.

He went on, reflecting about the tyranny of former kings —

that the lust of one man and his favrites was then only to be set up in the exercise of arbitrary power over persons and states; but now the tyranny over consciences is principally affected, and the civill powers are stretched unto this exorbitant height, for the establishment of popery.

He deplores the growing faintness of his countrymen, who had 'too deeply plunged themselves into worldly cares, and, soe that they might enjoy their trades and wealth, have lesse regarded the treasure that is laid up in heaven.' Gradually, in the closing passage, the resentment and litigiousness merge into a patriotic puritan prayer —

God will not suffer this land where the gospell hath of late flourished more than in any part of the world; he will not suffer it to be made a land of graven images; he will stirre up witnesses for the truth, and, in his owne time, spirit his people to stand up for his cause, and deliver them. I lived in this belief, and am now about to die in it. I know my redeemer lives; and, as he hath in a great measure upheld me in the day of my calamity, hope that he will still uphold me by his spirite in this last moment . . .

Clergymen came to see him, but he declined their services. The crowd outside the Tower was small and the ceremony brief. He made no speech, embarked on no prayers, but handed a sheet of paper to the Sheriffs with the remark that 'he had made his peace with God and had nothing more to say to men'. He neither read it aloud himself nor had it read for him, and said he would tear it up if they did not take it. 'He was ready to die, and would give them no more trouble.' Noticing the executioner seemed disappointed with three guineas, he asked Ducasse to give him two more. Then it was over. Some of the spectators pushed forward to dip handkerchiefs in the blood round the scaffold, but the dead man's remains were quickly gathered into a red cloth, carried to a hearse drawn up nearby, and driven to the hall of the Grocers' Company where the head and trunk were reunited. The hearse then drove on to Penshurst where Algernon was buried under a non-controversial inscription in the church that had once seen Hammond's learned sermons and Maudit's denunciations of the Earl of Leicester. One defiant aristocratic gesture was made: despite the Act of Parliament requiring all corpses to be laid to rest wrapped in the national product, wool, he was wrapped in linen, and a donation in excuse was made to the poor of the parish.

His undelivered final speech, having been handed to the Sheriffs, was transmitted the same day to the King and the Duke of York, who no doubt based his remark about Algernon's dying as a stout republican on it when he wrote that evening to the Prince of Orange.[5] There was, of course, a spare copy in the keeping of Ducasse, which was immediately given to the press and was on the streets within a day or two. It was the best thing he ever wrote, and the solemn personal note struck by the words 'That Old Cause in which I was from my youth engag'd', introduced chivalry into the Parliamentarian tradition. After a career of almost uniform failure the man who had made heroes of others became a hero himself, and was to have a long and adventurous posthumous existence.

Consequences

GOVERNMENT pamphleteers[1] fired a hostile volley over his grave, but even their productions were affected by Sidney's stoicism. The author of *Algernon Sidney's Farewell* condemned him to eternal torment but reflected that

> No braver champion, nor a bolder son
> Of thunder ever graced your burning throne . . .
> We stopt at naught that souls resolv'd dared do
> And only curse the weak and falling blow,
> Whilst, like the Roman Scaevola we stand
> And burn the missing, not the active hand . . .
>
> A stouter hardier murmurer ne'er fell
> Since the old days of stiff-necked Israel.[2]

Some pamphleteers concentrated on refuting suggestions of irregularity at the trial – 'managed with as much coolness and temper as any tryal I have seen' said one – and when Sidney's dying paper came out it was subjected to analysis sentence by sentence. Even its opening remark about the cold season was seized on as 'something that should have put him in mind of a much sharper, which will attend all heinous and unrepenting criminals.' It was a 'virulent and declamatory Harangue against the Magistracy of the Nation ... a perfect appeal to the People to avenge his blood.' His protestations of innocence were 'so awkwardly and lewdly put together that half an eye of sense cannot but see through the falsity of them.' The whole paper could be summed up as 'a Prodigy of Infatuation of this departing Enthusiast.' What more could be expected from a man 'who made choice of Tully for his Evangelist?'

Filmer's publisher Bohun put out a pamphlet explaining he would never have entered the controversy but for Sidney's unjustifiable attack on *Patriarcha* (of which he had just issued a new edition). The rev. William Assheton, later to gain fame as a pioneer of life insurance, saw the death of Sidney as the denouement of a conspiracy mounted jointly by Catholics and Dissenters against the English Reformation in which the Gunpowder Plot, the Civil War, the Popish Plot, and the Rye House Plot had been successive episodes, and annexed a table showing that the Jesuit Parsons, Bradshaw who presided at the trial of Charles I, and Algernon Sidney, had all used the same quotations from scripture.

But the underlying note of the hostile obituarists was deeper and hoarser. What mattered was what Sidney had stood for: 'If this were the Cause wherein he was engaged from his youth, if he employ'd his time and wit, his pen and sword, to propagate and defend the practice, what need have we for further witness?' The question whether he was technically guilty, or even whether there had been a plot at all, was secondary to the fact that he was an inveterate opponent of the established order. This at last was the day of retribution for the 1640s and 1650s which expediency had restricted at the Restoration. Now the most eminent survivor of that evil time had been exterminated, still scheming and defiant, the man who to his last moment boasted of having fought against the father of the King who presided over 'the best government under the sun'. He had sat among the regicides and declared himself 'Manus haec inimica tyrannis'. 'This crafty rogue pulled off the whole vizard.'

It is not surprising that published opinion was unanimous. Possible objectors were watched and examples were made. Sidney's solicitor, a lawyer named Gwynne, was overheard remarking that 'the jury were loggerheads and gave a verdict contrary to the evidence', and heavily fined for contempt of court. The veteran East India director and opposition M.P. for Suffolk, Sir Samuel Barnardiston, wrote to an acquaintance that a reprieve had been denied to Sidney because 'the contrary party prevailed.' The letter was intercepted and Barnardiston was fined £10,000 for seditious libel, Jeffreys remarking that he was lucky not to be charged with treason.

The silence of the opposition and of 'God's People' is therefore no evidence of acquiescence. But there was a deeper reason for it, which extends to the whole failure of the opposition since 1678, and of the Cause to which Sidney had committed himself. Year after year, ever since the Restoration, 'God's People' had been abandoning England for New England and majority rule. There they developed, as Sidney argued societies always would, their own institutions, even though still technically subject to the English monarchy. By 1683 Boston and the Commonwealth of Massachusetts were very much what Charles II had feared London might become, and he had taken steps against the Massachusetts charter as part of his general programme assaulting municipal autonomy.

The fate of Sidney was therefore a matter of considerable interest to Americans. Within two days of his execution a detailed account of it was sent across the Atlantic to Increase Mather, the President of the only university in North America, Harvard College, and leader of the resistance to Charles II's action against the Massachusetts charter.[3] Mather's father Richard had crossed the Atlantic only just before Harry Vane, in 1635, and had experienced Vane's governorship. Increase, though born in America, had spent the latter part of the 1650s in England and Ireland hoping to make a career there, and Sidney would have been known to him.

In America the people's creation of their country was visible fact, the King's sovereignty a legal theory. Sidney's own understanding of this is shown by the comment he made about Penn's elaborate constitution for Pennsylvania, which produced a breach between them. Penn's approach, Sidney said, was far too patriarchal, and sought to bestow institutions on people from above instead of enlisting those they had already worked out for themselves. In his English tradition Sidney was to be a partisan hero, but in America he matched the future of a new nation.

As a life-long admirer of Dutch republicanism and opponent of William of Orange, he would not have welcomed the Revolution Settlement of 1688. His old friend Ludlow emerged from exile to look once more at England, did not like it, and retired to die in

Switzerland. The rev. William Assheton, however, who had so heartily denounced Sidney five years earlier, published a laborious pamphlet explaining why he thought it right, whatever loyalties he had adopted before, to take the required oaths of allegiance to William and Mary. Algernon, if he had survived, would probably have acknowledged the decision of Parliament giving William legitimacy, but he would have stayed in Gascony.

In 1689 an enquiry was held into his trial, and as a result Parliament unanimously enacted that his conviction should be cancelled 'and to the end that right may be done to the memory of the said Algernon Sidney deceased ... all records and proceedings relating to the said attainder be wholly cancelled and taken off the file, or otherwise defaced and obliterated to the intent that the same be not visible in after ages.' The initiative did not come from the Government but from Algernon's surviving brothers, Henry, one of the engineers of the Revolution, now an earl in his own right, and the fourth Sidney to govern Ireland; and Philip, now third Earl of Leicester who is described in the Act as Algernon's heir. So Philip won in the end, the removal of the attainder on Algernon much simplified the Leicester House development question, and the 'deare and honoured kinsman' in whose favour Algernon had made his will was not mentioned.

Algernon now began to be acclaimed as a sage as well as a political hero. In 1689 a pamphlet appeared entitled *Sidney Redevivus: or the Opinion of the Late Honourable Colonel Sidney as to Civil Government,* with the epigraph *Tandem Bona Causa Triumphans* followed by words which touch all the notes in the theme by which Sidney was to be invoked for more than a century:

> The Blood of the Saints is the Seed of the Church and the Blood of Patriots is the Seed of the Asserters of the People's Liberty.

The myth of Algernon Sidney brought the conflict of the mid seventeenth century (in whose language these words are couched) to bear on the liberalism of the late eighteenth.

In 1698, fifteen years after his execution, the pedestal of the martyred sage was completed by the publication of *Discourses Concerning Government.* Then his strange, solitary, and stormy life, the injustice of his condemnation, and his dignified, heroic end, which all might have merged into the story of his generation, became part of a lasting memorial. Sidney stood beside Hampden, Locke, and

Milton, in the Whig Pantheon, yet clearly distinguishable from all three, for he had wielded both sword and pen. Hampden had died in the field, but he had written nothing. Locke and Milton had written with greater genius than Sidney, but it was by their writings that they survived: though they had both been politicians, it had been the politics of the study.

What was more Sidney's book was inseparable from the story of its author's life and death, not a separate manifestation of his intellect. It is usually possible to consider the work of an author without much knowledge of his life, however much such knowledge may add to understanding and appreciating it: but with Sidney it is impossible to read *Discourses Concerning Government* without knowing he died for writing it. The impression was the greater because, till then, not a word of Sidney's writings had been published except the single sheet of his dying declaration.

One would like to think that the *Discourses* as published came from the manuscript which had passed through the hands of the infamous Jeffreys, but the printed edition conspicuously omits the passages which were read at the trial; and does include many which would have suited Jeffreys even better than those chosen. The Act rehabilitating Sidney had in any case ordered the destruction of all papers connected with the trial; and the Preface to the 1698 edition assures us its text was taken from an original manuscript '*put into the hands* of a person of eminent quality and integrity' by the author himself: a pointless and rather risky boast if it were not true. We are not told the name of the 'person of eminent quality' any more than that of the 'Deare and Honoured Kinsman' to whom Sidney wrote his last letter; but that they were one and the same seems highly probable, and such indications as there are point to Henry Neville as Sidney's literary executor.*

The editor of the 1698 edition does not give his name either, but it was probably John Toland, the young radical who had just made his scandalous debut with *Christianity not Mysterious*. Irish-born, Catholic-educated, Toland shone in a clique of iconoclastic young deists for whom the Civil War had passed into history. He had been only thirteen when Sidney went to the block, and as editor took great liberties with several works of republican heroes that he handled, modernising their style and clipping back their rambling

---

* This problem is examined in more detail in the Notes on Sources.

religious and mystical rhetoric.[4] Sidney may well have suffered grooming of this kind for an Augustan audience, but the rhetoric, irony and passion of his characteristic style survive and few of his other writings show any signs of emotional religious rhetoric: nor did his purpose in the *Discourses* require it.

Scripture and divine law are undoubtedly features of Sidney's structure, and so is a puritanical repugnance to the style of the Caroline political world, but the main weight of the book springs from its appeal to history and reason as demonstrated by experience. His lengthy assaults on Filmer, which seem so exaggerated to modern readers, have their source in impatient hatred of the mystification and nonsense in which *Patriarcha* decked out and concealed a reality of selfish cruelty and corruption.

Patriarcha, in his eyes, had been resurrected to assert that Charles, a man called to his office by Parliament, the lover of Algernon's own and his brother's cast-off mistress, the murderer of the man he most admired, a politician without principle, conscience or sense of responsibility, was half divine. There could be no general rule conferring lawful authority on such a man, or treating the benefit of the governed as merely incidental to the exercise of hereditary rights.

The *Discourses* attracted immediate attention. Benjamin Furly, we know, had a copy, as did William Penn, who sent one across the Atlantic in 1700. So did Locke, who recommended it to 'all gentlemen who hope to be fully educated', and Lord Somers, the architect of the Bill of Rights, who noted and approved Sidney's view that a member elected to parliament is not a mandated delegate of his constituency but a representative of the nation as a whole. Sir William Temple claimed to have read it from cover to cover, and reached the conclusion that Sidney himself hungered for absolute power.*

It soon achieved the dignity of a French translation (printed,

* *A Collection of Several Pieces by Mr John Locke* (1720) p. 244. Locke, however, said on another occasion that he had never read it himself (Karsten. 186), but then he was extremely cautious on such matters, and never even fully acknowledged his authorship of his own two *Treatises of Government*. For Temple's opinion see Dartmouth's note on Burnet i 538. The passage on which Temple relied does not entirely support his view, but only asserts one of Sidney's favourite themes that virtue, not birth, is the qualification for public authority. One cannot doubt that Sidney thought he had this qualification, but his whole life shows that power itself was not his main passion. For Somers see *Somers Tracts* iii 81.

of course, in the Netherlands) in 1702 and a second English edition in 1704. The French edition also included a translation of the letter which has come to be known as 'Mr Sidney's Letter against Corruption', and has had a wide readership ever since it appeared in a collection of letters vaguely associated with the Earl of Rochester. It took Sidney's message to a great many more people than ever worked their way through the four hundred pages of the *Discourses*; it belongs to the time he was still in Denmark, just after the Restoration, and refused the pleas of his friends to return home and make his submission to the new regime. The government of Charles, he declares, is 'corrupt'. In Sidneian language 'corruption' is not limited to venality, nepotism, and the trading of favours: most men of his time would have seen 'corruption' in that sense as the inevitable accompaniment of social life, carrying little if any stigma. It meant the monopolization of power and influence at the expense of those who were rightfully independent, was what one witnessed in the France of Louis XIV, and was the aim of Charles and his brother. It led to selfish and irresponsible rule through a dependent, parasitic class, and in Acton's famous apothegm about absolute power it is in this sense that the word 'corrupt' is used. The absolute ruler does not necessarily become venal, but he neglects the interests of the people for the sake of the state machine that sustains him.

The enemy of corruption was 'the Patriot' – the title Sidney's admirers soon conferred on him. Here again one must beware of more recent usage which makes 'the patriot' the champion of his own country against others. No one was more aggressively English than Dr Johnson, and his famous denunciation of patriotism as the last refuge of scoundrels can only be understood as aimed at the professional critic of domestic government. In the modern sense Caesar was as patriotic as any Roman; it was his threat to the institutions of his own country that made patriots of Brutus and Cassius in destroying him. The Sidneian patriot is not the defender of his country against the foreigner, but the champion of its liberties against the oppressor.

But Sidney's reputation as a martyr and hero was never fully incorporated in the broad stream of authority sustaining the system that flowed from the Revolution Settlement. That he had been the most outrageous victim of the replaced regime was granted, and his sufferings gave him admission to the Whig Pantheon: but it was, as perhaps he himself would have wished, in a niche still reserved for a deity of opposition, not, like Locke's, of the established order. So it was as Cassius, not Brutus, that James Thomson decided on reflection to commemorate him, 'bleeding for the unpublish'd page', in *The Seasons*.*

Sidney's first appearance as an icon of dissident whiggery can be traced to the career of one of his successors as ambassador in Denmark, the opinionated Robert Molesworth, who wrote a book about his embassy, emphasising Denmark's shocking transformation to absolutism in 1660, and retrieving or perhaps inventing, the story of the French ambassador's destruction of Sidney's now famous album entry.[5] Molesworth's book attained an extraordinary popularity, not only in England but in America, and his reputation for independence, symbolised by steady refusal of office, came into its own when in 1721 he led the forces of retribution against the corruption and self-seeking after the collapse of the South Sea Bubble. For some time he was credited, though mistakenly, with the polemical series of *Cato's Letters* which, in a deliberately Sidneian style, denounced the ministers and were read long after the South Sea affair was history.

It would not be too much to claim that the desire to explain and justify the present by systematic study of the past – in short, the study of history – was first stimulated on a large scale by the appetite of Englishmen in the eighteenth century to debate the seventeenth.

The works of Eachard, White Kennett, Rapin, Oldmixon and Boyer, all of which appeared in the first two decades of the new century, are now forgotten, but they had a voracious reading public in their time and did much to establish a new legitimacy as well as create a history-reading public. As the century continued authors who are remembered for quite different achievements – Hume, Smollett, Goldsmith, Macpherson, even Fox – found it interesting and profitable to devote time and effort to satisfying the guaranteed readership for histories of England. In all of them Sidney was assured of a respectful, if not always uncontroversial treatment.

Alongside, and integrated with, the production of historiography on an unparalleled scale went an activity which had never previously occurred and which is an unsung tribute to Whig

* In the earliest editions Sidney is apostrophized as Brutus, but Thomson later altered it: an interesting comment on the sensitiveness still felt on the subject. (See J. Logie Robertson's edition of Thomson (Oxford 1951) p. 109.)

England: the quest for original materials and their systematic publication. The treasured and secretive archives of great seventeenth-century families began to be opened to the unwearying industry of Archdeacon Coxe, the reverend Thomas Birch, Arthur Collins, and many other specialists in the publication of 'Original Papers'. One of the results was that more and more information about Sidney became generally available.

In 1742 Thomas Birch, the greatest seventeenth-century scholar of his time, published the seven volumes of the Thurloe Papers containing Sidney's despatches from Denmark, and in the same year his correspondence with his friend Savile was printed. Two years later the vast miscellany of the *Somers Tracts* gave the public Sidney's juvenile *Essay on Love*, and the indefatigable Arthur Collins displayed the fruit of his work in the Penshurst archives, which include most of Sidney's letters to his father, though not, oddly enough, the Earl of Leicester's remarkable diary. By the middle of the century, history was a far sharper and more formidable weapon in current debate than it had ever been before.

In 1742 'Corruption' and 'Patriotism' were the slogans of the great assault on Walpole's two decades' engrossment of power, and although Bolingbroke is often described as a Tory his idea of a Patriot King with its image of a disinterested ruler has much in common with Sidney's admiring attitude to Charles X of Sweden. Bolingbroke and his political ally George Bubb Dodington subsidised two works which invoked and helped to perpetuate the memory of Sidney as the hero of opposition. One of these, *The Use and Abuse of Parliaments*, attacked the manipulation of Parliament as practised by Walpole, and professed to include a contribution by Sidney himself.* The other was the much more impressive *History of England in the Reigns of King William, Queen Anne, and King George I, with an Introductory Review of the Reigns of the Royal Brothers Charles and James in which are to be found the seeds of Revolution. By a Lover of Liberty*.

Both were the work of a journalist named James Ralph, and the *History*, which was a product of shrewd and careful reading,

---

* The claim that the opening chapter, entitled *A General View of Government in Europe*, is a newly discovered work by Sidney is not only spurious but is given away by the irony of the opening paragraph where Sidney is made to say that since he has been asked to make this contribution from retirement he hopes 'a performance with a kid will be accepted when I cannot sacrifice a hundred bulls.'

long maintained its influence, for at the end of the century Charles James Fox was relying on it as a work of reference. Its panegyric of Sidney was one of the most eloquent he had yet received:

> So dyed one of the best and bravest men who ever did honour to the English name: a patriot indeed, however mistaken (as he certainly was) in hoping and endeavouring to graft the virtues of antiquity on the rotten stock of modern depravity. May his ashes rest in peace! May his name be ever dear to rememberance! When his failings are recollected may it be remembered that he was also a man! When the liberties of the people are threatened, may they never lack a Sidney to lay down his life in their defence![6]

Altogether Ralph devoted fifteen of his folio pages to Sidney's story.

Although Ralph had been living in England for twenty years when he wrote this, his origins were transatlantic. He was a native-born Pennsylvanian, son of one of Penn's original colonists and a boyhood friend of Benjamin Franklin with whom he had set out as a young man to try his chances in England. Their ways soon parted, but Ralph's enthusiasm for Sidney – more marked than anything that had so far appeared – must surely have been of early implantation. America, not England, was the soil in which Sidney struck root.

About three decades usually elapse between the serious reading of future revolutionaries and the revolutions in which they take part; and recent research into the range of works on political theory accessible to enquiring young Americans from 1740 onwards shows Locke's *Treatises* and Sidney's *Discourses* as almost equally predominant over all others.*

By 1760 there were copies of the *Discourses* at Harvard, The College of New Jersey (predecessor of Princeton), the New York Society Library, the Charleston Public Library, and many other collections. When Franklin planned his Academy in Philadelphia in 1749 he insisted the *Discourses* should be on its shelves. Sale catalogues show that the book was in many private libraries, and although by 1760 an American edition had appeared, booksellers' orders from Boston and Philadelphia for the improved English editions continued to cross the Atlantic in considerable quantities all through the sixties.

The book was not only accessible to Americans; it was read. The Boston clergy, who did so much to lay the foundations of

---

* See H. Trevor Colbourn, *The Lamp of Experience;* Louis Shores, *Origins of the American College Library 1638–1800* and Karsten op. cit. I owe many of the examples that follow to these works.

the independence movement, were especially enthusiastic, and the reverend Andrew Eliot, minister of Boston South Church, declared that Sidney was the first to teach him 'to form any just sentiments of government'. Jonathan Mayhew, the most outstanding Boston minister of the mid-century, drew almost verbatim from Sidney when he told the Governor of Massachusetts in a sermon in 1754 that 'Monarchical government has no better foundation in the oracles of God than any other'. Josiah Quincy, father-in-law of John Adams, solemnly directed in his will that his copy of Sidney's works, along with those of Locke, Bacon, and Tacitus, should be presented to his eldest son on his fifteenth birthday so that 'the spirit of liberty should rest on him'.

John Adams himself was perhaps the most influential of all Sidney's American readers, for he played a considerable part in framing the Constitution and became in due course Washington's deputy and successor as President. He venerated Sidney all his life. He read the *Discourses* with enthusiasm when he was twenty-four, and, in a letter to Jefferson, describes how he read it again with undimmed pleasure when he was over eighty. He kept a copy in his office to draw on for political and oratorical inspiration, often repeats how much the institutions of the new republic owed to Sidney's ideas, and carried his passion to the point of composing an epitaph for Sidney's tomb. Through him Algernon's entry in the Copenhagen album, which had caused so much trouble, found its way into the coat of arms of Adam's native state of Massachusetts.

Two years before the Declaration of Independence Sidney was triumphantly paraded in America by the author of a pamphlet arguing that the British Government had betrayed the principles of the Revolution of 1688 – 'I mean the principles which such men as Mr Locke, Lord Molesworth, and Mr Trenchard maintained with their pens, Mr Hampden and Lord William Russell with their blood, and Mr Algernon Sidney with both.' The pamphlet went to seven printings.*

In mid-eighteenth-century England, however, attitudes to Sidney's myth depended very much more on individual temperament. Impressionable and romantic men like Boswell and Horace Walpole responded to it. Walpole's friend George Montagu, who shared

---

* Bernard Bailyn, *The Ideological Origins of the American Revolution*, p. 132. Dr Bailyn's judgment (p. 299) that Sidney 'had no feeling whatever for the shifting possibilities of political life' seems to me erroneous.

ancestral connections with the Sidneys, made 'daily orisons' to Algernon's portrait. 'O Sidney!' wrote William Johnstone Temple to his friend Boswell in 1764, 'Thou friend to mankind, thou foe to oppression, thou scourge of tyrants and guardian of liberty, citizen, philosopher, hero, what can atone for thy sufferings, what expiate thy blood? The souls of departed patriots still call aloud for justice on thy inhuman murderers. And they shall be revenged ...'

Sceptical and robust natures thought otherwise. Boswell was quite shocked when Johnson bluntly dismissed the irregularities at the trials of Russell and Sidney by saying they were rascals anyway.* Hume, in his History of England conceded that Sidney was 'gallant' and 'illustrious' and (from Hume an even greater tribute) 'in no way tainted with enthusiasm'; Sidney's trial had indeed been irregular. But, he went on to reflect, Charles II could hardly be blamed for letting the law take its course on a man who 'tho otherwise possessed of great merit, was undoubtedly guilty.' To pardon him would have been, perhaps, 'an act of heroic generosity, but can never be regarded as a necessary and indispensable duty.' The passage so upset John Adams that, as he told Jefferson, he felt Hume's history had been 'the bane of Great Britain', and had destroyed the best effects of the Revolution of 1688.[7]

The Englishman who did most to sustain Sidney's memory and spread his influence was not a literary figure though he shared the high-minded seriousness of Bostonians (with many of whom he corresponded) and was himself descended from 'God's People'. Thomas Hollis came of a Baptist family of Sheffield whitesmiths, and inherited a fortune when he was in his early twenties. Finding himself free to devote himself to anything he pleased, he decided to be the patron and propagandist of what he called 'true whiggism' as expounded by the intellectual fathers of the English Revolution – Locke, Milton, and above all Algernon Sidney, and to demonstrate in his own life what he took to be their principles.

He did many of the things young men in his position did – he travelled, collected books and antiques, acquired a considerable

---

* Johnson may have felt even more strongly than usual. Wilkes had made great use of Sidney's story, and even threatened to write a biography of him. Wilkes's friend Churchill paid tribute in one of his worst couplets, in *The Duellist*:

> An everlasting crown shall twine
> To make a Wilkes and Sidney join

measure of connoisseurship and moved in smart society. At the early age of thirty-seven he was elected a Fellow of the Royal Society. But all these activities were subordinated to his central passion. On his travels he conversed with ministers and officials, making extensive notes about the government of their countries. The books and pictures he bought were presented to universities and colleges, notably Harvard, of which his father had also been a major benefactor. Sidney Sussex received a portrait of Cromwell from him, Trinity one of Newton. He considered acquiring a seat in Parliament, but rejected the idea of belonging to what he regarded as having become a corrupt institution. There is much that Hollis had in common with serious Americans of his own day and later.

Hollis carried his obsession to eccentricity. From an early age he refused not only alcohol, sugar, spice and salt, but all dairy products. When a public subscription for a statue of the Duke of Cumberland as victor of Culloden was abandoned after failing to raise more than five and a half guineas, he put a notice in the newspapers pointing out that he had given five of them. His habits became more and more reclusive, and when he was fifty he left London altogether for a farmhouse in Dorset where he died four years later in 1774.

During that comparatively short life he edited and published new editions of Neville's *Plato Redivivus*, Toland's *Life of Milton*, and Locke's two *Treatises*; but his devotion to Sidney was conspicuous. He organised three editions of his works, the first in 1751 and the last, for which he employed a scholarly editor, the reverend John Robertson, in 1772.* In them were included not only the text of the *Discourses*, the text of the trial, and many letters culled from the Thurloe and Penshurst collections, but a completely new work, the so-called *Apology*, which Algernon had written in the last weeks of his life.†

Hollis (or perhaps his assistant Robertson) also provided the first attempt at a biography of Sidney, for which he personally searched the records of the Tower of London for particulars

---

* Robertson had been a curate to Dr Arthur Ashley Sykes, a formidable Low Church divine, and correspondent of Birch. The references to a Dr Robertson working at Warwick Castle and copying Ludlow's memoirs refer, I suspect, to him, not to Principal Robertson of Edinburgh University.

† He gives no explanation of the source of this discovery, but probability points to Warwick Castle.

of Sidney's end, paying the substantial fees demanded by the custodians. He even had a gem struck showing Liberty on one face and a portrait of Sidney on the other surrounded by the answer he had made on being reproached with the guilt of the regicides: 'Guilty! Do you call that Guilty?'

Hollis died four years before the Declaration of Independence, and when, in 1781, a memorial volume to him appeared, its editor Archdeacon Blackburne reflected that,

> when it began to be visible that the management of our public affairs was consigned to the hands of men notoriously unfavourable to Liberty, the principles on which those men acted who sacrificed Sidney, and the most incurable prejudice against our Patriot will, we apprehend, be grounded upon his affection for *our late* American colonies; and Mr Hollis will undoubtedly class, in the estimation of the vulgar, among the first encouragers and abettors of their disobedience.[8]

The great realignment of English politics induced by the American Revolution brought Sidney's reputation once more into the battlefield, for in it the ghost of dissidence still survived. And now that he had found his way into the new transatlantic Pantheon, and was acclaimed as an inspirer of its revolution, his republicanism could no longer be overlooked, and his qualifications as an English Patriot were suspect. No complete edition of his works in English has appeared on this side of the Atlantic since 1772.

At this point the association of historical research and the movement of political opinion provides one of the most curious episodes in Sidney's posthumous career. Two historians, both Scotsmen, gained access to completely new material on the later Stuart period. Sir John Dalrymple published the results of his research in the archives of the French Foreign Office in 1771; and in 1775 James Macpherson produced his *History of England* and the original documents supporting it, which included the journal kept by James, Duke of York in the early 1680s. From the despatches of Barillon which Dalrymple printed (expressing as he did so the dismay he felt on their discovery) a horrified public learned that the stainless hero had accepted money from a foreign power. Macpherson showed how seriously Charles II and his brother had taken the threat to their rule in 1682–3. As a result he offered this portrait of Sidney. Compare it with James Ralph's forty years earlier:

In his political opinions he was harsh and austere: and even in his private conversation commanding and haughty. He was admired by many for his integrity and abilities; but he never was an object of love. His principles suited neither a people accustomed to the government of a single person, nor the profligacy of the times. In Rome or Athens, in the days of their simplicity and freedom, he might have arrived at the fame of their first patriots; but he was a visionary politician, and even a dangerous citizen under a monarchy. In the extravagance of his views seems to consist the greatest defect of his judgment. He dreamed perpetually of an ideal fabric of a republic, without considering the wretched materials out of which it was to be made.[9]

There is a tinge of irony in the fact that these words appeared only a year before the Declaration of Independence.

Dalrymple's revelations did the most lasting harm to Sidney, even though the sensible Hume said he did not see that subsidies from France really mattered very much. Everybody took them, including Charles II himself. But in the growing consciousness of nationhood they did matter, even in retrospect. Horace Walpole became exceedingly agitated, and tried to organize a reply to Dalrymple. One pro-Sidney pamphleteer stoutly maintained that Dalrymple had either forged the Barillon papers himself or had them planted on him by the French. The *Virginia Gazette* warned its readers in September 1775, to beware 'pamphlets' by Sir John Dalrymple which 'were calculated almost solely to extirpate the very idea of patriotism.'

The glory Sidney achieved in America permanently damaged his esteem among the English governing classes. One could not have a national hero who had contributed so much to the rival republican nation, where in due course eighteen towns in fourteen different states came to bear his name. On the eastern side of the Atlantic his ghost, exiled from the English Pantheon, began to descend on causes one can now recognize as clearly belonging to the Left.

On 18 January 1789 Thomas Jefferson, then United States envoy in Paris, asked his colleague in London to find modestly priced busts of Bacon, Locke, Newton and Sidney as ornaments for his legation. The first three were readily available but Sidney was not. Yet only a little later, in April 1792, Jefferson could have seen one carried in a revolutionary procession by some young English sympathizers among whom were James Watt the younger, son of the great Birmingham industrialist, and William Wordsworth, then aged twenty-two and in Paris to sit at the feet of Tom Paine. In the following year – Year Two of the Republic – the French translation of the *Discourses* reappeared after ninety-one years. It bore the epigraph from Sidney's own work:

> La Liberté est la mère des vertus, de l'ordre, et de la
> durée d'un état. L'esclavage, au contraire, ne produit que
> des vices, de la lâcheté, et la Misère.

Of Liberty, indeed, he had always been the champion, but one must hesitate about his commitment to the other two ideals of the French revolutionary trilogy. Equality he rejected on grounds of both his birth and his common sense; and his whole life was plagued by fraternal strife. The Girondins are said to have reflected as they awaited their fate that Sidney would have been in their company. But in Kiel the young Berchtoldt Niebuhr celebrated the anniversary of Sidney's execution in that same year describing it in a letter to a friend as 'a consecrated day ... even with such a death the virtue and holiness of his life would not be dearly purchased.'*

Wordsworth, however, had read the *Discourses* and possessed a copy which was spirited away in the luggage of two literary friends who stayed with him in the year *Lyrical Ballads* was published – 1794. Only a few months earlier, he had included Sidney in a projected series of essays on 'eminent men distinguished for their exertions in the cause of Liberty'; and at the end of that year he wrote an enthusiastic letter of congratulation to John Thelwall on his triumphant acquittal on a charge of high treason, as a result of which Thelwall came to stay in the little community of radical poets in North Somerset, which now also included Coleridge.

Thelwall marks a further stage in the evolution of Sidney's influence. Like Sidney's, his early years had been marred by the oppression of an elder brother. A life-long detestation of corporal

---

* *Notes and Queries* May 1852. Niebuhr laments that far more of his German contemporaries had heard of Sidney than had read him. The same thought was expressed by the editor (not Lord Stowell, despite the British Library Catalogue's attribution) who in 1795 published an abridgement of the *Discourses* (*The Essence of Algernon Sidney's Work on Government*, by a Student of the Middle Temple, London 1795). 'The work in itself is of such magnitude that few, except those who vainly call themselves THE LEARNED have it in their possession and among the learned I find none who would be thought ignorant of the works of Sidney, but I also find the numbers very small who actually have read them.' The European tradition was to have an attitude to Sidney's story: the American to read his works.

punishment, and perhaps also the serious speech defect from which he suffered, may be traced to his oppressed childhood. As one of the chief animators of the London Corresponding Society, he overcame his stammer to become a celebrated revolutionary orator, and found himself charged with treason. Though he was defended by one of the greatest advocates of the day, Henry Erskine, he vowed to make Algernon Sidney the model of his defence, and was acquitted after suffering no more from the bench than a lecture about the advantages of an attentive jury and the dangers of impetuousness. Almost as he left custody his wife bore him a son, whom he promptly christened Algernon Sidney Thelwall.* His friendship with Wordsworth and Coleridge spread to Hazlitt and Lamb, but though he remained a radical his achievement of middle life was as a pioneer of speech therapy, in which he had lasting success.

The English romantic radicals might invoke Sidney's ghost but their eyes were also on causes to which the real Algernon would have been indifferent – the reform of Parliament, the extension of the franchise, and, with Shelley and Byron, a retreat from piety. But what most eroded the link between the image and the man was the growing national consciousness which had revised the significance of the word 'Patriot'. At first Wordsworth tried to bridge the gap:

> Great men have been among us; hands that penned
> And tongues that uttered wisdom – better none:
> The later Sidney, Marvel, Harrington,
> Young Vane, and others who called Milton friend.
> Those moralists could act and comprehend;
> They knew how genuine glory was put on,
> Taught us how rightfully a nation shone
> In splendour: what strength was that would not bend
> But in magnanimous meekness . . .

But then comes the transposition to his own vision of patriotism –

> France, 'tis strange
> Hath brought forth no such souls as we had then . . .

Rousseau, Voltaire, Montesquieu, Diderot, vanish as he reflects on

---

* Algernon Sidney Thelwall's career was a sad one. He obtained a good degree at Cambridge and became a clergyman, but preferment did not come his way. He held a series of temporary posts, but never a living, and a pathetic circular signed by him and some clerical friends survives to describe his merits and appeal for a permanency in the Church.

the way his contemporaries have sunk in relation to the giants of seventeenth-century English puritanism –

> Plain living and high thinking are no more;
> The homely beauty of the Good Old Cause
> Is gone; our peace, our fearful innocence
> And pure religion breathing household laws.

Sidney's creed certainly included plain living and high thinking, but the idea of liberty to which he devoted his life was not seen by him as peculiarly English, and except at the height of the Rump Parliament's triumphs over the Dutch he would hardly have chimed on his return with the lines Wordsworth wrote on landing at Dover in 1802 –

> Thou art free,
> My Country! and 'tis joy enough and pride
> For one hour's perfect bliss to tread the grass
> Of England once again.

One can see how Sidney's lack of patriotism in its modern sense of national solidarity was diminishing his heroic status if one watches another traveller who passed through Dover on his way back from the Continent that same autumn of 1802. Charles James Fox had been visiting the French archives with two research assistants to work on his own projected History of the years preceding the Revolution of 1688,* which would redress the distortions produced by Macpherson, Dalrymple, and others. It was to be authoritative Whig history, and Fox deplores Hume's commonsensical view that it would have been too much to expect Charles II to spare Sidney. But in discussing the Rye House affair Fox places Russell on a far higher pedestal than Sidney. While considering them both equally courageous, and hoping both 'will be for ever dear to every English heart', he maintains that 'the fortitude of Russell, who was connected with the world by private and domestic ties, which Sidney had not, was put to the severer test', a curious if unconscious echo of Sidney's own caustic joke that

---

* *A History of the Early Part of the Reign of King James the Second with an Introductory Chapter by the Rt Hon Charles James Fox,* London 1808. It was originally intended as a major work on the whole Revolutionary period before and after 1688, but only a fragment had been completed at the time of his death. The work (apart from its authorship) is chiefly interesting as an early attempt to do what Macaulay later achieved with such remarkable effect, and for the extensive transcripts from Barillon's despatches.

if anyone had to be selected for execution he was probably the most suitable in view of his advanced age and the absence of wife and children to lament him.[10]

Fox himself, in the very year his History was published, was posthumously elevated to the rank of Patriot alongside Nelson and Pitt in the elegy with which Sir Walter Scott introduced the first Canto of *Marmion*:

> If ever from an English heart,
> O, *here* let prejudice depart,
> And partial feeling cast aside,
> Record that FOX a Briton died!

Lord William Russell was finally established as the leading figure in the resistance to later Stuart tyranny by his descendant the future Whig Prime Minister Lord John Russell in 1823; and Wordsworth, in the vast sequence *Ecclesiastical Sonnets*, composed when he was over sixty to review the whole history of England as an Anglican panorama, decided that the Seven Bishops had been the real heroes:

> Thy sons who for thy civil rights have bled!
> How like a Roman Sidney bowed his head!
> And Russell's milder blood the scaffold wet;
> But these had fallen for profitless regret
> Had not thy holy church her champions bred ...

Nevertheless, in the age of reform Sidney still had his admirers, among them Hazlitt, who rebuked the radical habit of stringing together heroic names without knowing much about either their acts or their writings. 'Mistaken Whigs!' he exclaims, quoting one journalistic daisy-chain of Sidney, Cromwell, Pym, Somers, Luther, Wyclif, Hampden and Milton, 'Thoughtless reformers!' He had read Sidney's *Discourses* and recommended them 'to every reader of whatever party, not only for the knowledge it contains, but for the purity, simplicity, and noble dignity of the style. It smacks of the old Roman elevation.'[11]

The first effective biography of Sidney was produced during these years. Its author, George Wilson Meadley, was a Unitarian, 'amiable but not prepossessing, and somewhat fanatical in his liberalism', and although he wrote as an admirer and defender of his hero's reputation, his research was thorough and he ferreted out much that had hitherto been unknown – a task in which he was supported by that patron of Whig history, Lord Holland. Meadley's verdict, though the language is heightened in accordance with his political beliefs and the style of his time, is not unjust:

> Let those who calumniate his character and revile his principles, remember that to the practical assertion of them at the Revolution, England had owed her best superiority over the nations of Europe. If he formed too favourable an opinion of the dignity of human nature, and recommended a freedom too lofty for the passions and prejudices of mankind, it was the error of a mind sublime and generous ... And if, in the revolving annals of her history, that day shall ever arise, when the despotic prince, and the profligate minister, shall again prompt the patriot of noble birth to do or die for his country; then may the image of Algernon Sidney rise up to his admiring eye.[12]

Nevertheless one senses the gallant effort to scumble over the two senses of patriotism. Almost the last major national celebration of Sidney was in the early 1830s when the historical painter S. P. Stephanoff produced his much admired picture of Sidney's trial, showing all the persons mentioned in the record down to the maidservants, presided over by a scowling Jeffreys and addressed by a saintly orator whom one can hardly believe is a prisoner. Even Mr Gladstone, as a rising young minister in Peel's government, felt himself bound in 1844 to steal time from the pressures of a massive revision of tariffs to read the *Discourses* and reduce their four hundred pages to four neatly written sheets of notepaper – a striking tribute to his gigantic mental powers.[13] He strongly objected to Sidney's assertion that unjust laws need not be obeyed, and his interest may have been stimulated by the Chartist agitation, one of whose heroes Sidney now was. Revolutionaries, especially English ones, love to recall patrician heroes of the past to set against patrician oppressors of the present, and by the middle of the century 'Sid' had become a popular working-class name. As late as 1854 the left-wing *People's Paper* serialized Sidney's trial.

But six years before that, as the age of reform merged into true Victorianism, Sidney had been authoritatively banished from English History. In the tones of a headmaster expelling a promising boy for an unforgiveable offence, sorrowfully yet firmly, Macaulay wrote in the first volume of his fabulously successful *History of England*:

> Among those who cannot be acquitted of this degrading charge [the acceptance of French money] was one man who is popularly considered as the

personification of public spirit, and who, in spite of some great moral and intellectual faults, has a just claim to be called a hero, a philosopher, and a patriot. It is impossible to see without pain such a name in the list of the pensioners of France. Yet it is some consolation to reflect that, in our time, a public man would be thought lost to all sense of duty and of shame, who should not spurn from him a temptation which conquered the virtue and the pride of Algernon Sidney.[14]

So Sidney's myth of stainless patriotism was employed to destroy the man, and as Macaulay himself confessed, the morality of a later age was set up to judge a man who had never known it.

Foreign gold was not the real point. The English republicans have never been fully digested into the English tradition, and Sidney, who maintained republicanism with iron consistency and quixotic gentlemanliness, could never have a secure place among the statuary. His permanent contribution to English society lies not in his myth of purity and sacrifice for an ideal which was rejected but, at unascribable levels, in the way people talk about politics: as the Duke of St Bungay, in Trollope's *Phineas Redux*, tries to console the new Duke of Omnium on having to give up the House of Commons. 'I do think that the England we know would not be the England that she is but for the maintenance of a high-minded, proud, and self-denying nobility.' And when in the same novel Violet Effingham says she fully understands the Constitution – 'one can criticise the nobility, the bishops, the monarchy, the civil service, everything except the House of Commons'. With both these observations Sidney would have entirely agreed. But they are drained of passion. In America it was otherwise, and somewhere in the eighteenth century the Sidney tradition became autonomous. His pluralism, distrust of central authority, mystical veneration for elected assemblies, respect for local self-determination, insistence on due process as essential to law, all fitted into the way America had grown and the instincts of God's People.

It is a safe general rule to suspect that an interested motive underlies all writing intended for another eye during the dissimulating times of Algernon Sidney. Diaries, being intended for only one eye, are different; and perhaps the seventeenth century is the golden age of the diary because it provides the writer with a refuge from the oppressive world of dissimulation in which he moved. So, even with the great number of Sidney's letters that have survived it is not easy to form any just idea of the man himself. The record of his life has episodes in it which can be claimed as stains on the heroic consistency, 'sans peur et sans reproche', with which he was credited in his story, and which he asserted with almost his last words: the ambiguities of his return from Ireland in 1643, the signs of sympathy with the defeated after the 'Second Civil War', the allegations (whatever they were) of Captain Cannon, the dealings with French (and for the matter of that Dutch) authority between 1663 and 1666 and again after 1677, his apparent willingness to be reconciled to Charles II in 1672, and (in the non-political field) his possible hopes of quarrying something for himself from Strangford's estates. None of these would have counted against him in human estimation in his own time. His trouble was that a legend, to which he himself consciously contributed, claimed to put him above his own time.

But all this does not help to explain his true character, and in the large body of evidence there seem to be two statements which are particularly telling because they are widely separated in time and made by witnesses who cannot have collaborated. One is Montagu's record of the meeting at Elsinore, and the other Howard's description of the meeting of the 'Cabal' in the spring of 1683. In both conflicts Algernon, certain he was right, behaved in precisely the same way. First he spoke at length and with passion, and then, finding himself opposed by a majority, retired into himself, muttered words that could hardly be caught, and wrapped himself in sullen isolation.

Even his bitterest enemies never accused him of timidity, and few have fought more bravely at the end or died better. Nor was he a cold man in personal relationships: if anything his affections outran his discretion, as in the cases of Lady Carlisle and Howard of Escrick. Despite his apparent isolation he himself had a tendency to make heroes of others in his imagination: the great Sir Philip, whom he had never met, and Harry Vane, whose depths he never understood. Conscious of his own talent, oppressed by his elder brother, shadowed by his arrogant but indecisive father, his head buzzed with self-justifying certainties. Yet at the same time he found it difficult – perhaps too much for him – to influence those surrounding him, as his youngest brother Henry could do so well.

A worship of honour, therefore, coalesced with a deeply independent sense of religion to dominate his life, and provides the genuine foundation for his heroic myth. His attachment to the Cause has in it a good deal of the feudalistic personal loyalty to the Roses plucked two centuries before his time. But, that said, it led him, with his considerable intellectual gifts, into the effort of explanation which made him the lasting hero of dissidence and opposition.

This in turn gives him his historiographical importance. Although the British were for a time impressed by his self-sacrifice it was in America that his story and his doctrines chimed in with the experience of living in a new world. His assertion that liberty should make all things possible, which was both a strength and a weakness for him in his own time, was built into the institutions of the transatlantic republic; and if the sun of nationalism as it rose in the nineteenth century, may have melted his image even there, his contribution to its foundations has been lasting. If one discounts the exaggeration of the myth one finds that in many respects the man behind it was indeed the stuff of which heroes are made, and attempts to represent him as a fabricated hero-saint are not convincing. One discovers a personality reminiscent perhaps of de Gaulle or George Orwell, which corresponds to no conventional profile or grouping, a man whose reactions are not dictated by external events and influences but by inner compulsion and independent insight. He was, in a literal sense, a seeker. For him the struggle of the imperfect individual towards morality, and of society through the infinite permutations which were necessary to its health, could neither of them be helped by imposed and organized ideologies: both required liberty, moral in one case, political in the other; and those who by internal discipline achieved virtue qualified themselves to guide a society on its endless quest. His best epitaph is Coleridge's exclamation after reading the *Discourses*: 'What a gentleman he was!'

References

A.S.	Algernon Sidney
BL	British Library
DCG	Discourses Concerning Government
DLP	De L'Isle Papers
HMC	Historical Manuscripts Commission
SPD	Calendar of State Papers Domestic
SPD Ireland	Calendar of State Papers Ireland
SPD PRO	Domestic State Papers in the Public Record Office

Chapter I pp. 1–26

1 The most recent and convenient edition is that of W. A. Bradley (Boston 1912) but it is much abridged and a scholarly edition giving both the Latin text and a translation in full is much to be desired. The correspondence has a curious history. Languet's side of it, which must originally have been at Penshurst, exists only in the Frankfurt edition of 1633, and it is reasonable to infer, from the disappearance of the originals, and the fact that Algernon's father the Earl of Leicester had gone as ambassador to Denmark only a year previously that the Sidneys were behind the Frankfurt publication. This would be natural in a newly appointed ambassador seeking to establish his family's European standing and sympathy for the Protestant cause in the Thirty Years War. Philip's letters to Languet, and some other items in the correspondence, did not come to light until the nineteenth century.

2 Sir Ernest Barker in *The Proceedings of the Huguenot Society of London* xiv 37–61.

3 Sir Henry Sidney to Lord Treasurer Cecil 1 Oct 1587 quoted in *Proceedings of the Huguenot Society of London* x 473.

4 Countess of Leicester to the Earl of Leicester, 15 Apr 1632. A. Collins, *Letters and Memorials* ii 456.

5 Clarendon, *History of the Rebellion* vi 201.

6 DLP U 1500 A 14 (14 May 1634).

7 SPD Charles I 1638–39 400.

8 DLP U 1475 F 25 (Undated memorandum by the Earl of Leicester).

9 BL Add. MS 35,589 f. 228.

10 HMC De L'Isle vi 403.

11 HMC De L'Isle vi 520, Northumberland to Leicester 19 March and 7 May 1640.

12 Sir John Temple to the Earl of Leicester 7 Feb 1639, Collins ii 592.

Chapter II (no references)

Chapter III pp. 27–37

1 Gilbert, Sir John, *History of the Irish Confederation and the War in Ireland* (London 1882) i 1.

2 Hogan, James, *Letters and Papers Relating to the Irish Rebellion between 1642 and 1646* (Dublin 1936) 84. The letter in question is dated 20 July 1642; HMC Ormonde i 124.

3 Hogan, Lords Justices to the Commissioners of Irish Affairs 29 Sept 1642.

4 SPD Ireland 1642 11 November and 22 December.

5 HMC De L'Isle vi 419–428; Gilbert i 124 and ii 257.

6 Gilbert ii xlviii.

7 SPD 1644–45 486.

8 Vicars, John, *Parliamentary Chronicle* iii 268. Watson, Leonard, *More Exact Relations of the Late Battaile neare York.*

Chapter IV pp. 38–53

1 Macpherson, J., *Original Papers* (1775) 76.

2 BL Sloane MS 1619 f 112.

3 SPD 1643–44 182.

4 SPD Ireland 1633–47 462–478.

5 SPD Ireland 1633–47 586.

6 DLP U 1475 f 24. It is included in Blencowe and (a fuller text) in HMC De L'Isle vi.

7 Inchiquin to the Speaker of the House of Lords 10 March 1647, LJ ix 108. Lisle to the Speaker of the House of Lords on the same day LJ ix 94. See also Gilbert 19–25 and Blencowe 13–19.

Chapter V pp. 54–70

1 DCG III xiv.

2 'Court Maxims' XV.

3 *Memoirs of Edmund Ludlow* ed. C. H. Firth (1894) i 69.

4 Ludlow i 85.

5 See Gardiner, *Great Civil War* iii 408. These leaders included both the Earl of Holland and the Duke of Buckingham.

6 A.S. to William Aylesbury 4 Oct 1648, *Clarendon Papers* ii 241.

7 A.S. to the Earl of Leicester 12 Oct 1660, Blencowe 255.

8 A.S. to the Earl of Leicester 10 Jan 1649. BL Add. MS 21,306 f 55. The letter is catalogued as 1648, which was correct at the time of writing, since 1649 was not due to begin till 25 March. A reference in it to 'The Great Business ... which all men's minds are full of' clinches the dating as 1649.

9 See Blencowe 281–84. Sir James Mackintosh's note.

Chapter VI pp. 71–80

1 A.S. to the Earl of Leicester 12 Oct 1660, Blencowe 238.

2 Ludlow i 247.

3 CSPD 1650 101 13 April 1650.

4 CSPD 1650 101, 226, 251, 284, 359, 399, 435; and CJ vi 523, 526, 554. The episode starts rather earlier than Dr Worden suggests (*The Rump Parliament* 249) but the whole story confirms his view that the root of the affair lies in Algernon's opposition to the Army in 1649.

5 The main source for the Strangford story is Algernon's own long memorandum addressed to his legal adviser, Sir William Jones, in 1679 (BL Eg 1049), but there is also ample material in the De L'Isle MSS and in the PRO, all of which is skilfully analysed by Dr Jonathan Scott in his *Algernon Sidney and the English Republic*.

6 A.S. to the Earl of Leicester 28 July 1660 Blencowe 192. The spelling (if it is accurately copied) varies from Algernon's usual style. This is odd, but can hardly impugn the letter's genuineness.

Chapter VII pp. 81–90

1 BL Egerton MS 1049.

2 HMC De L'Isle vi 614.

2 Blencowe, Leicester Diary, 139–140.

Chapter VIII pp. 91–101

1 Dorothy Osborne to William Temple ? 24 April 1653.

2 BL Add. MS 15,194 f. 118. DLP U 1500 14–16 contain full accounts between Algernon Sidney and Kellerby for timber showing a substantial business.

3 A.S. to van Beverning 8 August (NS) 1654, Thurloe ii 501.

4 De Witt to van Beverning 28 August (NS) 1654, De Witt *Brieven* I 224.

5 A.S. to the Earl of Leicester (transcript) 14 August (NS) 1654, Thurloe ii 503.

6 John Milton, *Pro Populo Anglicano Defensio Secunda* (London 1654), *Works* (1738) ii 346.

7 23 Feb 1657 and 14 June 1658 HMC De L'Isle vi 500, 501.

8 SPD 1657 3, 4.

9 Leicester to Northumberland 17 February 1658. HMC De L'Isle vi 500.

10 Philip Lisle to the Earl of Leicester 17 June 1656, Meadley 314–316.

11 Ludlow ii 89.

Chapter IX pp. 102–119

1 For Whetstone's mission see *Clarendon Papers* iii 493, 565, 570 and 703.

2 'Mrs Harrison' to Charles II 19 March 1660. *Clarendon Papers* iii 703.

3 Pepys, 15 May 1660. See also du Terlon's *Memoirs* 475 where Montagu's departure from the Sound is specifically attributed to a decision to support a Restoration.

4 A.S. to the Council of State 10 August 1658. Thurloe vii 724.

5 *Journal of Edward Montagu, 1st Earl of Sandwich*, ed. R. C. Anderson. Navy Records Society lxiv.

6 A.S. to Thurloe 12 Sept. 1659, Thurloe vii 741.

7 A.S. to the Earl of Leicester 3 Nov 1659, Collins ii.

8 A.S. to Bulstrode Whitelocke 13 Nov 1659, Blencowe 169.

9 Ludlow ii 129.

10 A.S. to Bulstrode Whitelocke 1 March 1660, Blencowe 176.

11 A.S. to the Earl of Leicester 22 Feb 1660, Blencowe 174.

12 A.S. to Thurloe 2 April 1660, Thurloe vii 741.

13 A.S. to the Earl of Leicester 21 Sept 1660, Blencowe 214.

14 A.S. to the Earl of Leicester 28 May 1660, Blencowe 184–75.

15 A.S. to Bulstrode Whitelocke 1 Mar 1660, Blencowe 176.

16 A.S. to the Earl of Leicester 22 May 1660, *Collins* ii 686.

17 A.S. to the Earl of Northumberland 28 May 1660, Blencowe 182–183.

18 A.S. to the Earl of Leicester 28 July 1660, Blencowe 192.

Chapter X pp. 120–135

1 Earl of Leicester to Algernon Sidney 30 August 1660, Blencowe 207. The Earl was so concerned that he made a private memorandum of 'Peddicombe's allegations' – BL Add. MS 32, 680 f. 11.

2 Southwell to Sir John Percival 23 Dec 1660, HMC Egmont i 615–616.

3 A.S. to the Earl of Leicester 19/29 November 1660, Blencowe 243.

4 A.S. to the Earl of Leicester 15/25 April 1661, Collins ii 708.

5 A.S. to the Earl of Leicester 15/25 April 1661, Ibid.

6 A.S. to the Earl of Leicester 3 and 23 June 1661, Collins ii 718–721.

7 A.S. to the Earl of Leicester 29 Dec 1660/8 Jan 1661, Collins ii 702–704.

8 A.S. to the Earl of Leicester 14/24 July 1661, Blencowe 251.

9 A.S. to the Earl of Leicester 23 June 1661, Blencowe 247.

10 Charles II to Clarendon, Howell's *State Trials* vi 187–188.

11 *Apology* p. 1.

Chapter XI pp. 136–148

1 A.S. to Furly? 1666, Blencowe 258.

2 Ludlow ii 346.

3 'Riardo' to the Secretary of State from Pontarlier 8 August 1664, SPD 1663–6, 671.

4 A.S. to the Earl of Leicester 1/11 December 1663.

5 SPD 1663–64, 463. An alternative interpretation of Algernon's portrait in armour is that it was connected with the prospect of fighting on the Danube, and funded as such from Penshurst.

6 'L.B.' to the Secretary of State 19 August 1664, SPD 1663–64, 671.

7 Ludlow, ii 376.

8 Nicholas Arthur to the Secretary of State 13 May 1666, SPD 1665–66, 377. Aphra Behn's reports are in the PRO and printed in N. J. Cameron: *New Light on Aphra Behn* (Auckland 1961).

9 De Witt *Brieven* ii 205 and 207.

10 Ludlow ii 329.

Chapter XII pp. 149–161

1 SPD PRO 29/172 81/II, August 1666. Aphra's report is based on information from Scot.

2 Aphra Behn to Whitehall 5 Oct 1666.

3 William Temple to Algernon Sidney 29 April 1667, *Works of Sir William Temple* ii 31.

4 SPD 1667–68, 331, 529. Robert's passport was issued on 6 April 1668, and the regiment 'of the late Robert Sidney' assigned to Sir Walter Vane on 12 August.

5 Archives Nationales R2 82. It was discovered by the local historian Lagrange-Ferrègues whose research papers, now in the archives of the Department of the Lot, (Série J) contain useful information about Algernon's stay in Nérac. I owe this hitherto unknown source to the Librarian of the Nérac public library and Mlle Lucille Bourrachot.

6 DCG I. ii.

Chapter XIII pp. 162–183

1 DLP K, F32.

2 A.S. to Furly 20 Nov 1677, Forster, Thomas, *Original Letters &c* 79.

3 PRO Chancery Papers C 33/252/41, C 33/254/258, C 33/254/221 all bear on stages of AS's litigation with his brother or Strangford.

4 A.S. to Furly 29 Jan 16 78, 3 Apr 1678, Forster 82–86.

5 Barillon to Louis XIV 14 Dec 1679, Dalrymple i 337.

6 D'Avaux Négotiations I 9.

7 A.S. to Furly 29 Jan 1678, Forster 82.

8 A.S. to Furly 3 Aug 1678, Forster 85.

9 A.S. to Henry Savile 10 July 1679.

10 Barillon to Louis XIV 24 Oct 1678, Dalrymple I 249.

11 Collins 153; Meadley 332–335; CJ viii 578.

12 Penn to AS 1 Apr 1679, Meadley 331–332.

13 Gilbert Spencer to Henry Sidney 1 Sept 1679, *Sidney Diary* I 115.

14 *The Case of Algernon Sidney Esq as it appeared before the Committee Nov 10* 1680.

15 See James Welwood's *Memoirs* (2nd Ed. 1700 p. 134). Welwood, who was later William III's doctor and a careful observer of politics, writes of this time that 'The Parliament had in their view the Princess of Orange; and it was she and the Prince her husband who were to have filled the throne on the death of their uncle [Charles]'.

16 For a full discussion of *Patriarcha*, including its bibliography and manuscripts, see Laslett's edition (Blackwell 1949). There were clearly several manuscripts in existence during the 1680s, and they vary considerably. Algernon's edition, being the earliest, has the worst text. The best text came to light only in the twentieth century not far from Penshurst, which makes it tempting to suppose Algernon knew of a better one.

17 George Spencer to Henry Sidney 7 Jan 1680, *Sidney Diary* i

18 Dorothy Spencer to Henry Sidney 16 April 1680, *Sidney Diary* ii 40.

19 Barillon to Louis XIV 30 Sept 1680, Dalrymple i 379–80.

Chapters XIV and XV (no references)

Chapter XVI pp. 205–222

1 All these facts are established, and in most cases corroborated, by the evidence given at the trial (Lloyd, Ducasse, and the servants), Algernon's own *Apology*, and Ducasse's subsequent evidence to the House of Lords Committee of Enquiry into the case in 1689.

2 Altogether there were 32, between 25 June and the end of September (SP 1683, 385).

3 See *A Display of Tyranny* (London 1689) ii 281. The author is anonymous, but is generally held to be Titus Oates, which detracts from the book's authority. But the connection between Oates and Smith, and the intrinsic probability of the Crown's approaching Smith, make the report credible, and it is supported by the record of the enquiry itself.

4 Meadley 347.

5 Meadley 351.

Chapter XVII pp. 223–230

1 It was duly made, and was printed, which suggests its purpose was primarily propagandist. A copy (probably an intercept) is in PRO SPD Car II xxix.439.96. It is addressed to 'Mr Marlow, a clothier, at Witham in Essex'.

2 See in particular the minutes of Monmouth's surrender in PRO SP Dom xxix.434.128. It is particularly interesting that Monmouth denied that assassination formed any part of the conspiracy, and included many of the sectarian leaders, such as Dr Owen, in the conspiratorial circle. The initial offer of terms of surrender was made on 15 November, but negotiations had begun before that.

3 SPD PRO Car II xxix.434.114 (also printed in Meadley 370). It is drawn up in a legal hand. No decision is endorsed on it.

4 Evelyn, 5 Dec 1683.

5 James Duke of York to William of Orange, 7 Dec. 1683, Dalrymple i 116.

Chapter XVIII pp. 231–253

1 *A Defence of Sir Robert Filmer against the Misrepresentation of A. Sidney; Mr Sidney, his Self-Conviction; Reflections Upon Col. Sidney's Arcadia; Some Animadversions on the Paper & c; The Royal Apology; Remarks on Col. Sidney's Overthrow; An Elegy on the Death of Algernon Sidney; A Funeral Sermon on the Occasion of the Death of Algernon Sidney Esq.; Algernon Sidney's Farewell.*

2 *Anthology of Poems on Affairs of State*, ed. G. de F. Lord. (Yale 1975) p. 361.

3 Anonymous newsletter to Increase Mather London 10 Dec. 1683 (*Collections of the Massachusetts Historical Society 4th Series* viii 636). The writer corrects a still earlier letter, and gives much the most

careful description of the execution. He was particularly anxious to report Sidney's religious stance in the presence of death, and emphasised his refusal to accept the ministrations of any clergyman.

4 See A. B. Worden's commentary on Ludlow's 'A Voyce from the Watchtower', Camden Soc. IV xxi.

5 Molesworth, R., *Account of Denmark as it was in the Year 1692.*

6 Ralph, J., *History of England* (London 1742) 185.

7 Temple to Boswell 7 Feb 1764 *Boswell in Holland*, ed. Pottle (Yale 1952) 146; *Boswell for the Defence*, ed. Pottle (Yale 1960) 166. Hume, *History of England* (London 1762) vi 356.

8 *Memoirs of Thomas Hollis*, ed. F. Blackburne (London 1780) 5.

9 Macpherson's *History of Great Britain* (London 1775) i 405.

10 Letter to Increase Mather, see 3 above.

11 Hazlitt, *Works* ed. Henley (London 1902) iv 250 and 81.

12 Meadley, last paragraph.

13 BL Add. MS 44729 f. 19.

14 Macaulay, *History of England* (1864) i 109.

Note on Sources

A full bibliography for the life of a man who played an active part in politics throughout the Civil War, the Commonwealth, and the reign of Charles II, and in the course of it spent long periods in Denmark, Rome, and Gascony, not to mention Sweden, Germany, the Netherlands, and Switzerland, would be too extensive, and what follows concentrates on the sources available for Sidney personally. It is divided into four parts: his works, his letters, other personal MS sources, and a small selection of secondary works. As can be seen from my references in support of the text it does not include all the works that have been consulted.

A. Sidney's Works

Sidney has the distinction of being a voluminous writer, not one of whose works was published in his life-time. They have come to light in haphazard order during two and a half centuries since his death, so I have listed them in order of presumed composition.

1 *Essay on Virtuous Love*. Written before 1650. An autograph MS exists – BL Add. MS 34, 100. Printed in Somers *Tracts* viii 3 (1813).

2 *A Character of Sir Henry Vane*. Probably written in Italy soon after Vane's execution in 1662. The MS, in the hand of a copyist, found its way to the Cowper Papers and is now in Hertfordshire County Record Office as DIEP F 45. It was discovered by Dr Violet Rowe and is printed as an Appendix to her *Sir Henry Vane the Younger* (Athlone Press, 1970).

3 *Court Maxims*. Written 1665–66; The MS, in the hands of two copyists (one of them Benjamin Furly) was discovered by Dr Blair Worden in Warwick Castle and is now in the Warwickshire County Record Office as MS CR 1886. For a discussion of its history and its place in Sidney's career see my article in *Historical Research* for February 1989. It remains unpublished, but an edition is projected by Dr Jonathan Scott.

4 *A Prophecy*. Written 1666. Autograph authenticated by Furly in Bodleian MS Engl. Letters C 200 ff 24–5. Printed by Furly in London and Rotterdam in 1689.

5 *Discourses Concerning Government*, written mainly 1679–1683 but some passages may be earlier. No MS authority has been found, though the first published edition (1698) claims to be taken from 'a manuscript which in the judgment of all who knew him best, was all written in his own hand', and was 'put into the hands of a person of eminent quality and integrity by the author himself'. It was several times

reprinted in the eighteenth century (1704 Darby,) making a possibly significant change in the earlier title page from 'the' original manuscript to 'an' original manuscript, and adding the text of 6 below; 1750, G. Hamilton and J. Balfour, Edinburgh 2 vols 8 vo; 1751, 1763, and 1772, Strahan, London. These 3 last editions were masterminded by Thomas Hollis, who had the assistance of the Rev. J. Robertson for at any rate the last of them, and probably the two earlier ones as well.) There are also two French editions, the first printed in Holland in 1702 and the second (with identical text) in Paris in 1794. A modern edition is being prepared by the Liberty Foundation of Indianapolis.

There are compelling reasons for rejecting any idea that the 1698 text is based on the Sidney autograph produced at his trial. It significantly omits passages used against him in the indictment; its Section numbers differ from those quoted at the trial; it contains passages which would have been far more damaging to Sidney than those which were actually used; and it seems inconceivable that Sidney, after his conviction, would have been able to recover it for presentation to a friend. Moreover the Act of Parliament rehabilitating Sidney in 1689 directed that the whole record of his trial should be destroyed.

It is just possible that when that destruction took place the MS of the *Discourses* was spared and passed to 'the person of eminent quality and integrity' referred to in the preface to the 1698 edition, but if so it is surprising it was not preserved afterwards. My view is that there was a duplicate, probably in Ducasse's hand, and that this passed soon after Sidney's execution to the 'Dear and honoured kinsman' to whom he wrote his last letter making him his heir. The 'Dear and honoured kinsman' and 'the person of eminent quality and integrity' are therefore likely to be one and the same. The person who fits this composite profile best is Henry Neville, who was not only a cousin of Sidney's and a person of quality (his father was a knight, and his name one of the most glorious in English genealogy) but had been a life-long political colleague from the time Algernon brought him into Parliament in 1645 until the 1680s, when he issued a republican pamphlet *Plato Redivivus*. That pamphlet was republished in the same year, and by the same publisher, as *Discourses Concerning Government*. Neville died in 1694, and the interval between that time and 1698 is hardly too long for the editing and printing of so massive a work, especially as it could have been delayed by the survival of the censorship till 1697. A copy in Ducasse's hand would not have had the same association value as an autograph, and its fate afterwards would have been less important.

Nevertheless there are good grounds for supposing the MS had a subsequent history and may even still be in existence. Warwick Castle, once the seat of the Nevilles, passed in the sixteenth century to Fulke Greville, first Lord Brooke, whose monument there commemorates his celebrated friendship with Sir Philip Sidney. His successor, the second Lord Brooke, was a contemporary of Algernon and an enthusiastic Parliamentarian who, but for his death in a skirmish early in the war, would have played a conspicuous part in what followed. Algernon would certainly have known him. He married a Russell (aunt of Algernon's fellow-sufferer in the Rye House business), and his sister married that great parliamentarian Arthur Heselrige.

At the end of Algernon's life the Grevilles were represented by Fulke, fifth Lord Brooke, youngest son of Algernon's contemporary the second Lord, who survived till 1710. He cannot be described as prominent politically, though he served as an MP for thirteen years and attended the House of Lords after succeeding a series of elder brothers. But there is one odd feature about him: although he had no known connection with the House of Percy he christened his second son by the unusual name of Algernon, which continues to recur in his descendants.

There are other reasons for supposing that the links between the Greville and Sidney families brought Algernon's surviving manuscripts to Warwick Castle early in the eighteenth century. 'Court Maxims' was found there; in 1763 the head of the family (by then Earl of Warwick) wrote to Dr Thomas Birch inquiring about the source of Algernon's inflammatory motto (BL Add. MS 4321 f. 30). In 1751 the *Apology* makes its wholly unexplained appearance in Hollis's edition of the *Discourses*.

6 *Algernon Sidney's Apologie in the Day of His Death*. Dictated to Ducasse in November 1683. First printed in the Hollis edition of the *Discourses* in 1751 as 'from Sidney's original manuscript' – a claim later modified in recognition that the text was in Ducasse's hand from Sidney's dictation.

7 *The Copy of A Paper Deliver'd to the Sheriffs on the Scaffold at Tower Hill, on Friday Decemb. 7 1683*. The last of Sidney's works and the first to be printed. It was written early in December 1683 and the earliest editions appeared before the end of the year.

B. Sidney's Letters.

A very large number of Sidney letters have been preserved, and many have been printed in various collections:

Blencowe, R. W. (ed) *Sydney Papers*, 1825

Collins, A. W. (ed) *Letters and Memorials of State*, 1746

Forster, Thomas (ed) *Original Letters of John Locke, Algernon Sidney &c.*, 1830

Historical Manuscripts Commission: De L'Isle Papers vol vi. 1966.

Rochester: *Familiar Letters Written by John late Earl of Rochester and Several Other Persons of Honour and Quality*, 1697

Savile: *Letters to the Honourable H. Savile in the year 1679 &c Now first printed from the Originals in Mr Sidney's own Hand*, 1742

Thurloe Papers, 1742

The originals of these are in various collections, notably the De L'Isle Papers, and those using Blencowe and Collins should note that these editors frequently suppressed what they considered unsuitable passages.

Many letters, however, remain unprinted, the chief MS collections concerned being:

British Library Additional MSS
Glynde MSS East Sussex Record Office
Archives Départementales du Lot et Garonne
Bibliothèque Nationale.

C. Other Original Sources

Adams, John, *Diary and Autobiography*, Cambridge Mass, 1961–66
The Adams–Jefferson Letters 1777–1826, Chapel Hill, 1959
British Library, Egerton MSS
Sloane MSS
Additional MSS
Additional Charters
Burnet, Gilbert, *History of His Own Time*, Oxford, 1833
Clarendon, Edward Hyde, Earl of, *History of the Civil Wars in England*, Oxford, 1731
State Papers, Oxford, 1767–68
Dalrymple, Sir John, *Memoirs of Great Britain and Ireland*, Edinburgh and London, 1771–78
D'Avaux, Count, *Négotiations*, London, 1754
De Witt, Johann, *Brieven &c*, ed. Fruin, 1906
Resolutien de Heeren Staaten van Holland ende Vest-Vriesland, 1653–1668, Utrecht, 1706
Du Terlon, Chevalier Hugues de, *Mémoires &c*, Paris, 1681

Evelyn, John, *The Diary*, ed E. S. de Beer, Oxford, 1955
Ferguson, James, *Robert Ferguson*, Edinburgh, 1887
Filmer, Sir Robert, *Patriarcha and other Political works*, edited and with an introduction by Peter Laslett, Blackwell, 1949
Gilbert, Sir John, *History of the Irish Confederation and the War in Ireland*, 1882
Grey, Forde, Lord Grey of Wark, *Secret History of the Rye House Plot*, 1754
Historical Manuscripts Commission:
MSS of the Duke of Ormond
MSS of the Earl of Egmont
Howell's *State Trials*
Huguenot Society Proceedings
Journals of the House of Commons
Journals of the House of Lords
Louis XIV, King of France, *Memoirs of Louis XIV Written by Himself*, London, 1806
Ludlow, Edmund, *Memoirs of Edmund Ludlow*, edited by C.H. Firth, Oxford, 1894
A Voyce From the Watchtower, edited by A. B. Worden, Camden Society Fourth Series xxi, 1978
Macpherson, James, *Original Papers Containing the Secret History of Great Britain &c.*, 1775
Montagu, Sir Edward, *Journal*, Navy Records Society lxiv
Pepys: *Diary*, ed. Latham and Matthews, 1968–76
Public Record Office:
Chancery Papers
State Papers Domestic
State Papers Foreign
State Papers Ireland
Savile Correspondence, Camden Society lxxi, 1858
Sidney, Henry, later Earl of Romney,

Diary of the Times of Charles II &c., 1843

Sidney, Sir Philip, *Correspondence with Hubert Languet*, edited by W. A. Bradley, Boston, 1912

Temple, Sir William, *Works &c.*, 1720

Welwood, James, *Memoirs of the Most Material Transactions of the Last Hundred Years &c.*, 1700

D. Secondary Sources

Bailyn, Bernard, *The Ideological Origins of the American Revolution*, Cambridge Mass, 1967

Blackburne, F., *Memoirs of Thomas Hollis*, 1780

Cameron, N. J., *New Light on Aphra Behn*, Auckland, 1961

Clarke, J. S., *The Life of James II &c.*, 1816

Colbourn, H. T., *The Lamp of Experience*, North Carolina, 1965

de Fonblanque, E. B., *Lives of the Lords Strangford &c.*, 1873

Ewald, A. C., *The Life and Times of the Hon. Algernon Sidney &c.*, 1873

Faber, Sir Richard, *The Brave Courtier*, 1983

Fink, Z., *The Classical Republicans*, Chicago, 1945

Hull, W., *Benjamin Furly and Quakerism in Rotterdam*, Philadelphia, 1941

John, L. B., 'The Parliamentary Representation of Glamorgan', (University of Wales Unpublished Thesis) 1934

Jones, J. R., *The First Whigs*, Oxford, 1961

Haydon, Bridgit, 'Algernon Sidney 1623–1683', *Archaeologica Cantiana* lxxvi, 1961

Karsten, Peter, *Patriot Heroes in England and America*, Wisconsin, 1978

Kenyon, J. P., *Robert Spencer, Earl of Sunderland*, 1958

The Popish Plot, 1972

Macpherson, James, *History of Great Britain from the Revolution to the Accession of the House of Hanover*, 1775

Meadley, G. W., *Memorials of Algernon Sidney*, 1813

Ralph, James, *History of England in the Reigns of King William III &c.*, 1745

Robbins, Caroline: *The Eighteenth-Century Commonwealthsman*, Cambridge, Mass., 1959

'Algernon Sidney's Discourses on Government: Text-Book of Revolution'. *William & Mary Quarterly*, Third Series iii. 4, 1947

Rowe, Violet, *The Life of Sir Henry Vane the Younger*, 1970

Sachse, Julius F., *Benjamin Furly*, Philadelphia, 1895

Santwoord, G. V., *Life of Algernon Sidney &c.*, New York, 1851

Scott, Jonathan: *Algernon Sidney and the English Republic*, Cambridge, 1988

Sidney, Richard Chase, *A Brief Memoir of the Life of the Honourable Colonel Algernon Sidney*, 1833

Shores, Louis, *Origins of the American College Library*, New York, 1935

Thelwall, Stella, *The Life of John Thelwall*, 1837

Underdown, David, *Pride's Purge*, Oxford, 1971

'Recruiter Elections 1645–48', *English Historical Review*, lxxxiii, 1968

Whitelocke, Bulstrode, *Memorials of English Affairs*, Oxford, 1853

Worden, A. B., *The Rump Parliament*, Cambridge, 1974

'The Commonwealth Kidney of Algernon Sidney', *Journal of British Studies* xxiv, 1985

Index